P9-ECW-346

"Sufficiently Radical"

"Sufficiently Radical"

Catholicism, Progressivism, and the Bishops' Program of 1919

Joseph M. McShane, S.J.

The Catholic University of America Press
Washington, D.C.

LIBRARY OF CONGRESS CATALOGING-IN-PUBLICATION DATA

McShane, Joseph Michael, 1949–
Sufficiently radical.
Revision of thesis (Ph.D.)—University of Chicago, 1981.
Bibliography: p.
Includes index.
1. Church and social problems—Catholic Church. 2. Catholic Church—United States—History—20th century. 3. Radicalism—United States—History—20th century. I. Title.
HN39.U6M39 1986 261.8'3 86-9735
ISBN 0-8132-0631-6

To my mother and to the memory of
my father.

"The mouths of the just tell of wisdom,
and their tongues utter what is right.
The law of God is in their hearts,
and their steps do not falter."

Contents

Acknowledgments

In the last entry in his diary, Bernanos' country priest declares that grace is everywhere. Certainly my own experience confirms the insight of that fictional hero. In writing this book, I have been aware of grace and human graciousness at every turn. Therefore, I would like to express my gratitude to all who have helped me in this work.

Part mentor and part pastor, Martin E. Marty ministered to me academically and spiritually throughout this ordeal. With patience, wit, and insight he directed and challenged my thought; and with unfailing grace he encouraged me. My words here do not adequately summarize either his talents or my debt to him. Robin W. Lovin and Arthur Mann were the sources of both valuable insights into my project and personal encouragement. They were thus more than merely readers of this work. They became collaborators whose assistance I gratefully acknowledge.

Anthony Zito and Ann Crowley, S.N.D., the archivists of the Catholic University of America, unlocked the secrets of the Ryan Papers and the Archives of the National Catholic War Council to me, and were unfailingly patient with my questions and kind in their responses to my requests for assistance. The Paulist Fathers' archivist, Lawrence McDonnell, C.S.P., made John J. Burke's personal papers available to me; and the archivists of the Archdioceses of Boston, Baltimore, and San Francisco, and of the Dioceses of Toledo, Brooklyn, and Cleveland were helpful to me in my work. Scott and Peggy Appleby encouraged me with both laughter and prayer.

My debt to the Society of Jesus is immeasurable. The New York Province has provided me with the leisure and the financial backing necessary for this undertaking. Among the brethren, I wish especially to acknowledge the assistance offered me by the communities at LeMoyne College, Fordham University, Gonzaga College High School, and Hopkins Hall.

Finally, and most important, I wish to thank my parents, Catherine Veronica and the late Owen Patrick McShane, whose living faith in God and His love first taught me the meaning of life, and whose love and support have been as sustaining as they have been unflagging.

Laus Deo semper.

Abbreviations

Archives of the Archdiocese of Boston	AAB
Archives of the Catholic University of America	ACUA
Archives of the Diocese of Toledo	ADT
Committee on Special War Activities	CSWA
National Catholic War/Welfare Council/ Conference Archives	NCWC
File of the Chairman of the War Council, Most Rev. Peter J. Muldoon, Bishop of Rockford	NCWC Rockford
File of the Chairman of the Committee on Special War Activities, Rev. John J. Burke, C.S.P.	NCWC-CSWA, Burke
File of the Executive Secretary of the Committee on Special War Activities, Mr. Walter Hooke	NCWC-CSWA, Ex. Sec.

Introduction

The American Catholic Church was slow to develop a unified and effective strategy for dealing with the problems of industrialization. There is, of course, a spectacular irony contained in this situation. In the late nineteenth century, when the pace of America's industrialization was accelerating, the church's members were mostly poor men and women who were the victims of the deleterious effects of industrialization and the laissez-faire thought that undergirded it. In such a situation, one would have expected the church to rush to the aid of her beleaguered people and become devoted to the criticism and relief of industrial abuses. In point of fact, although the church was not entirely ignorant of the needs and sufferings of her people, her responses to their problems were timid and ineffective.

Although it would be tempting to suggest that the church's leaders failed to address social problems because their attempts to provide for the strictly spiritual needs of their rapidly expanding congregations left them with little time to articulate a clear, principled, and unified approach to the social questions of poverty, exploitation, and industrial unrest and violence, there were in fact other problems or forces that, either singly or together, conspired to block the development of a realistic and unified social strategy. The church was in a difficult position both in her American environment and in the universal church; she was a mission church composed of a bewildering diversity of ethnic groups in an exceedingly hostile environment. In addition, she possessed no intellectual apparatus that would help her either to understand fully the problems of industrial life or to reconcile her ethnic Catholicism with American ideals and mores.

Because of her divided pedigree (ethnic, Catholic, and American), the church had to deal with and juggle three often conflicting sets of expectations: as a mission church under the supervision of the Congregation for the Propagation of the Faith, she had to be conspicuously loyal to Rome and its directives; as a suspect church in a hostile host culture, she had to be conspicuously American; and as a church of ethnics, she had to endeavor to answer the needs or demands of a multiplicity of different groups that were as often at odds with each other as they were with the host culture. The conflicts arising from attempts to respond to this range of expectations colored every aspect of American Catholic life in the nineteenth century, including social concern. Rome's fear and censure of secret societies and socialist thought and intrigue, both of which were thought to be present in the labor movement, made the American church leery of unions at the same time that her impoverished members were flocking to the unions for protection against the power of big business.[1] To make matters worse, American Nativism caught the church in a triple bind: if she condoned union activity, some Nativists would accuse her of fomenting insurrectionist radicalism; if she forbade Catholics to join unions, other Nativists would find her guilty of an autocratic tendency that denied the free exercise of choice and offended American ideals.[2] Moreover, the thinly veiled proselytizing that normally accompanied American Protestant charitable endeavors made Catholics wary of joining hands with reform-minded Americans who were actively addressing industrial problems during the period. In such a vexing situation, it is not surprising that the American church was confused, timid, and frightened about confronting social issues. Any stance was sure to anger some group: if she condemned unions, she would run afoul of the immigrants; if she condoned them, she was sure to offend Rome and the Nativists; and if she attacked laissez-faire capitalism, she would appear completely radical. In addition, her own charitable endeavors, undertaken partly to

1. For discussions of the way the church's fear of secret societies influenced her thinking on unions, see James E. Roohan, "American Catholics and the Social Question 1865–1900: A Survey" (Ph.D. dissertation, Yale University, 1952), pp. 73–87; and Henry J. Browne, *The Catholic Church and the Knights of Labor* (Washington: Catholic University of America Press, 1949).

2. See Aaron I. Abell, "The Catholic Factor in Urban Welfare: The Early Period, 1850–1880," *Review of Politics* 14 (1952): 289–324, for a treatment of the way fear of Nativism directed Catholic social action.

blunt Protestant missionary work among her members, were largely unequal to the task of alleviating industrial abuses both because conservative Catholic attitudes could not conceive of the social causes of poverty (they saw it as a personal problem) and because ethnic jealousies and internal ideological divisions prevented the church from addressing the problems of the age in a unified and effective manner.[3] In the face of such problems, the leaders of the church pursued a strategy of "masterly inactivity" with regard to social questions and assumed a low profile in the hope that by offering no offense to any group, the church would be left in peace.

Such a strategy meant that most Catholic social or charitable activities were confined to fairly traditional enterprises run by ethnic groups and religious orders and that the only real advances made in American Catholic social thought and action were somewhat scattered and occurred in crisis situations when the pressure from one group, force, or set of expectations was so great that timidity was forced to give way to decisive action or creative thought. For instance, following the Molly Maguires affair and the rail strikes of the 1870s, reform-minded Catholic newspaper editors such as John Boyle O'Reilly, George Dering Wolff, and Patrick Ford began to respond both to the complaints of the workers that the church and the nation were sacrificing them to the power of big business and to the charges of the Nativists that the Catholics were fomenting insurrection by examining the systemic causes of industrial unrest and formulating a sophisticated critique of laissez-faire capitalism[4] (which was unfortunately ignored by the church as a whole). Rome's condemnation of the Knights of Labor in the 1880s brought

3. Consult Donald P. Gavin, *The National Conference of Catholic Charities, 1910–1960* (Milwaukee: Bruce, 1962), p. 2; and Aaron I. Abell, *American Catholicism and Social Action: A Search for Social Justice, 1865–1950* (Garden City, N.Y.: Hanover House, 1960), pp. 25–38, for discussions of the retarding influence of conservatism and internal divisions on Catholic social action.

4. For treatments of the contributions of the editors, see Roohan, "American Catholics," pp. 174–203; James P. Redechko, *Patrick Ford and His Search for America: A Case Study of Irish-American Journalism, 1870–1913* (New York: Arno, 1976); and Francis G. McManamin, "John Boyle O'Reilly: Social Reform Editor," *Mid-America* 43 (1961): 36–54. The work of the editors continued beyond this period, most notably by the *Boston Pilot*'s labor correspondent, Phineas.

forth a defense of unions from some members of the hierarchy led by James Cardinal Gibbons, who succeeded in having Rome reverse itself.[5] In both of these cases, however, the church's social progress was largely reactive, and in the case of the Knights of Labor Memorial, it was guided chiefly by a defensive fear on the one hand and expediency on the other. (An analysis of Gibbons's Memorial reveals that it was prompted both by the fear of losing the affections of the working classes and of appearing autocratic and un-American in the eyes of the Nativists. A passionate and principled attitude toward the need for social reform is conspicuously absent from the document.[6]) Moreover, even when crisis-fostered advances in social thought were made, they could not be sustained either because they lacked unified hierarchical approval (as in the case of the work of the reforming editors) and hence lacked moral authority in the church; because they were based on fear and expediency rather than principle; because ethnic or ideological divisions among the hierarchy or the Catholic people made it impossible to unite the church behind a single program;[7] or because the crisis that had prompted them had passed and another crisis calling for a different strategy developed. The sterility of such an approach became particularly apparent in the last decade and a half of the century, when the hierarchy's mildly prolabor stance of the Knights of Labor crisis evaporated in the face of internal ideological differences among the bishops (Archbishop John Ireland of St. Paul, for instance, vocally opposed unions), and the resurgent Nativism of the American Protective Association, which associated union activity with radicalism and both with Cathol-

5. The classic study of the Knights of Labor affair is Browne's *Catholic Church and the Knights of Labor.*

6. See Roohan, "American Catholics," p. 323. There is some irony connected with the Knights of Labor Memorial. Gibbons managed to create the impression that he was a real social liberal; actually, he remained a conservative all his life and consistently opposed the unions' use of strikes and boycotts.

7. The problems of ethnic and ideological fragmentation that troubled the church during the period are chronicled in standard histories of American Catholicism. The church was further hampered in her search for a unified strategy for dealing with social problems because between 1884 and World War I, there were no plenary meetings of the American hierarchy, which might have helped to define a unified approach to the questions of the day.

icism.[8] Thereafter, the hierarchy became so dedicated to demonstrating the church's conservatism as to construe *Rerum Novarum* in an almost strictly antisocialist light and to ignore its criticism of capital and support of unions. This stance was calculated to still the cries of the Nativists and endear the church to the "better classes," but it angered the working-class men and women, who came to doubt the church's devotion to their cause.[9]

Thus at the end of the nineteenth century, the church's social mission was confused, ineffective, and devoid of passion and intellectual depth. As a result, the American church was unable either effectively to respond to the needs of her own people or to contribute to the working out of solutions to the industrial problems that plagued the nation. If she ever wished to become a partner in effective reform activity, she would have to overcome the problems of ethnic and hierarchical fragmentation, intellectual shallowness, and fear of Nativism that had marred—indeed stunted—her social activity in the nineteenth century. More positively, the church would have to develop a

8. Consult Edward G. Roddy, "The Catholic Newspaper Press and the Quest for Social Justice, 1912–1920" (Ph.D. dissertation, Georgetown University, 1961), p. 16; Charles H. Shanabruch, "The Catholic Church's Role in the Americanization of Chicago's Immigrants, 1833–1928," 2 vols. (Ph.D. dissertation, University of Chicago, 1975), 1:117; and John Higham, *Strangers in the Land: Patterns of American Nativism, 1860–1925* (New Brunswick: Rutgers University Press, 1955), p. 82.

9. Some Catholics, of course, saw the full critical potential of *Rerum Novarum*. For treatments of laborers' and social activists' use of it, see Aaron I. Abell, "The Reception of Leo XIII's Labor Encyclical in America, 1891–1919," *Review of Politics* 7 (1945): 464–95; and John A. Ryan, "Some Effects of *Rerum Novarum*," *America*, 25 April 1931, pp. 58–60. For explanations of the way the encyclical came to be viewed as antisocialist, see also Neil Betten, *Catholic Activism and the Industrial Worker* (Gainesville: Florida State University Press, 1976), p. 12; Marc Karson, *American Labor Unions and Politics, 1900–1918* (Carbondale: Southern Illinois University Press, 1958), p. 228; William Stang, *Socialism and Christianity* (New York: Benziger, 1905); and Roddy, "Catholic Newspaper Press," pp. 14–15. For the response of business to the image created by this stance, see Robert D. Cross, *The Emergence of Liberal Catholicism in America* (Cambridge, Mass: Harvard University Press, 1958), p. 34. For an analysis of Leo's thought in the context of papal social thought in both the nineteenth and twentieth centuries, see Richard L. Camp, *The Papal Ideology of Social Reform: A Study in Historical Development, 1878–1967* (Leiden: E. J. Brill, 1969). Camp praises the boldness and originality of Leo's program (p. 13) for reconciling the church with the modern world.

solid intellectual basis that could both ground and unify her social criticism (and thus protect her social mission from charges that it was motivated by expediency) and provide a base for replacing her servile fear of Nativism with a real sense of belonging in America; and she would have to develop a greater sense of internal hierarchical unity that would endow her words with moral authority within the church and overcome the fragmentation that had compromised her social action in the past if she wanted to respond creditably to the problems of the industrial world. Surely the challenges were great. The dangers inherent in continuing to pursue the hopelessly fragmented social ministry of the past, however, were greater.

Chapter 1

John A. Ryan and Openings to Progressive Thought

While the American Catholic Church of the late nineteenth century was struggling with a notable lack of success to come to terms with the problems resulting from industrialization, the nation as a whole had to face the same complex of challenges. The nation's response took the form of a fervor for reform that was channeled into a variety of movements. The early reform impulses, such as Populism and the Greenback movement, had only tenuous connections with the fortunes of Catholicism because they were essentially rural movements and the great majority of the Catholic faithful lived in urban centers. The Progressive and Social Gospel movements, however, occurred within an urban context, and their connections with American Catholicism were both numerous and momentous. Unfortunately, the relations between the church and the urban reformers were hostile.

The Progressive movement was a direct and rather idealistic response to industrial change in America. Industrialization transformed American society from a rural and agrarian culture to an increasingly urban and industrial one. To be sure, this change brought with it some blessings, for as Samuel P. Hays points out, "industrialism opened vistas of vast human achievement." In the face of industrial might and awesome technological expertise, the world seemed plastic to man's touch. Destiny and the future seemed to be playthings responsive to human dreams and human power. The more perceptive, however, realized that the same industrial might that seemed capable of creating a bright future for humanity also "produced a restless and strife-torn society." As a result of reflection upon social unrest, tender consciences began, as Philip S. Foner says, "to realize that the rushing industrialization and urbanization which had been brought about by the expansion of American business during the previous half-century had been accomplished at a great cost in human suffering." Reflections upon the evils of industrialization in turn gave rise to a nostalgia for a more stable, innocent, preindustrial life and to a passion for reform of those new conditions that mocked the American dream and the ideals upon which the republic was founded.[1]

The discrepancy the Progressives perceived between American ideals and values and the strange new industrial world spurred their activity: misery cried out for correction, and the revitalization of the founding ideals of the nation served as the transcendent goal toward which they strove. Hence Progressivism rested on an idealistic basis. Hays, however, points out that the Progressives combined their idealism with a desire to devise concrete measures for realizing their idealistic goal: "Concerned citizens gave increasing attention to coping concretely with the new conditions. Patrician reformers dropped their reliance on negative government and asserted the need for positive actions to give direction and order to social change; labor and agriculture, accepting their new economic condition, strove to construct the power to advance their welfare within society; those concerned with social tension examined more closely its causes and proposed more concrete and immediate solutions."[2] Thus the Progressives reacted to industrial reality by proposing immediate steps to return traditional values to American life.

Since the industrial titans of the Gilded Age had benefited substantially from the rise of unbridled capitalism, it is not surprising that Progressivism found little favor among their ranks. It is surprising, though, that initially the lower classes of industrial society, who had suffered the most from laissez-faire capitalism, were also conspicuously excluded from the Progressive fold. By and large the Progressives were drawn from the broad and relatively heterogeneous ranks of the middle class, who saw the rise of industrialism as a threat to American values and

1. Samuel P. Hays, *The Response to Industrialism, 1855–1914* (Chicago: University of Chicago Press, 1957), p. 3; Philip S. Foner, *History of the Labor Movement in the United States*, vol. 5, *The American Federation of Labor in the Progressive Era, 1910–1915* (New York: International Publishers, 1980), p. 39.

2. Hays, *Response to Industrialism*, p. 47.

harmony.[3] To these middle-class citizens, it seemed that industrial growth undermined the nation's political and social stability because it had created two groups at either end of the social scale (the immensely wealthy and powerful industrialists on one hand and the desperately poor and exploited urban workers on the other), whose respective brands of selfishness gave rise to aggressive—even belligerent—behavior toward each other which showed a shocking disregard for national order and the common good. In response to these threats to the health of the republic, Progressives adopted democracy as their ideal and set about the hard work of bringing reality into line with the ideals of human rights and human dignity enshrined in the concept of democracy and in their favorite American document, the Declaration of Independence.

It must not be assumed, however, that the reformers were naive in their understanding of the founding documents of the republic. Quite the contrary; as fairly sophisticated revisionists, the Progressives understood that the Declaration and the Constitution were historically and socially conditioned documents, and part of their contribution to the cause of reform was their exposure of the classbound thinking of the framers of the Constitution.[4] Moreover, they understood and decried the Lockean interpretation of the nation's fundamental documents which had guided American political, social, and economic life in the nineteenth century and had allowed a ruthless laissez-faire capitalism to savage the working classes in the name of the natural right of each man to liberty. In the face of the (to them) patent evidence that the Constitution had been conditioned by the class interests of its framers and the equally obvious evidence that its interpretation throughout the nineteenth century had been similarly skewed by self-interested parties, the reformers

3. Richard Hofstadter sees the movement as a reaction to a loss of status and power on the part of the middle class (*The Age of Reform: From Bryan to F.D.R.* [New York: Vintage Books, 1955]).

4. See Charles A. Beard, *An Economic Interpretation of the Constitution of the United States* (New York: Macmillan, 1914); and J. Allen Smith, *The Spirit of American Government* (New York: Macmillan, 1907). For interpretations of these works, see Eric F. Goldman, *Rendezvous with Destiny: A History of Modern American Reform* (New York: Vintage, 1977); and Alan P. Grimes, *American Political Thought* (New York: Holt, Rinehart and Winston, 1955), chap. 15.

boldly and frankly went about the work of revising the meaning of the Declaration and the Constitution. The fruits of the work of these Reform Darwinians were startling and refreshing. To be sure, they did not jettison the notion of democracy. Indeed, they insisted on the inviolable dignity of man and, as Alan P. Grimes puts it, the "assumed equality of rights" that flowed from that dignity.[5] Because nineteenth-century economic liberals had defended their laissez-faire thinking by appeals to inviolable natural rights, however, they balanced their emphasis on individual rights with a complementary insistence on the need for a sense of social responsibility that could mediate the claims of individual rights and the common good. According to their thinking, a reformed and more democratically responsive government would be the agent for mediating these claims. What emerged from the pens of the reformist thinkers of the latter part of the nineteenth century, then, was a startling interpretation of the meaning of American values. Reacting against a laissez-faire system gone wild and itself based on a patently self-interested interpretation of natural rights and civic responsibility, the Progressives did not choose so much to reappropriate the now disgraced (in their minds) thinking of the Fathers of the Republic as they sought to reinterpret the meaning of democracy and responsible government for their times.[6]

As Robert Wiebe points out, the Progressive prescription for an effective reform of the social order that would reinvigorate American democracy was threefold: "regulation of the economy to harness its leaders and to distribute more widely its benefits; modification in government to make elected representatives more responsive to the wishes of the voters; and assistance for the dispossessed to open before them a richer life."[7] The Pro-

5. Grimes, *American Political Thought,* p. 355.

6. The Progressives' isolation of the inviolability of human dignity and the radical equality of human rights flowing therefrom and their insistence on assigning to the state an active role in securing the rights of the poor were key points in the reform platform which were picked up by John A. Ryan in his attempts to prove the essential congruence between American and Catholic reform thinking.

7. Robert H. Wiebe, *Businessmen and Reform: A Study of the Progressive Movement* (Cambridge, Mass.: Harvard University Press, 1962), p. 6. See also Hays, *Response to Industrialism,* p. 47.

gressives hoped that reforms in these three areas would create a classless society and a neutral government (that is, free from domination by special interests), which "would act as umpire among contending special interests in the spirit of fair play" and would bridle the centers of power that threatened to disrupt American life.[8]

Although the Progressives ardently believed that their program would reform and reinvigorate American society in a relatively short time, the movement suffered from several flaws that lessened its effectiveness. First, the movement was somewhat formless. It consisted of a chaotic collection of patricians, passionate intellectuals, conscience-stricken humanitarians, and radicals who had varying and sometimes conflicting views of reform and the course it should take.[9] The openness of the coalition to a diverse membership could and did provide the movement with a wide base for reform fervor, yet this very diversity points out its lack of the true cohesion that only a totally unified ideological base could provide. As a result, the movement did not possess the internal integrity that alone could enable it to survive frontal assaults by more unified and better-organized groups. The movement was destined to disintegrate.

Progressivism suffered from other defects as well. The idealism upon which the movement was based and the ideals toward which its programs were directed sometimes blinded the reformers to the necessity of dealing forcefully and realistically with the exigencies of power. As a result, in their schemes for political reform, the Progressives overestimated the effective-

8. Irwin Yellowitz, *Labor and the Progressive Movement in New York State, 1897–1916* (Ithaca: Cornell University Press, 1965), p. 83.

9. Foner, *History of the Labor Movement*, p. 57. John Buenker maintains that "the patrician reformers 'made little or no sense as a democratic phenomenon.' They sought to make the lower and middle classes politically ineffectual in order that the city and state could be run in the interests of those who owned it. This alienation of government from the mass of citizens in turn, led to the neglect of pressing socioeconomic problems until they had become crises or worse" (*Urban Liberalism and Progressive Reform* [New York: Charles Scribner's Sons, 1973], p. 132). See also Lewis L. Gould, *The Progressive Era* (Syracuse: Syracuse University Press, 1974), p. 1; Hays, *Response to Industrialism*, p. 76.

ness of their proposed reforms and underestimated the ingenuity of the political bosses and industrial leaders against whom their proposals were aimed. Finally, and perhaps most important, the Progressives were possessed of a narrow, middle-class consciousness and sensibility that circumscribed and sometimes undercut their actions. As John Buenker hints, an undercurrent of patronizing paternalism marked and marred the Progressive program. In a spectacular irony, the classbound vision of the reformers prevented them from fully understanding and sympathizing with the very people they hoped to help with the reforms they were advocating. As Foner points out, this paternalism combined with their fear of concentrating power in the hands of special-interest groups to make the Progressives especially leery of the labor movement:

> Many reformers were not interested in including labor in the alliance of the groups that made up the reform movement . . . the "better classes" were not interested in having organized labor as an ally. Even many of the Muckrakers, much as they wanted to end corruption in American life, were frightened by the prospect of an alliance with organized labor to accomplish this, and they were especially alarmed at the prospect of unity with the more militant elements in the labor movement. In the minds of most upper-and-middle-class reformers, militant unionism meant mob violence and in many respects was a greater danger to the nation than the trusts.[10]

It must not be assumed that because the Progressives were paternalistic, they were unconcerned with ameliorating the working conditions of the laboring classes. Quite the contrary. The Progressives were vitally interested in such issues. The problem that grew out of their prejudiced attitude was a procedural one. As Melvyn Dubofsky summarizes the situation, it would appear that the Progressives were captivated by the idea of disinterested benevolence as the only trustworthy platform and motivation for reform: "As long as the middle and upper classes led, the laborers were allowed to share in the benefits; when labor proposed through its own organizational or political power to redistribute wealth and reorder the American social structure, reformers balked, deeming organized labor a threat to

10. Buenker, *Urban Liberalism*, p. 26; Foner, *History of the Labor Movement*, p. 61.

true American values."[11] Noblesse oblige was acceptable—even praiseworthy. Self-interest was suspect.

Class-consciousness was, however, not the only barrier to close cooperation between labor and the reform movement. Although labor and the reform movement were able to work together on issues of common concern such as laws for the protection of women and adolescent workers, such unity was both rare and fleeting. More often than not, the Progressives and organized labor parted company on questions of both method and substance. The method labor preferred was to wrest concessions from capital through such weapons as the strike and boycott, whereas the reformers placed more trust in legislation which placed the reform process safely beyond the reach of special-interest groups. More important and substantial, however, even when labor was eager or willing to follow the Progressives' lead and seek legislative reforms, the Progressives were not interested in the issues that concerned labor. There was no "identity of interests" between the two groups.[12] Thus, although the reformers worked on behalf of the "people," they lacked understanding or sympathy for either the aspirations or the problems of the people they so loudly championed. Their prejudices were invisible to themselves but glaringly obvious to their enemies and their nominal beneficiaries. The resultant gap between the reformers and the laboring classes contributed to the poisoning of relations between the Progressives and American Catholics. It was not, however, the only barrier that divided the two camps.

Because of the overwhelmingly middle-class nature of Progressivism, the movement was almost necessarily Protestant and tinged by Nativist beliefs concerning Catholicism. The Progressives believed that they had justifiable grounds to distrust the church. First, as Charles H. Shanabruch points out, "The Catholic Church was viewed as an obstacle to the reform movement that was sweeping the nation. Progressives hoped to solve the problems of industrial society and bring about innovations that would give fuller freedom to all peoples and limit the power

11. Melvyn Dubofsky, *When Workers Organize: New York City in the Progressive Era* (Amherst: University of Massachusetts Press, 1968), pp. 25–26.

12. Yellowitz, *Labor and the Progressive Movement*, pp. 125–26.

of monied interests. . . . When the reform expectations were not realized, there was need for a scapegoat. The Catholic Church and its historic identification as a conservative force in the modern world bore the brunt of some frustrated reformers' anger."[13] Second, and consequently, in the social unrest that marked the Progressive era, the immigrants were seen in some quarters as being at least in part responsible for the social evils from which America suffered. Because many of the immigrants were Catholic, the church was thought to be responsible for these social ills. This point of view gave rise to strenuous efforts on the part of humanitarian reformers and Social Gospellers to wean the immigrants away from the un-American influence of Catholicism and transform them into responsible Americans. This eagerness for proselytization bespoke a residual distrust of the church. Third, because of their attachment to unions and political machines, both of which seemed selfish and disruptive of good order, the Catholic immigrants were perceived as dangers to the ideal of a classless society treasured by the reformers. Thus Nativist fear and prejudice fueled a hostile attitude toward the church among the Progressive ranks.[14]

It would be wrong to assume that the church was any less hostile to the reformers than the Progressives were to the church. Although Thomas T. McAvoy attributes the church's conspicuous absence from Progressive ranks to her preoccupation with internal questions of doctrinal discipline,[15] other problems prevented her joining with the Progressives to combat the evils of industrialization and urbanization from which her largely lower-class flock suffered. The suspicion Progressives felt for Catholicism was returned in kind. Churchmen felt

13. Shanabruch, "Catholic Church's Role," 1:311.

14. Higham, *Strangers in the Land,* 176, 122. As time went on, the hostility increased (see ibid., p. 178–79). See also Shanabruch, "Catholic Church's Role," 1:317–18.

15. Thomas T. McAvoy, "The Catholic Minority after the Americanist Controversy, 1899–1917: A Survey," *Review of Politics* 21 (1959): 77. David O'Brien seems to agree with McAvoy's contention and enumerates several reasons for the Catholic hesitancy to become involved in social reform: "Fearful of liberal attacks from without and modernist accommodation within, the Church reacted by overemphasizing its role as a vehicle of salvation, obscuring the mysterious character of its life and ignoring the inevitable effects of its temporal, historical involvement" (*American Catholics and Social Reform: The New Deal Years* [New York: Oxford University Press, 1968], p. 4).

threatened by the taint of Nativist hostility which they perceived behind the actions and programs of the reformers. Therefore, in the early years of the Progressive Era, Nativism and the church's fears of its strategies and effects continued to guide and circumscribe her involvement in the work of social reform. The thinly veiled proselytizing carried on by the humanitarians in their settlement houses, for example, seemed to present a subtle but serious threat to the faith of the poorer members of the Catholic flock. The church reacted to this humanitarian challenge in two contradictory ways: by condemnation and imitation. As Richard Krickus notes, the church "chastised those clergy or laymen who cooperated with the 'socialists' and Protestants who sought to alleviate the plight of the Catholic poor"; at the same time she encouraged and supported the growth of her own set of competitive humanitarian agencies lest the humanitarians "succeed in . . . their supposed intention to 'draw our children from the Church.'"[16] The church's hostile and defensive attitude toward Progressive reform ironically seemed to substantiate the reformers' belief that she was an implacable foe of social reform.

Mutual suspicion was not the only barrier that separated the two parties. During the Progressive era, Catholic leaders were deeply concerned with the threat of socialism. To the church, the Progressive platform's emphasis on reform by legislation and the creation of a welfare state had an alarmingly radical tinge. As Edward Roddy notes, the paralysis born of these fears heightened the church's isolation from the reform movement and threw the sterility of her own approach to social issues into sharper relief: "Catholic opposition to welfare state legislation . . . points up an essential weakness in the Church's understanding of the problems confronting the nation. Her anti-restriction, anti-welfare legislation attitude was too strongly emotional and unreigned of any deep analysis of and commitment to, alternative measures of reform."[17]

16. Shanabruch, "Catholic Church's Role," 2:338, 1:109; Richard Krickus, *Pursuing the American Dream: White Ethnics and the New Populism* (Garden City, N.Y.: Doubleday, 1976), p. 83.

17. Elizabeth McKeown, "War and Welfare: A Study of American Catholic Leadership" (Ph.D. dissertation, University of Chicago, 1972), p. 36; Roddy, "Catholic Newspaper Press," p. 193.

The church thus confused Progressivism with socialism. Although her final judgment was faulty, the church was not altogether wrong in perceiving some common basis for the analyses of social ills advanced by these two ideologies. It was at this fundamental analytical level that the church parted company most decisively with both socialism and Progressivism. The reformers believed that poverty and misery were products of environmental factors and forces. Hence both parties believed, to some extent at least, in economic determinism. The church, however, believed that poverty was essentially a personal problem, and though willing to deal with the problems resulting from the rise of industrialism and the growth of the cities, she continued to view poverty from a personalist religious point of view. Thus the church worked through agencies that were designed, as Aaron Abell notes, "to protect individuals against the effects of urban evils, not to remove the evils themselves."[18] The church's adamant refusal to acknowledge the environmental nature of the causes of poverty caused her to expend her energies on traditional charitable enterprises that were unequal to the challenges of the day. The sterility of the Catholic approach to social relief led the Reverend William J. Kerby, father of the National Conference of Catholic Charities, to remark: "Every unpleasant effect of provincialism was in evidence. Relations between our relief work and civil movements were usually remote and without distinction. The units of our Catholic charities displayed a spirit of offishness that made them to some degree socially ineffective. A defensive attitude on the part of our charitable agencies made criticism unwelcome and they were satisfied at times with ineffective or futile work."[19]

Of these three obstacles to the creation and maintenance of a close and fruitful alliance between the church and the Progressives, however, the most serious was the "almost wholly Protestant-Yankee ethos of some reform groups and programs, with their underlying vein of implicit nativism."[20] The leaders of the

18. Aaron I. Abell, "The Catholic Church and Social Problems in the World War I Era," *Mid-America* 30 (1948): 141.

19. Even the traditional charities' effectiveness was hampered by the duplication caused by ethnic jealousies. See Gavin, *National Conference of Catholic Charities*, p. 5; Kerby quoted in ibid., p. 14.

20. Roddy, "Catholic Newspaper Press," p. 17.

church could neither ignore nor forgive the crusading anti-Catholicism evident in practically all the words and actions of the reformers. The hierarchy responded by pursuing a timid and defensive course of action that further isolated the church from the American reform camp. There is, of course, a peculiar and cruel irony to this situation. Clearly, both the church and the Progressives were faced with the same pressing problems and should have been able to form an alliance to address them. Prejudice and fear on both sides unfortunately rendered vain the hope of forging such a bond.

The hierarchy of the church, however, were not the only American Catholics put off by the crusading spirit of the Progressives. From ethnic and class points of view, the laity had ample reason to distrust or hate the reformers.[21] Ethnic Catholics harbored tremendous resentments toward the reformers. The Irish, for example, resented the patronizing tone of their rhetoric.[22] In addition, the Irish, who were well on their way to political power in the urban centers of the country, found the reformers' stress on the reform of government both insulting and threatening. Since politics seemed to be one of the few avenues for social advancement open to them, the Irish were particularly incensed by the civil service reform movement, which they perceived as "a device to shut them out of office."[23] They therefore opposed all civic reforms,[24] and as Oscar Handlin reports, developed a healthy distrust of the meddlesome reformers (especially muckrakers) who attacked the machine bosses, whose brand of social action seemed to the Irish to be both more reasonable and more effective than that advocated by the reformers. The immigrants had little use for the ideals of democracy cherished by the reformers. Rather, they wanted the

21. Although the ethnics were hostile to reform, Melvyn Dubofsky, J. Joseph Huthmacher, Irwin Yellowitz, and others argue that the political machines were key elements in pushing through much of the Progressive program. Richard Krickus further contends that the pragmatic politics of the machines, shorn of ideological apparatus and the idealism of Progressivism, was the breeding ground for a later, more realistic form of American reform: urban liberalism.

22. Lawrence J. McCaffrey, *The Irish Diaspora in America* (Bloomington: Indiana University Press, 1976), p. 6.

23. Thomas N. Brown, *Irish-American Nationalism, 1870–1890* (Philadelphia: J. B. Lippincott, 1966), p. 140.

24. Hays, *Response to Industrialism*, p. 189.

material benefits of life in America for themselves, which was what the ideals of democracy translated into in practical terms. As Handlin points out, the practical bent of the immigrants caused them to view the reformers and their crusades with amused incredulity. This clash of values and world views reveals the futility of Progressive hopes. The reformers hoped to change social structures to benefit the "people," but they did not realize that their patronizing tone offended and outraged their intended beneficiaries. As J. Joseph Huthmacher says, "When, during the Progressive Era, certain old-stock, Protestant, middle-class reformers decided that the cure for social evils lay not only in environmental reforms, but also necessitated a forcible 'uplifting' of the lower-class immigrants' cultural and behavior standards to one hundred percent 'American' levels, the parting of the ways came."[25]

The bulk of the Catholic population was increasingly joining labor unions. The labor leaders who led and represented the workmen did not care about broad ideological reforms that aimed at the renovation of society at large. They were realists who were interested in the bread-and-butter issues of hours, wages, and working conditions. In short, they were concerned with effective and immediate power. Such practical aims were in stark contrast to the idealistic goals of the reformers. As a result, the labor leaders were cool toward and critical of the reformers; they resented the Progressives' paternalism and were frustrated by their refusal to become involved in their causes or committed to their demands.[26]

To make matters worse, the church, motivated by fear and expediency, cautiously drew closer to organized labor, thereby increasing her isolation from the reform movement. Following the Molly Maguires affair and the adverse publicity the church

25. Oscar Handlin, *The Uprooted: The Epic Story of the Great Migration That Made the American People* (Boston: Little, Brown, 1952), pp. 218–19; J. Joseph Huthmacher, "Urban Liberalism and the Age of Reform," *Mississippi Valley Historical Review* 49 (1962): 238.

26. Dubofsky, *When Workers Organize*, 26–27. As Yellowitz points out, "Organized labor and the social Progressives also disagreed on the desirability of arbitration as a means for solving industrial disputes. In those between the special interests of organized labor and organized capital, the social Progressives demanded arbitration by representatives of the impartial public" (*Labor and the Progressive Movement*; p. 142).

suffered as a result, and because the socialist cause advanced during the Progressive Era (peaking with Eugene Debs's strong showing in the election of 1912), the church was ever more solicitous about the kinds of unions to which the faithful belonged. Thus, at the turn of the century, in a move that was at odds with the Progressivist dream of a classless society, the church embraced, however reservedly, the cause of unionism merely because she feared socialism and saw the unions and their activities as a strong antidote to socialist agitation and contagion.[27]

Official American Catholic support for the cause of labor during the Progressive years was therefore devoid of passion. Indeed, it could be said that Catholic leaders supported unions only by default. A double compromise was implicit in this new Catholic advocacy of labor. From the point of view of church leaders, the optimal hedge against the socialist threat would have been the formation of confessional labor unions (if there had to be unions at all) founded on Catholic social principles and responsive to church direction. Since American Catholic laborers displayed a marked coolness that bordered on an aversion to such unions, however, the church followed the pragmatic course of enduring the nonsectarian unions that American Catholics did join and which Pope Leo XIII had implicitly approved in *Rerum Novarum.* The contingent nature of this approval, however, was not forgotten for, as Catholic representation in the American Federation of Labor (AFL) grew, so also did the watchfulness of the Catholic leadership.[28] As Marc Karson

27. Betten, *Catholic Activism,* maintains that the church's alliance with labor was in advance of the "fashions of the day" (p. 10). In searching for an explanation for the church's labor advocacy, Betten says, "From the late nineteenth century, a major segment of the American Church looked toward labor as an aid to the laboring classes. Catholics held working class status in greater proportion than other religious groups" (p. 146).

Abell, *American Catholicism and Social Action,* maintains that this stance marks an advance over late nineteenth-century Catholic thought (pp. 54–55). It seems to be a minor advance.

28. Roddy, "Catholic Newspaper Press," pp. 97–98. For various estimates of the Catholic strength in the labor movement, consult Karson, *American Labor Unions and Politics,* p. 221, who follows the estimates of Selig Perlman and says that Catholics formed the majority of the membership of the unions, and Roddy, who says that Catholics accounted for between 40 and 50 percent of the unions' membership. Although the estimates differ, all three men seem to agree that Catholics were a force to be reckoned with in the unions.

notes, the church presented the union leadership with what amounted to ultimatums: if the AFL countenanced any flirtations with socialism, the conditional approval of the hierarchy would be removed.[29] Since moderate union leaders shared Catholicism's fear and loathing of socialism, they welcomed the church's support and agreed to the conditions upon which it was contingent.[30]

On the whole, then, the church's concern for labor and consequently for the social question was still motivated by fear and limited to expedient measures "calculated to combat socialism and to influence the behavior of Catholic labor leaders."[31] There was no passion in her stance and no intellectual commitment to the cause of reform. Even this unimpassioned prolabor stance, however, put the church out of step with the Progressive reformers, who continued to view unions as a threat to the ideal of a classless America devoid of the disruptions of special-interest groups.

Thus there were many and cogent reasons for the gulf between the Catholic Church and the Progressive movement. Although by the turn of the century it was clear to all but the

29. Karson, *American Labor Unions and Politics,* p. 239.

30. Thus, the church's advocacy for the cause of labor was motivated by an expedient desire to counter the influence of socialism among the faithful. There were other indications of the church's lukewarm attitude toward labor. Cardinal Gibbons advised Catholic workingmen to avoid the use of strikes (ibid., pp. 225–26), and Catholic editors roundly condemned strikes in general and the sympathetic strike in particular as being immoral (see Roddy, "Catholic Newspaper Press," p. 140). Further, even though in 1912, Catholic unionists begged the church's leaders to state their support for labor publicly and forcefully, the hierarchy "refrained from making any official pronouncement on the labor problem until 1919. As a result, organized labor, while not hostile to the church, was less than enthusiastic about her failure to endorse her program" (Roddy, "Catholic Newspaper Press," p. 91). Although antisocialism was the basis for the general Catholic attitude toward the unions, some Catholics supported unions for their own sake and some combined a real passion for the cause of labor with a typical Catholic fear of socialism. The *New World of Chicago* (see Shanabruch, "Catholic Church's Role," 2:399–400) typified the first group. The Reverend Peter E. Dietz represented those Catholics in the second group (see Mary H. Fox, *Peter E. Dietz, Labor Priest* [Notre Dame: University of Notre Dame Press, 1953], p. 30). Appalled by the lack of direction provided for Catholic unionists by the church, in 1910 Dietz formed the Militia of Christ for Social Service to advance the knowledge of Catholic social teaching. Dietz was joined in this endeavor by John A. Mitchell of the United Mine Workers of America (ibid., p. 51).

31. Krickus, *Pursuing the American Dream,* p. 84.

most insufferably blind or the most invincibly ignorant that crushing urban poverty and chronic industrial unrest were common features in the lives of the working classes, and although it would have made good sense for the church to join in the reforming crusade of the Progressives, she could not do so. The real barrier to fruitful collaboration was the church's overly cautious and defensive attitude, which resulted from her long and painful experience of Nativism. Before she could join hands with the Progressives, the American church had to substantiate and defend her claim that she could be both Catholic and truly American, or show that there was a congruence between American and Catholic values.

Of course, the attempt to demonstrate a similarity or compatibility between Americanism and Catholicism was not entirely new.[32] In the late nineteenth century, the liberal Americanizers had sought to show the compatibility of Catholicism with American political institutions. Accordingly, they praised America, defended democracy to an incredulous Roman Curia, and stridently exhorted the immigrants to renounce all traces of ethnicity so that they could more easily be absorbed into the American community. Understandably, this approach was convincing neither to the non-Catholic American populace nor to the immigrants. Although the liberals were convinced of the essential goodness of America, their arguments and their program were defensive in tone and motivated by fear. They did not adequately present a firm foundation for their arguments, much less for their conclusions. Their arguments were intellectually shallow, although pastorally and practically wise. The continuing force of Nativism showed that America was unconvinced. The conservative reaction among some members of the hierarchy indicated a less than heartfelt commitment on the part of the American church to the liberal arguments about the compatibility of American and Catholic institutions. *Testem Benevolentiae* resoundingly denied Roman approval for the liberal stance. Clearly, fear, expediency, and shallow enthusiasm for American values could not and did not provide an adequate

32. I do not employ the term *Americanism* in the technical historical-theological sense used in the Americanist controversy. Rather, I refer here to American nationalism.

foundation for the task of reconciling the American and Catholic traditions in such a way as to make collaboration between Catholics and reformers possible.

Yet another approach to the task of reconciling the apparently conflicting traditions which was tried at the turn of the century was ingenious and passionate but hopelessly tortured. This was the attempt to demonstrate that the American political system was derived directly from Catholic sources, especially the thought of Saint Thomas Aquinas and Saint Robert Bellarmine. Such an approach led to sometimes ludicrous attempts to track down the reading material available to and used by the Founding Fathers as they composed the documents upon which the nation's political system rested. Such inquiries unfortunately relied on conjecture, tenuous connections, and tortured logic. This approach, too, was unconvincing to non-Catholics, however comforting it was to the Catholic population.[33] Although the argument presented by scholars engaged in this "proof" of the Catholic foundations of the republic was farfetched and based on the existence of lines of influence that could never be proven conclusively, it did rehabilitate the concept of democracy on specifically Catholic grounds. Thus, John Rager could say, "If democracy is a government primarily for the people; if it is conscious of the dignity and equality of every man as a human being; if it recognizes the rights and liberties of the private citizen; then again the defense of these principles by Cardinal Bellarmine is another proof that the Christian Church,

33. See William M. Halsey, *The Survival of American Innocence: Catholicism in an Age of Disillusionment, 1920–1940* (Notre Dame: University of Notre Dame Press, 1980); John S. Zybura, *Present-Day Thinkers and the New Scholasticism* (St. Louis: B. Herder, 1926), especially Moorhouse F. X. Millar, "Scholasticism and American Political Philosophy," in ibid., pp. 301–41; John C. Rager, *Democracy and Bellarmine: An Examination of Blessed Cardinal Bellarmine's Defense of Popular Government and the Influence of His Political Theory upon the American Declaration of Independence* (Shelbyville, Ind.: Qualityprint, 1926); and Sylvester J. McNamara, *American Democracy and Catholic Doctrine* (Brooklyn: International Catholic Truth Society, n.d.). The burden of the arguments of these Catholic apologists was that the true cradle of Western democracy was to be found in the thirteenth century (see James J. Walsh, *The Thirteenth Greatest of Centuries* [New York: Catholic Summer School Press, 1907] and that the democratic spirit of that age was communicated to the Founding Fathers through their exposure to authors who were familiar with the writings of Saint Thomas Aquinas, Saint Robert Bellarmine, and Francisco Suarez.

while upholding rightful civil obedience and loyalty did not oppose but rather did defend and promote the just rights and liberties of the common people."[34] By calling attention to the basis of the church's political philosophy and the originating and normative national documents on similar, if not identical, natural law assumptions, the advocates of this approach identified the foundation of a fruitful reconciliation of the American and Catholic traditions.

Yet a third approach to the problem also proceeded from the perception that since the republic's and the church's political and social thought were both based on natural law thought, a reconciliation between the two traditions was possible. This approach argued that the two traditions had a common heritage. The American natural law tradition of the eighteenth and nineteenth centuries, however, was so clearly Lockean, stressing self-interest and negative government, that it would be difficult if not impossible to square it with Roman Catholic thought, or the points in common would be very few indeed, and the reconciliation would be tangential at best.

The only truly salvific course to follow in the attempt at reconciling the two traditions had to be the enunciation of a fourth approach, which was a combination and a refinement of the others. It derived a confidence in and commitment to American values and institutions from the liberal Americanizing prelates of the late nineteenth century but wisely toned down their unquestioning enthusiasm. From the group that could be called the "ideological genealogists," the new approach to the task of reconciling the Catholic and American traditions derived a confidence in the wisdom of the church's traditional political and social thought and the keen perception that the key to the solution of the American Catholic conundrum lay in realizing that natural law thought underlay both the American and Catholic traditions of social thought and ethics. The Catholic chauvinism of the genealogists had to be stilled, and the ludicrous attempts to demonstrate direct derivation had to be replaced by the more flexible and ultimately more useful and neutral idea of congruence or intellectual convergence. Of course, the demonstration of a useful and fruitful congruence between the two

34. Rager, *Democracy and Bellarmine,* pp. 131, 118.

traditions necessarily involved the honest admission that the Lockean cast of thought of the Founding Fathers ruled out a wholehearted Catholic embrace of their version of natural law. To have any meaning, this congruence would have to be based on an American interpretation of natural law which was more congenial to the Catholic tradition. Clearly, then, a closer examination and appreciation of the revisionist thought of the Progressives and their understanding of the meaning of American political and social thought, with their insistence on maintaining a balance between natural rights and social responsibility, offered the American Catholic Church the possibility of effecting a reconciliation with her American environment without compromising her own tradition. Catholicism could thereby meet Americanism on a revisionist plane.

Many benefits accrued to the church in her attempts both to make a home for herself in America and to enunciate a positive social position. First, if Catholic scholars could demonstrate to the satisfaction both of Catholics and non-Catholics the existence of an intellectual or ideological congruence between Catholic and American political and social thought on the basis of a shared understanding of natural law thought, the Catholic Church would be able to assert her claim to a place in American life with more persuasive and intellectually respectable force than hitherto. Second, such an intellectual base would allow the church to put behind her the reactionary and defensive attitude toward American life and problems that had plagued her relationship with the host culture throughout most of the nineteenth century. Intellectual grounding and respectability would allow principled commitment to reform to replace mere expediency. Third, the demonstration of the church's possession of a natural law social ethic would allow the church freely to converse with and make common cause with the reformers, who framed their programs in terms of their own revisionist understanding of the natural law concepts contained in the nation's founding documents. Finally, once the intellectual congruence between the two traditions had adequately been demonstrated, Catholic scholars and social critics could use the insights and prescriptions of either of the two traditions to correct, inform, or complement those of the other. In short, the discovery and demonstration of an intellectual convergence between the

Catholic and American traditions of political and social thought would enable Catholic scholars to liberate the American church from the paralysis resulting from her strenuous and exhausting attempts to live up to the conflicting expectations of the universal church and the American majority, for if both traditions were in fact predicated upon similar natural law foundations, then American churchmen could present their social thought to Americans in terms that were both comprehensible and congenial to the American majority; conversely, it would enable the American church to represent American reform dreams and strategies to Rome and to her American flock in terms that were fully and undeniably Catholic.

At the end of the nineteenth century and the beginning of the twentieth century, however, the American church was a long way from achieving the reconciliation of the American and Catholic traditions to which she was heir. The success of this endeavor rested upon the American church's confident possession of and appreciation of universal Catholicism's natural law political and social thought. At the end of the nineteenth century, however, the American church lagged behind her European sisters in social matters precisely because she lacked a firm intellectual footing. As a result, the American church was not at one with the Leonine vision of the church's mission in an industrial world. On the basis of Leo's natural law thought the universal church had left behind her formerly negative attitudes and had become committed to and supportive of the reform of social structures either through union activity, regulatory legislation, or state intervention. The American church, however, had essentially truncated the message of *Rerum Novarum* by interpreting the encyclical as a purely antisocialist document. For this reason, American church leaders shied away from the legislative reform platform of the Progressive movement because such a platform seemed to countenance the establishment of a socialist system. Further, the narrow reading of *Rerum Novarum* blinded the American churchmen to Leo's strong endorsement of unions as instruments of social amelioration. They chose to follow the old "tolerari potest" attitude of 1888 and merely tolerated unions as an expedient hedge against socialism. As a result, the American Catholic response to social problems during the early years of the Progressive period was bloodless, unimpassioned, timid, and strangely out of step with both Leonine Catholicism and the American reform tradition precisely because the American church lacked an intellectual basis for creative social thought. Therefore, the first task the American church and American Catholic scholars had to address in their brave attempts to reconcile the two poles of the church's hyphenated identity was that of reappropriating, or, more correctly, of discovering the natural law moral theology which Pope Leo XIII had rehabilitated for the universal church in the late nineteenth century. Only if the church's scholars could accomplish this first appropriative task could they ever hope to accomplish the difficult subsequent tasks of demonstrating a convergence between the American reform and Catholic traditions of political thought and of proving to the satisfaction of both Progressives and Catholics that they could and should make common cause against the social problems of industrialization. The challenges facing the scholar who dared to undertake these tasks were great. The potential benefits to the church that would follow a successful meeting of these challenges were also great: if the American church appropriated the natural law thought of Leo XIII, this body of thought could be used both to redeem the Catholic place in American life and to infuse passion and intellectual conviction into the church's social ministry. Expediency, fear, and timidity would be emotions of the past.

In large measure the man to whom fell the awesome tasks of recovering the Leonine natural law tradition, of showing the modern critical social utility of that tradition, of demonstrating the essential unity of American reformist and Catholic social thought, and of moving the church into a position of sympathetic collaboration with reformist schemes for social reform was John Augustine Ryan.

John A. Ryan was born in the rural Minnesota town of Vermilion on 25 May 1869 of immigrant Irish parents.[35] He re-

35. If Oscar Handlin's thesis (*The Children of the Uprooted* [New York: George Braziller, 1966], p. xx) is accepted, Ryan's being a second-generation American may have been a key to his development of a sensitivity to social injustice. Indeed, Handlin includes Ryan in his collection of representative second-generation writers.

ceived his early education at the Christian Brothers' school in Saint Paul, and upon graduation from high school, he enrolled at Saint Thomas College in Saint Paul, from which he was graduated in 1892. Upon leaving college, he entered Saint Paul Seminary and received ordination at the hands of Archbishop John Ireland in 1898. With the approval of Ireland, he was sent to the fledgling Catholic University of America in Washington, D.C., to study moral theology and thus prepare for a teaching post at Saint Paul Seminary, which post he assumed in 1902, four years before the completion of his doctorate. His career, however, was intertwined with the Catholic University, to which he returned as a professor in 1915, and where he continued to teach until his forced retirement in 1939. During his years in Washington, he also taught at Trinity College, headed the Social Action Department of the National Catholic Welfare Conference, and served as the editor of the *Catholic Charities Review.*[36] He was a man of seemingly boundless energy and endless causes. At his death in 1945, he was still the dominant American Catholic social theorist.

The influences upon Ryan's thought were both numerous and diverse, both Catholic and American. Indeed, the very catholicity of these influences may have equipped him for the mediating task he shouldered. In his early years, Ryan was exposed to the Populist platform by Patrick Ford's *Irish World and American Industrial Liberator.*[37] Through the *Irish World,* Ryan became acquainted with the Populist rhetoric of Ignatius Donnelly and

36. The purpose of this study is not to provide a full biography of Msgr. John A. Ryan. For full biographical treatment, see his autobiography, *Social Doctrine in Action: A Personal History* (New York: Harper and Bros., 1941), and Francis L. Broderick, *Right Reverend New Dealer: John A. Ryan* (New York: Macmillan, 1963).

37. William V. Shannon, *The American Irish* (New York: Macmillan, 1966), p. 320. Ryan's acquaintance with the Populist platform began with and was sustained by his family's subscription to Patrick Ford's *Irish World and American Industrial Liberator.* It is also possible that his exposure to Ford's editorial policies accounts for the link between Ryan's rural background and his later passionate association with the essentially urban Progressives. For a discussion of Ford's American odyssey, which led him from radicalism to Progressivism, see Redechko, *Patrick Ford and His Search for America.* In many ways, Ford's ideological development offers striking and illuminating parallels to Ryan's development.

the land reform and single tax schemes of Henry George,[38] with both of which he had great sympathy, as well as with Ford's own editorial insistence that the church become more involved in social issues and the work of reform. Even in his boyhood, then, Ryan was exposed to and became intensely interested in the work of social reform and convinced of the wisdom of the American reform movements' attempts to reinterpret the fundamental meaning of American democracy.

Ryan's early heroes, who had an enormous influence upon his intellectual formation, were not all drawn from the ranks of the Populist movement, although all seemed to share a passion for the work of reform. Among economists, he revered the Social Gospeller Richard T. Ely[39] and William S. Lilly. Of the two, Ely was clearly the more important influence upon Ryan's intellectual development. Ryan subscribed to Ely's position (in contradiction to the code of classical economists) that because economic activity was a human endeavor, it was subject to moral judgment. In addition, Ryan approved of Ely's advocacy of a positive, active role for the state in the search for social justice. From Lilly, he derived further intellectual warrant for the lesson he learned from Ely that economic life and activity had to be subjected to moral reflection and judgment.[40] Thus, from secular and specifically American sources, the young Ryan derived and developed an abiding interest in social and economic reform and was exposed to the Progressives' thinking on democracy and civic and political responsibility. By the time he was a

38. Patrick W. Gearty, *The Economic Thought of Monsignor John A. Ryan* (Washington: Catholic University of America Press, 1953), p. 3; Thomas Becnel, *Labor, Church and the Sugar Establishment* (Baton Rouge: Louisiana State University Press, 1980), p. 53.

39. Gearty, *Economic Thought of Ryan*, p. 19. Ryan said of Ely, "I came upon Dr. Richard T. Ely's book 'Socialism and Social Reform.' This was, I am confident, the first work by an American economist which made any systematic or vital contribution to the discussion of modern economic evils and maladjustments" (John A. Ryan, "Seventieth Anniversary Address," p. 2, Ryan Papers, Writings 1935–40, Box B2-28, ACUA).

40. He stated his debt to Lilly: "His writings on economic subjects were radical in the true sense, for he tried to go to the roots of every matter that he handled, and his methods and habits of thought were fundamental and philosophical. . . . For him, the supreme values of life were ethical, and he tested all social institutions by that standard" (*Social Doctrine*, p. 47).

young man, Ryan's interest in reform had become a consuming passion.

In the church, Ryan readily admitted that he was deeply influenced by two of the great Americanizers of the late nineteenth and early twentieth centuries, James Cardinal Gibbons of Baltimore and Archbishop John Ireland of Saint Paul.[41] With these two men, Ryan shared a belief that American culture could and indeed should be reconciled to the Catholic tradition. His principal reason for admiring Gibbons, however, was for his having prevented the papal condemnation of the Knights of Labor in 1886–88,[42] for in Gibbons's action Ryan saw and applauded an instance of Catholic social concern in action. Ryan was destined, however, to go beyond the merely expedient approach to social questions evident in Gibbons's actions. In Ryan, the American church found a man who was more intellectually grounded in and committed to social reform principles than Gibbons ever was. His intellectual foundation, conviction, and passionate commitment finally allowed the church to become reconciled to Leo XIII's social vision and to the American Progressive crusade.

As a result of his exposure to these diverse influences, by the time he was a student at Saint Paul Seminary, Ryan was obsessed with the social question precisely because he believed that for modern man in an industrialized social order, salvation had to be seen, interpreted, and addressed in terms of social justice and human rights: "With each succeeding year of my theological studies, my desire and determination increased to devote as much time and labor to the study of economic conditions, institutions and problems as would be possible and permitted after my ordination. I wanted to examine economic life in the light of Christian principles, with a view to making them operative in the realm of industry. It seemed to me that the salvation of millions of souls depended largely upon the economic opportunity to live decently, to live as human beings in the image and likeness of God."[43] In enunciating this mission

41. Ibid., pp. 18, 21.
42. Ryan, "Seventieth Anniversary Address," pp. 1–2.
43. Ryan, *Social Doctrine*, p. 59.

of bringing the church into the economic marketplace, Ryan was admittedly facing a grave challenge. He acknowledged that the church's innate conservatism and predilection for a theocratic order made the success of such an undertaking improbable. Nonetheless, he hoped that by cooperating with—even baptizing—the spirit of reform, the church could make her peace with the age and enter into a critical relationship with the forces at work in the world: "Theocracy is a thing of the past; the Church must henceforth depend upon her own worth and her own intrinsic adaptability for her successes. How is she most likely to succeed? Why, by taking advantage of the permeating tonic of the age, by appreciating its aspirations, and by making these her own in so far as they are conducive to the glory of her Divine Master."[44] In other words, the Populist boy from Minnesota was longing for a way to reconcile the church and the America of the reformers. The past record of the church in America, however, offered scant hope for the realization of Ryan's dreams.

For Ryan, the indication of the way out of the social action impasse created by the burden of the American Catholic past and present situations came not from an American but from a Roman source. As Ryan relates in his autobiography, in 1894,

> One of our professors assigned to his class in post-graduate English the task of writing an essay on the encyclical of Pope Leo XIII entitled "On the Condition of Labor." As the encyclical had been published May 15, 1891, it was then almost three years old; nevertheless, this was the first occasion when it was brought formally to the attention of the students of Saint Thomas Seminary. I recollect very clearly the portion of the encyclical to which my own essay devoted most time and emphasis. . . . It was Leo's discussion of the state and the very large scope that he assigned to legislation as an instrument of reform. . . . The doctrine of state intervention which I had come to accept and which was sometimes denounced as "socialistic" in those benighted days, I now read in a Papal encyclical.[45]

This exposure to *Rerum Novarum* was tantamount to a confirmation of his own personal and Populist-permeated vision of the church's role in industrial society and a great commission

44. John A. Ryan, "The Social Question," Journal entry, 21 November 1894, Ryan Papers, Box B2-32, ACUA.

45. Ryan, *Social Doctrine*, pp. 43–44.

for Ryan's life work: "I had before me the specific exhortation and command of Pope Leo XIII: 'At this moment the condition of the working population is the question of the hour, and nothing can be of higher interest to all classes of the state than that it would be rightly and reasonably decided.'"[46]

From his encounter with *Rerum Novarum* in 1894 and from his lifelong study of Leo's work, Ryan learned a threefold lesson, each component of which would be vitally important for his task of moving the church toward a social stance that was both intellectually respectable and religiously grounded and was at one with the American reform tradition. First, from Leo's statement that "it is the opinion of some, and the error is already very common, that the social question is merely an economic one, whereas in point of fact, it is first of all a moral and religious matter, and for that reason its settlement is to be sought mainly in the moral law and the pronouncements of religion," Ryan gained the assurances both that religion had a place in the field of economics and that the church's pronouncements were the final critical word in social matters.[47] Ryan derived a great deal of confidence from Leo's insistence upon involving the church in social matters, and since the American church at the turn of the century was all too willing to maintain a low social profile, Ryan repeatedly used Leo's words and ideas both to goad his coreligionists out of their social laxity and to defend himself against charges that his social involvement was a radical betrayal of the gospel.[48]

Second, in Leo's thought, as it was enunciated in *Rerum Novarum*, Ryan discovered a method for bringing traditional moral reflection to bear upon modern industrial questions, a method

46. Ryan, "Seventieth Anniversary Address," p. 2.

47. Leo quoted in John A. Ryan, *Declining Liberty and Other Papers* (New York: Macmillan, 1927), pp. 180–81. Ryan remarked, "Into this world of pagan industrialism, the great pontiff of the Workingman hurled his thunderbolts of authoritative doctrine. The responsibility of the Apostolic office and the right which was his to interpret the moral law impelled him, he said, to lay down the principles which truth and justice dictate for the settlement of the question" (John A. Ryan, "Pope Leo's Rerum Novarum," in his *Seven Troubled Years, 1930–1936: A Collection of Papers on the Depression and on the Problems of Recovery and Reform* [Ann Arbor: Edwards Bros., 1937], p. 138).

48. Ryan, "Some Effects of *Rerum Novarum*," p. 58. See John A. Ryan, "Catholic Laymen and the Labor Problem," address, Ryan Papers, Writings Miscellaneous, Box B2-24, ACUA.

of adapting scholastic principles to modern situations: "This great pontiff enunciated no new principles of justice or charity in relation to industry. The general principles which he laid down had long been commonplaces of Catholic moral theology. The new thing which he did was to consider comprehensively the facts of present-day industry and to apply the traditional principles specifically to these facts."[49] In Ryan's hands, this Leonine method became surprisingly supple and effective as a basis of criticism of economic affairs. Further, since the Leonine approach to current problems was based on natural law ethics, it seemed to Ryan to represent an area of congruence between Catholic and reformist American political and social thought. Thus in his demonstration of the necessity and desirability of reconciling the two traditions, Ryan frequently called attention to this similarity.

Finally, Ryan derived from Leo's encyclical a belief in the principle of state intervention for social amelioration that served as a further basis for effecting a reconciliation of the church with the ideas and programs of the Progressives.[50] As a result of his exposure to *Rerum Novarum,* and especially the three elements described above, Ryan believed that on the basis of Leonine thought, he could not only justify his own reformist leanings but also move the American church into a position of greater intellectual sympathy and practical collaboration with the American reform tradition.

Although Ryan staunchly insisted that his thought was fully derived from Leo, his autobiography shows that he was an adherent of the American reform tradition before he ever read Leo. As a result, his encounter with Leonine thought was colored by

49. John A. Ryan, *Questions of the Day* (1931; rpt. Freeport: Books for Libraries Press, 1967), p. 223. For an evaluation of the importance of this discovery, see Richard Purcell, "John A. Ryan: Prophet of Social Justice," *Studies* 35 (1946): 157: "Ryan struck the keynote of his lifelong labors—the integration of the principles of scholastic philosophy and moral theology into an interpretation of current social and economic problems."

50. Karl Cerny maintains that because of his own American reform sympathies, Ryan read *Rerum Novarum* from a prejudiced point of view and hence assigned a greater role to the state than Leo would have favored. See Cerny, "Monsignor John A. Ryan and the Social Action Department" (Ph.D. dissertation, Yale University 1954), p. 146; see also Broderick, *Right Reverend New Dealer,* pp. 152–53.

Progressive ideas. This Progressive conditioning in Ryan's intellectual development is vitally important for understanding his thought and for evaluating his achievement for two reasons. First, Ryan's reformist sympathies led him away from the approaches to a Catholic reconciliation with America pursued by the ideological genealogists who sought to prove the direct derivation of the thought of the Founding Fathers from Catholic sources and from those who wished to argue for a common heritage. In both of these approaches, Catholic scholarship almost necessarily had to canonize, at least by implication, a Lockean natural law ethic. As a Progressive, Ryan had nothing but disdain for such thought. He did not wish to prove that the entire American tradition of political thought was identical to the Catholic tradition but merely to demonstrate a congruence between American reformist thought on social and political matters and the Catholic (Leonine) tradition. (For him, the point of contact between American and Catholic thought was located in the Progressives' frankly revisionist understanding of the meaning of American values.) In a sense, then, Ryan's goal was more modest than that of other Catholic scholars. Second, his reformist background undeniably led him to downplay differences between Leo and the Progressives in areas such as state intervention. In a sense, then, Ryan was as selective in his reading of Leo as were his conservative contemporaries who derived an exactly opposite lesson from *Rerum Novarum.* This selectivity was the negative result of his Progressive conditioning. Both of these aspects of his intellectual background made Ryan a double revisionist: as a Progressive, he insisted on redefining the meaning of the republic's founding documents; and as a Progressive he was led to read Leo XIII from a distinctly American point of view. Ryan himself was blind to this conditioning. He firmly maintained that his thought was truly derived from that of Leo XIII.

Ryan derived immense encouragement from his reading of Leo's works. He also discovered a challenge that was to consume a lifetime of labor: the double task of bringing the American church into line with Leo's insights and coincidentally of increasing its sympathy for reform. In 1894, however, Ryan's fascination with the positive reform ideas of *Rerum Novarum* was purely personal, for the American church as a whole construed the document in a fairly narrow, antisocialist light and thus ignored the enormous potential it contained for formulating a positive American Catholic social program. The loneliness of Ryan's position is readily apparent. It was one thing for a seminarian to be personally convinced that the church should be concerned with social justice but quite another to convince a laggard national church first, that she should embrace this mission and second, that she could do so through a collaboration with the Populist and/or Progressive reformers whom she feared and distrusted. Therefore, before 1919 (and indeed until his death), Ryan devoted himself to persuading the church to assume her rightful and critical role in industrial society. To accomplish this twofold work, Ryan had squarely to face the fundamental challenge of helping the American church recover her own natural law heritage. In addressing himself to this challenge, Ryan turned for guidance and encouragement to the man in whose works and method he had discovered a convergence between the Populist orientation of his youth and the Catholic tradition, Pope Leo XIII. Taking his cue from Leo, he resolved to immerse himself in the study of Thomist philosophy, in the hope of freeing the church from the sterility of her recent social thought. Thereafter, using the language of Thomas and Leo, Ryan outlined the bases for moral judgment, demonstrated the flexibility of traditional norms of morality when these were stated in contemporary terms, and exhorted the church to assume a critical, Leo-inspired mission in industrial society. As he developed his arguments, Ryan hoped coincidentally to bring the church to see its common ground with Progressivism, a realization that he arrived at through the use of the church's own heritage of social and political thought.

To illustrate Ryan's approach to these multiple challenges, one must understand his recovery, understanding, and articulation of the main points of the church's natural law heritage; his Leo-inspired translation of these concepts into contemporary terms that would facilitate the church's mission of social criticism; and his use of his own understanding of Leo's works to invite the church to a full and fruitful collaboration with America's reformers.

Since Leonine Thomism was the source of Ryan's method and the basis of his social criticism, it is important to understand the distinguishing characteristics of this revitalized scholasticism. As William M. Halsey notes, neo-Thomism was anything but a slavish repetition of Saint Thomas's words: "Rather than a strictly literal interpretation of Thomistic philosophy, there appeared an adventuresome quality of mind among Catholics in both Europe and America. Though the appeal for this opening toward modern culture was based on papal encyclicals and orthodox authority, the results were often unexpectedly revolutionary." The reason for these revolutionary results was, as Gerardo Bruni points out, that the real legacy of Thomas cherished by the new Thomists was the spirit behind the text rather than the text itself: "For the rest, the return to Saint Thomas as desired by Leo XIII . . . should consist in a return to the teaching of Saint Thomas, but much more in a return to his spirit and his method of working."[51]

This distinction of letter and spirit may at first seem mundane—even obvious—but realizations consequent to it enabled the new scholasticism to liberate itself from deadening repetition and to soar above merely derivative thought. The separation of spirit and letter allowed the new scholastics to see that the specifics of Thomas's systematic thought were historically conditioned: "It is obvious that the Scholasticism which will achieve this work of renovation will be and at the same time will no longer be the Scholasticism of Saint Thomas. That is, the Thomistic system will continue to live in this renewed Scholasticism up to a certain point. The renewal of Scholasticism must inevitably bring with it a certain abandonment of the Thomistic system, but not the abandonment of the soul that upholds and confers a high historical significance on the entire work of Aquinas."[52]

The understanding that Thomas's works were conditioned by the historical circumstances of the thirteenth century was lib-

51. Halsey, *Survival of American Innocence,* p. 140; Gerardo Bruni, *Progressive Scholasticism,* trans. John S. Zybura (St. Louis: B. Herder, 1929), pp. 115–16. Josiah Royce acknowledged both the wisdom of the new Scholastic appeal to Thomas's spirit and the potency of the same spirit: "Saint Thomas' spirit is more potent than his letter, that the application of this spirit of inquiry to modern problems has indeed brought you into closer touch with the intellectual issues of the day" (quoted in Halsey, *Survival of American Innocence,* p. 140).

52. Bruni, *Progressive Scholasticism,* p. 125.

erating as well as challenging. If Thomas was thus limited, it would be patently absurd to repeat his directives to a radically changed world. Thus attention was shifted away (though not entirely) from the Thomistic corpus to Thomas the man and to his intentions. Hence Bruni postulated that Thomas would never have been so brash as to expect that his thought would stand unchanged: "Who will still dare maintain that Saint Thomas intended his system, marvelous though it was in its way and in its day, to be a rigid and a closed system? His synthesis, his doctrinal framework, is supple and open." The new scholastics thus distinguished two aspects of Thomistic method: a methodological predisposition and a procedural method. As for the first aspect, the new scholastics believed that Thomas showed an openness that allowed him to embrace and to baptize the philosophical currents of his day; hence they revered Thomas for his synthetic approach to knowledge. As for procedure, the new scholastics believed that Thomas used his synthetic system to confront contemporary problems; hence they honored him for what they believed to be his openness to the world and his practical approach to moral problems. In this way, the appreciation of the historical conditioning of Thomas's thought allowed the new Thomists to justify their program on the basis of a sophisticated appeal to Thomas's spirit of inquiry. Against this background, John Zybura enunciated the goals and methods of the neo-Thomists: "In a word, the aims and ideals of the Neo Scholastics is to penetrate ever deeper into the deep thought of the great Scholastics of the past, to re-think and reinterpret it, whenever necessary, in reference to the new conquests and new problems, with fine discernment to search out the true in the old and the true in the new, thoroughly to assimilate both, and then to labor earnestly to contribute his share toward the eventual elaboration of a richer and more fruitful synthesis than has yet been achieved."[53]

It must not be assumed, however, that these liberated neo-Thomists were willing altogether to jettison the thought or letter of Saint Thomas. Quite the contrary. Along with their papal patron, Leo XIII, they revered Thomas for his brilliant exposition and explanation of the principles of natural law. They clung

53. Ibid., p. xxv; Zybura, *Present-Day Thinkers*, p. 477.

tenaciously to his first and transcendent moral principles because they believed that such principles gave firm objective grounding to their reflections. Their freedom in Thomas's spirit was thus more in the areas of the translation of the meaning of these principles into modern parlance and their application to modern industrial situations than it was a complete liberation from the influence of Thomas's works. Indeed, James Ryan maintained that the grounding in objective first principles made the new scholasticism an especially potent lever of social criticism: "I do not think it too strong an assertion to contend that the New Scholasticism has more to offer philosophy in the field of ethics than in any other field. The theoretical basis of its formulations is essentially sound. The practical application of these principles to present-day conditions of industry, politics, social life, education and religious belief is easy to make. A large and respected wing of Neo-Scholastic thought is hard at work in Europe and America making such applications, following the lead of Pope Leo XIII."[54] Ryan embraced the program of the new scholastics. He was supremely confident that his use of its system and method would give him remarkable critical powers in social discourse and social reform.

For Ryan, as for his new scholastic colleagues, there were two poles to Thomism that made it attractive as the basis for social theory and civil discourse: the objective and universal principles of natural law and the elastic and creative application of these principles to modern social conditions. (This latter aspect involved the audacious translation of the principles into modern idioms that went as far as monetary quantification in the case of Ryan's own work on the living wage.) A brief exposition of Ryan's ethical thought will illuminate the ways he pursued his task of breathing life into the Thomistic system and the ways he arrived at a thoroughly Catholic understanding of the state's role in social welfare which was strikingly similar to the Progressive stance.

As did all the neo-Thomists, Ryan believed that the ultimate authority of the natural law was that it was rooted in God and that this foundation not only ensured an ultimate authorization

54. James H. Ryan, "The New Scholasticism and Its Contribution to Modern Thought," in Zybura, ed., *Present-Day Thinkers*, p. 367.

but also bestowed an incontrovertible objectivity and immutability on its commands. In Ryan's mind, this objectivity of natural law morality was especially attractive and useful for social criticism because its immutable principles alone were capable of rescuing humanity from the dangerous moral relativism of modern society and modern philosophy.[55]

Objectivity did not exhaust the potential practical benefits of the natural law morality of Thomistic thought. Although the ultimate source of morality is found in God, Ryan believed that the norms of morality were, as Patrick W. Gearty says, more proximately and indeed universally available to man through the revelatory medium of nature in general and human nature in particular: "The moral law—at least the main tenets of it—can also be known in another manner, for the divine reason and will of the Creator are expressed in the nature of the things which He created. Consequently, a thorough study of man's nature reveals the law of nature according to which man must act to be truly human. A close examination of man's nature reveals that man is a reasonable or rational being and that there exists in him a hierarchy of faculties that must be ordered by reason if man is to be true to his nature."[56]

As a result of his reflection on the nature of man, Ryan concluded that the goal of life and the end for which man was created was a right and reasonable life, and he canonized this norm of right and reasonable life as the criterion by which personal decisions and social actions might be judged: "Since man is a reasonable being, all his acts ought to be directed to an end which is reasonable."[57] This rather vague insistence that the morality of all human actions was to be judged on the basis of their promotion of reasonable life reveals the elasticity of Ryan's system. Canonizing the promotion of reasonable human life as the criterion for moral judgment bestowed and demanded a certain latitude of judgment within the natural law framework and demanded ingenuity and adaptability on the part of the ethi-

55. John A. Ryan and Morris Hillquit, *Socialism: Promise or Menace?* (New York: Macmillan, 1914), p. 1; John A. Ryan and Francis J. Boland, *Catholic Principles of Politics* (New York: Macmillan, 1940), p. 1.

56. Gearty, *Economic Thought of Ryan*, pp. 100–102.

57. John A. Ryan, *The New Norm of Morality: Defined and Applied to Particular Actions* (Washington: National Catholic Welfare Conference, 1944), p. 7.

cian. Ryan displayed sufficient creativity and elasticity to allow him to breathe life into the Thomistic morality he inherited from Leo XIII. He based his ethical prescriptions for the industrial world on his consideration of the contemporary meaning and content of those human rights which the natural law ethicians identified as aids to the achievement of man's end: a right and reasonable life.

In order that man might attain the life called for by his nature, Ryan maintained that man was endowed by nature (and by God) with certain rights which were the means to the attainment of his end and which he defined as follows: "Natural rights are the necessary means of right and reasonable living. They are essential to the welfare of a human being—a person. They exist and are sacred and inviolable because the welfare of the person exists—as a fact of the ideal order and is sacred and an inviolable thing." In a sense, Ryan's discussion of natural rights forms the basis of his system. Therefore, he devoted a great deal of time and energy to defining these rights and fencing them round with all the authority that natural law thought could provide. Ryan announced, in effect, that these rights are not negotiable. They are simply facts of the natural order. Further, because they inhere in man because of who he is by nature and by God's will, Ryan insisted that they could never be revoked or abridged by human will or by the actions of agencies erected by man. In this regard, Ryan said, "His [man's] worth and his place in the universe are to be measured with reference to himself, not with reference to other men, or to institutions, or to states. He is worth while for his own sake." Having thus provided strong natural and divine protection for human rights, Ryan then went about the delicate task of defining or enumerating man's natural rights. In this endeavor, Ryan was evidently of two minds. On one hand, he believed that human rights were as numerous and as extensive as the needs man experiences in his struggle for a right and reasonable life. On the other hand, because the strong have a tendency to abridge the rights of the weak and thus demean sacred human personality, all in the name of the promotion of their own natural rights, Ryan, following the line of thought of the Progressives, believed that natural rights had to be defined carefully: "Man's natural rights must not be so widely interpreted that the strong and the cunning, and the unscrupulous will be able, under the pretext of liberty, to exploit and overreach the weak and simple and honest majority."[58] Ryan resolved this tension between the desire to define natural rights extensively or expansively, and the desire to thwart the designs of the cunning, by establishing or recognizing a hierarchy of rights (according to which the basic right to life took precedence over the right to profit or property), which could be used in sorting out the various claims of contending groups.

In his fundamental thought, then, Ryan discovered and articulated the keystone of his ethical system: the nature of man was sacred because it was created by God and destined for life—reasonable life. From this fundamental truth followed the ethical principle that the universally equal dignity of the human person (his person and his rights) had to be preserved and fostered. Any actions that violated that dignity or abridged the rights supporting or ensuring its maintenance were to be condemned in the strongest possible way. At the most basic level, then, Ryan discovered a significant point of contact between the Catholic and American reform systems of thought: both were insistent that the dignity of the individual was inviolable.

Although Ryan's strong championship of the rights of the individual might lead one to suspect that he would advocate an atomistic existence for humanity, he believed (following the tradition of the church) that man was required by his nature to live a social life, for apart from society, man could not obtain the attributes necessary for reasonable life.[59]

Social living, however, is not possible without an agency of order and authority. Therefore, man must have a state. Since this impulse to live in a state comes from man's nature, the authority of the state comes ultimately from God, and this authority acts through laws that promote man's end: "The authority of the State to make laws is derived from God. He has endowed men with such qualities and needs that they cannot live

58. John A. Ryan, *A Living Wage: Its Ethical and Economic Aspects* (New York: Macmillan, 1906), pp. 44, 64; John A. Ryan, *The Church and Socialism and Other Essays* (Washington: The University Press, 1919), p. 59.

59. Leo XIII, "The Christian Constitution of States," in John A. Ryan and Moorhouse F. X. Millar, *The State and the Church* (New York: Macmillan, 1922), p. 2.

reasonable lives without the State. Therefore, He wishes the State to exist and function in such a way as to attain this end, to promote man's temporal welfare. It does so by means of law." For Ryan, then, the state was necessary, and its authority was both real and binding. This does not, however, mean either that the state is above the law or that the state is the final arbiter of right and wrong. Rather, the state stands under the law and can and must be judged according to the principles of the natural law.[60] This firm stance provided a lever of criticism against willful actions and irresponsible refusals on the part of the state to fulfill the functions assigned it by nature and nature's law. In addition, Ryan's natural law philosophical background informed his articulation of the duties of the state.

In entering into or establishing a society or state, a man does not, in Ryan's eyes, surrender any of his natural rights. Natural rights inhere in human nature and are inviolable. Hence, in the ontological order, they exist prior to and remain independent of the will of the state. Because of his insistence on the priority and independence of natural rights, Ryan assigned to the state the duty of promoting human welfare: "The purpose of government is to promote the common good, which means in the concrete, the welfare of all individuals";[61] and this promotion of

60. John A. Ryan, "The Moral Obligation of Civil Law," *Catholic World,* October 1921, p. 73. Ryan contrasted this situation with that of the amoral view of the state that informed American political theory: "The concept of sovereignty accepted in our tradition in political science derives mainly from the English writer, John Austin. In essence it declares that the sovereign power of the State is incapable of legal limitation. . . . The mischief begins as soon as the word legal in Austin's definition, is taken to include all kinds of law, moral as well as political or civil. . . . It means that the State is not subject to the moral law, nor bound by the laws of God" (John A. Ryan, "A New Theory of Political Sovereignty," *Catholic World,* November 1917, pp. 237–38).

61. John A. Ryan, "Assaults upon Our Civil Liberties," *Catholic Charities Review* 7, no. 2 (1923): 17. Elsewhere, Ryan reflected on the concept of the common good: "Taking then, the two words, 'common good,' as the most concise expression of the purpose for which the State exists and functions, let us ask ourselves first, what are the beneficial objects denoted by the term 'good'? They are all the great classes of temporal goods; that is, all the things that man needs for existence and development of this life. . . . That all these objects are conducive to human welfare is self-evident; that none of them can be adequately attained without the assistance of the State, is fully demonstrated by experience; that they all come within the proper scope and end of the State is the obvious conclusion" (John A. Ryan, "The Purpose of the State," *Catholic World,* March 1921, p. 811).

the common good boils down, not surprisingly, to a strenuous defense of man's natural rights: "The business of the State then is to protect men in their enjoyment of those opportunities that are essential to right and reasonable life. They may be summed up in the phrase, natural rights."[62] The implications of such a perception are clear and startling. By assigning the state the role of protecting human rights, Ryan was clearly going beyond a merely negative and juridical definition of the function of the state. Indeed, he opened up the possibility—even the necessity—of the state's engaging in the formulation of positive legislation for the promotion and not merely the protection of human rights, a stance he defended on the basis of Catholic teaching: "The positive promotion of general welfare is regarded by the Catholic writers as normal and necessary, because required by the fundamental needs of human beings."[63] Further, such a belief stood in marked contrast to nineteenth-century American Catholic fears of overweening state powers.[64] Finally, the assignment of such a large role to the state in the establishment and maintenance of a just social order was at one with the Progressive view of the function of the state.[65] Hence, on the purely personal philosophical level, Ryan was building Catholic bridges to the Progressive position.

In published articles, books, and numerous lectures, Ryan publicized his recovery of the neo-Thomistic foundations of Catholic political and social thought, and in this way he met the first and most fundamental of the myriad challenges confronting him in his attempt to bring the church into the social

62. Ryan, *Living Wage*, p. 301.

63. Ryan and Millar, *State and Church*, p. 224.

64. John W. Gouldrick, "John A. Ryan's Theory of the State" (Ph.D. dissertation, Catholic University of America, 1979), p. 177.

65. Ryan was not willing to surrender complete authority to the state, nor was his support of state activity unconditional. With many Catholics, he distrusted the tendency of the state to become omnicompetent. Therefore, he insisted that in any conflict between the claims of the government and the individual, the supreme value of the individual's sacred rights was to take precedence: "The 'common good' is not to be conceived in such a collective, or general, or organic way as to ignore the welfare of concrete human beings, individually considered" (Ryan and Millar, *State and Church*, p. 204). For Ryan, there was to be a careful balance of the common good and individual rights, with the balance always clearly in favor of individual rights, which are the foundation of human life and human society.

reformers' camp. This recovery of the foundations of Catholic social thought was, however, only the first step in a far more ambitious undertaking: Ryan had yet to demonstrate fully both the contemporary critical utility of traditional Catholic thought and the compatibility of the Catholic and American reform traditions.

Although Ryan was a moral theologian, he was not content to allow the natural law morality he derived from Leo and the new Thomists to remain an abstract system. The ultimate goal of his moralizing was application: the true test of the power and adequacy of any moral theology was its ability to judge and guide industrial life. In other words, a moral system's critical social utility was all-important.[66] Following the example of Leo, he sought to show how fundamental and generally accepted (dare I say self-evident) natural law principles, if translated into terms drawn from the conditions of industrial life, could be used to make moral judgments on and suggest solutions to contemporary problems. Although for genuinely intellectual (he truly admired Leo) and strategic (following the 1899 condemnation of Americanism and the 1907 condemnation of Modernism, it was prudent to call attention to the safe papal roots of all that he said) reasons, Ryan staunchly insisted that everything he said regarding practical solutions to industrial abuses was rooted in Leo's thought, actually his work was also informed by his own principle of expediency, which, as Charles Curran notes, he developed in response to his perception that social utility was an absolute essential for any moral theology: "Ryan added his own distinctive development to the basic natural law emphasis on harmony and balance—the principle of expediency. The ultimate test of the morality of any social system is its bearing on human welfare. In the matter of social institutions, moral values and genuine expediency are in the long run identical." As Curran points out, the enunciation of this principle grew out of a realization of the limits of philosophical theology adequately to equip the church for the work of ethical criticism in an industrial situation: "Ryan was an economist and acknowledged the limits of dealing with ethical problems merely in the light of philosophy and theology. The

66. O'Brien, *American Catholics and Social Reform,* p. 124.

acceptance of the public welfare as the determining criterion, the principle of expediency and the use of economics to determine what was expedient in practice all characterized his . . . understanding of natural law"[67] and a coincident realization that the ultimate good was probably never attainable. Thus the principle of expediency operates as a mediating, moderating element in his thought. An appreciation of its operation in Ryan's thought allows one to understand both his passionate commitment to the ultimate goal of the establishment of justice[68] and the ease with which he could shift his support from one means of achieving this goal to another. It also accounts for the pragmatic and gradualist approach that marked both his thought and his activities, for as Karl Cerny notes, "his interest was fixed upon what was feasible and would represent a partial step toward justice."[69] Significantly, in the Progressive era, his principle of expediency led him to highlight the ways in which concrete Progressive strategies answered the needs uncovered by his natural law–based analysis of the industrial world. As a result, it was at this second, more practically oriented stage of Ryan's work that the groundwork for greater cooperation between the church and the Progressive reformers was laid and Ryan's Progressively conditioned approach to the Leonine corpus is most evident.

Informed by his understanding of Leo and guided by the operation of his own principle of expediency, Ryan addressed himself to the task of demonstrating the critical social utility of traditional natural law thought. As a result of his reading of *Rerum Novarum,* Ryan isolated two key natural law ideas which he believed should inform the church's criticism of existing social structures and guide her choice of remedies to the evils arising from those conditions. The first principle, which

67. Charles E. Curran, "American and Catholic: American Catholic Social Ethics, 1880–1965," *Thought* 52 (1977): 57, 59. Hereafter, the term *expediency* will be used in Curran's sense.

68. According to Gearty, "The unifying factor in Ryan's entire treatment of economics was his practical objective—he had an intense desire to establish economic justice and defend the rights of the underprivileged, especially the rights of the propertyless wage earners of our present industrial system" (*Economic Thought of Ryan,* p. 298).

69. Cerny, "Monsignor John A. Ryan," p. 147.

Ryan spent a lifetime laboring to have recognized as a canonical principle of Catholic social teaching, was that of the living wage. For Ryan, the living wage doctrine translated the meaning of the human right to life into economic and industrial terms,[70] which translation, because it was at once rooted in an absolute belief in the dignity of the human person and an equally resolute insistence that this dignity be protected and promoted in a specifically industrial society, demonstrated both the contemporary critical leverage and the objective power of natural law morality. In all of Ryan's reflections and writings following his encounter with *Rerum Novarum* in 1894, this principle formed the basis of his critique of American industry, which, following the dictates of classical economic thought, treated labor as a commodity and set wage rates with reference to market forces but without reference to the laborers' right to a reasonable life.

In addition, from his reading of Leo's labor encyclical, Ryan came to believe that because the individual worker was no match for the power of capital in fighting for a living wage, he could have recourse to two major secular agencies that could help him protect his rights—labor unions and the state—and that the decision to use one and then the other of these agencies was to be made upon pragmatic considerations of expediency and optimal efficacy. It is clear that although he advocated that men first resort to unions to amplify their voices and make their demands stronger (reasoning that "it is better that men should do things for themselves than that the state should do things for them") Ryan favored the use of the power of the state to effect social change and secure social justice because "we know from abundant experience that the labor unions of the United States are not able to effect the reforms in industrial

70. Ryan pointed out that in an industrial society, the natural right to life could be actualized only by granting a living wage: "The laborer has a right to a decent livelihood; but in the present industrial order his sole means of realizing this lies in his wage; therefore, he has a right to a living wage" ("The 'Living Wage' Philosophy," in *American Catholic Thought on Social Questions*, ed. Aaron I. Abell [Indianapolis: Bobbs-Merrill, 1968], p. 239). Since the right to life is unconditional and ontologically prior to the employer's right to a profit, in any conflict of these rights, that of the laborer clearly takes precedence. This reasoning led him to believe that current wage strategies were in violation of natural law.

conditions which are urgently demanded. We must have recourse to the state."[71] Expediency led him to advocate state intervention as the final and sure cure for social ills.[72] Thus he called for the erection of a regulatory welfare state that would meet the needs of the time: "Let me point out the two great evils of the present situation: first, millions of the poorest paid laborers are insufficiently protected against the unjust conditions of life and employment, and second, immense masses of fortunately placed capital receive excessive and unnecessary profits or interest. Neither of these evils can be adequately met except by the action of public authority, the state."[73] Indeed, on the basis of a pragmatic evaluation of the ways of power and the needs of the day, Ryan wished to elevate the idea that the state should play a powerful positive role in social reform and welfare to semicanonical status in the Catholic tradition.

Because he realized that such an embrace of state intervention was at odds with the conservative sympathies of the American church of his time,[74] in his writings on this subject he justified all of his ideas proximately by appealing to the authority of Leo XIII's writings and ultimately by appealing to the general natural law understanding of the positive functions of the state. He argued that the demand of the natural law that the state protect natural rights and the common good translated in practical terms into a belief that the state assume a Progressive-sounding regulatory and welfare role in industrial society. Moreover, Ryan believed that Leo's enunciation of the principle of state intervention jettisoned forever the traditional Catholic idea that the works of charity could overcome social ills in an industrial world: "The authoritative refutation and overthrow of the assumption that industrial evils were to be overcome entirely by beneficence on the one hand and resignation on the other, is probably the greatest of the salutary effects of *Rerum*

71. John A. Ryan, "The Need of Legal Standards of Protection for Labor," *American Labor Legislation Review* 11 (1921): 222.

72. As David O'Brien puts it, "It was Ryan's preoccupation with the pervasive individualism of American society and his ever-increasing consciousness of the power of the business community that led him to deprecate the fears of his fellow Catholics concerning excessive government power" (*American Catholics and Social Reform*, p. 139).

73. Ryan, *Church and Socialism*, p. 45.

74. Ryan, *Social Doctrine*, p. 44.

Novarum."[75] Clearly, Ryan was using Leo's ideas to move the church toward greater sympathy with the environmental approach to poverty and its alleviation, a stance which coincided with that of the Progressives.[76]

Ryan thus met the second challenge that had confronted him at the outset of his career—he succeeded in demonstrating the power and ability of traditional natural law morality adequately—even powerfully—to criticize modern industrial conditions and to suggest approaches and agencies capable of correcting abusive practices. Moreover, he did so in a way that proved that the church could and should, on the basis of her own natural law political thought and moral theology, make common cause with the Progressives as they agitated for the erection of a regulatory and welfare state capable of furthering the cause of social justice. He was convinced of the congruence of the two traditions.

On the basis of these convictions, Ryan's personal concern for social justice developed quickly, and the hallmarks of his mature and Progressive-sounding program developed early. In his dissertation (1906) he dealt with the moral foundations of the living wage doctrine, and in 1911 he authored a minimum wage bill for the Minnesota legislature. In 1909 he wrote a two-part

75. Ryan, "Some Effects of *Rerum Novarum,*" p. 58.

76. Ryan's arguments for state intervention for the establishment of social justice were, however, markedly different from those of the Progressives. The Progressive reformers distrusted the unions because they represented a base of power that was selfish and at odds with the good of the "people." The Progressives hence placed all their trust in the neutral arbitration of a state that was above special interests and responsive to the needs of all the people. Ryan arrived at his advocacy of reform by legislation by a contradictory route. He did not shy away from the unions as instruments of reform because they were too powerful but because they were not powerful enough and hence unable to effect any real changes in the social order. In America's industrial society, only the state had the power effectively to control corporate avarice and protect the working poor. Therefore, it was on the purely pragmatic grounds of what Cerny calls his principle of expediency (see "Monsignor John A. Ryan," pp. 144–45) that Ryan opted for reform by legislation rather than through the activities of the unions: the state alone was powerful enough to counter corporate power. The lesser and voluntary agencies and individual actions advocated by Leo as the agents of first resort for the establishment of social justice were not so much thoughtlessly dismissed by Ryan as they were thoughtfully judged insufficient to accomplish the difficult task of forcing change upon reluctant capital. Circumstances and a keen appreciation of what was possible in any given situation dictated Ryan's choice of agencies for social change.

article for the *Catholic World* which summarized his thought on social concerns and advocated a program of reform by legislation. The article reveals that Ryan had already embraced an almost completely Progressive platform. In discussing the causes of the economic evils from which American society suffered, Ryan made the significant gesture of recounting and making his own the diagnosis offered by the Progressive John Graham Brooks, which centered on the disparity of wealth from which America suffered and the resultant degrading depression of the workers. Even more significantly, Ryan espoused legislation as the means for achieving two of the cherished Progressive goals of creating a regulatory and a welfare state. At the core of Ryan's Progressive program stood a demand for a legal minimum wage, which he defended on the basis of his usual natural law principles. Thereafter, Ryan proposed a variety of legislative measures for the establishment of social justice, among them legislation to effect an eight-hour day; laws governing working conditions for women and children that were justified on humanitarian grounds; the establishment of labor boards to ensure and enforce the implementation of fair labor practices; the creation of employment agencies; the adoption of "social insurance"; public housing for poor workers; and the public ownership of utilities and natural monopolies. In short, Ryan proposed a fully Progressive program for social reform. He contrasted this moderate program of reform with a socialist approach and defended it as a compilation of "all the legislative proposals that seem sound and worth striving for at the present time."[77] Ryan had entered the Progressive fold wholeheartedly.

In these early phases of his work, Ryan performed a twofold service for the American Catholic community as it struggled to locate itself in the American mainstream: one (and by far the more important) intellectual and the other practical and personal. Intellectually, under the spell (and protection) of Leo XIII's call for a revival of scholastic thought, Ryan had been forced to return to the wellsprings of Catholic social thought—natural law theory—to seek sustenance for his work and au-

77. John A. Ryan, "A Programme of Social Reform by Legislation," *Catholic World*, July 1909, pp. 433–44; August 1909, pp. 608–14. These articles formed the basis for Ryan's later thoughts on reconstruction of the social order.

thority for his words. As William Halsey points out, this return to Thomism was a surprisingly fruitful source for deriving a moral vocabulary for dialogue with American culture: "The relationship between Thomism, the American Enlightenment and the Scottish Common Sense Realism of the early nineteenth century was comfortable enough for Catholics to feel a spiritual and intellectual bond with the thinking of most of the founding Fathers and Protestant theorists before the Civil War. . . . The methodology and presuppositions of Scholastic and the new Thomistic philosophy provided the intellectual means for Catholics to appropriate large areas of the American experience without threat of appearing radical."[78] Ryan was encouraged by the congruence he discovered between the foundations of Catholic and American reformist social thought (which framed its proposals in terms of the natural law–natural rights language of the Founding Fathers and the fundamental, normative documents of the republic as they understood them), and on the basis of this perceived similarity he constructed an intellectual bridge between the two traditions.

His personal service to the reconciliation of the two traditions was also important. In a sense, he was an ambassador who shuttled between the Catholic and American reform traditions. Realizing, as Abell notes, that "Catholics alone, no matter how socially enlightened they might become, were powerless to transform the social order,"[79] Ryan joined men and women of other faiths and of no faith to bring about the realization of justice. In this common task, Ryan shared with his colleagues a belief in the efficacy of gradual reform, a faith in the power of the state to realize reform, and a hope for the establishment of a classless society.

While Ryan was making common cause with the reformers and demonstrating to the church that there was nothing to fear

78. Halsey, *Survival of American Innocence*, p. 4. Charles Curran says with regard to the discovery of the congruence between the two traditions: "Catholic theology itself provided an impetus to the approach which saw basic compatibility between the American ethos and environment and the Catholic understanding. Methodologically, Catholic social ethics especially from the time of Leo XIII had been developing in terms of natural law theory" ("American and Catholic," pp. 53–54).

79. Aaron I. Abell, "Monsignor John A. Ryan: An Historical Appreciation," *Review of Politics* 8 (1946):131.

and much to gain from such collaboration, his natural law training led him to lecture the church on its duties concerning social reform. In this way, he shouldered the last crucial challenge of his multifaceted task, that of moving the church into a position of sympathy with the American reform camp. It must be remembered that in the years following the turn of the century, the church was shy of involvement in social concerns. When she did involve herself in such matters, her approach was noticeably lacking in commitment and passion. To move the church off dead center on social issues, Ryan returned once again to the scholastic roots of the church's philosophical tradition. He reminded the church that according to this tradition, she was the guardian and authoritative interpreter of morality.[80] Therefore, Ryan told the church that it was her duty to apply the moral law to all human endeavors, especially to the human activities of the economic sphere:

> The mission of the Church is to teach and help men to save their souls, to make men fit for the Kingdom of Heaven. They save their souls not by faith alone (the Protestant notion) but by works, by conduct. They must not only believe correctly but live righteously. Now righteous living takes in the whole field of human action. It is not confined to those of man's actions which affect merely himself and his God. . . . It concerns those actions which have an economic character. . . . In a word, all free human actions . . . come under the control of the moral law; and the teaching and application of the moral law is the business of the Church.[81]

True to his own neo-Thomistic heritage, Ryan assured the church that she had a ready vehicle for this critical task in her own natural law vocabulary and tradition: "These doctrines of the sacredness of life, equality of rights, etc. have lost none of their efficacy or appropriateness. All that is necessary is that they be applied specifically and in detail to the new conditions."[82] Ryan reasoned that since the church had the mission to

80. Not even the state was immune to the critical judgment of the church, at least in Ryan's mind: "It is true that the actions of the State, whether in the field of legislation or administration, have moral aspects, inasmuch as they are human actions; therefore, they are in some manner subject to the Church as the interpreter of the moral law" (Ryan and Millar, *State and Church*, p. 42).

81. Ryan, *Declining Liberty*, p. 181.

82. Ryan, *Church and Socialism*, p. 52.

apply the moral law to all aspects of life, and since modern life was dominated by economic considerations, she was required to enter into a ministry of criticism with regard to industrial affairs. He went so far as to say, "If the Church did not provide guidance in this field, she would neglect one of her most important duties."[83] In essence, Ryan was reminding the church that if she failed to exercise her critical teaching mission, she would be liable to judgment. To this principled argument, Ryan added an ominously practical note: "Unless the clergy shall be able and willing to understand, appreciate and sympathetically direct the aspirations of economic democracy, it will inevitably become more and more unchristian and pervert all too rapidly a larger and larger proportion of our Catholic population."[84]

In goading the church toward a more active social ministry, Ryan expanded on his prescription for the church. He outlined a three-part mission that would allow the Church to enter confidently into her task of practical social criticism and social action. Building on his simple statement mentioned above, he maintained that the church could fulfill her mission "by applying the general principles of morality to particular economic practices; by passing judgment upon the morality of particular methods and measures of reform and by advocating and urging the adoption of certain methods and measures."[85] As time went on and Ryan became more and more convinced that the problems of poverty were environmental,[86] he became more and more insistent that the church allow his own principle of expediency to direct and mediate her choice and advocacy of reform measures: "It is quite natural and eminently desirable that the authorities of the Church should on opportune occasions urge

83. John A. Ryan, "The Teaching of the Catholic Church," *Annals of the American Academy of Political and Social Science* 103 (1922):80.

84. John A. Ryan, "The Church and the Workingman," *Catholic World*, September 1909, p. 782.

85. Ryan, *Declining Liberty*, p. 183.

86. As early as 1894, Ryan had come to believe that the church had to adopt an institutional and systemic approach to social questions. In his journal, he said, "She [the church] will make this universal longing for the brotherhood and better conditions of life her own, approving it where it is right, and pointing the way to the highest practical realization. To do this, she must deal with institutions and systems, not with individuals" (Journal entry, 21 November 1894, Ryan Papers, Box B2-32, ACUA).

the adoption of particular methods of reform which they know to be morally right and which they believe to be actually expedient. It is quite unnatural and not at all desirable that they should maintain a specious attitude of neutrality."[87] Through such arguments, Ryan hoped to move the church toward a realistic collaboration with any and all reforming groups that advocated measures that could be justified on the basis of Catholic natural law morality. In the Progressive era, this plainly meant that the church should join with the Progressives, whose platform called for the establishment of a social system that more closely approximated a just order than did that of autocratic capital. Realistic yet principled expediency demanded that the church not merely speak for reform, but that she do so with a Progressive accent.

Ryan was a lonely pioneer. In an address at Boston's Old South Church in 1917, he obliquely described his role in the church and summarized his dream: "The way in which any new social idea, or social application of an idea, or piece of philosophy becomes current in Catholic thought, is through the instrumentality of individuals here and there who take up these things and make the application. And after the sufficient time has elapsed and these applications seem to have stood the test of time, it is commonly accepted that the idea is all right and that there is nothing in it contrary to Catholic theory."[88]

These were the words of a pioneer with a touch of the visionary and a great deal of realism. In the years before 1919, Ryan was laying the foundation for a thoroughly Catholic approach to reform which grew out of an appreciation of natural law. This intellectual groundwork held great promise for the social mission of the American church. It could replace the fear-based motivation behind her prior social involvement with a basis of passionate conviction. Further, Ryan demonstrated on these same Catholic grounds not only that the church had urgent reason to espouse social justice crusades, but also that the Catholic care for natural rights should lead logically and pragmatically in an industrial society to greater and greater dependence on the

87. John A. Ryan, "The Church and the Social Question," address, n.d., Ryan Papers, Box B2-24, ACUA.

88. Quoted in Broderick, *Right Reverend New Dealer,* p. 109.

regulatory and welfare state as the proper agent for the protection and promotion of these rights. In other words, he provided a Catholic justification for two of the major concerns of the Progressive reformers. He offered the church an avenue to self-confident action in social matters through a program that was demonstrably Catholic and truly American. Thus, two of the great barriers to Catholic reform action—fear of Rome's displeasure and alienation from the American host culture—were removed. There remained only the barrier of the church's internal fragmentation. In this regard, Ryan was powerless.

Although John A. Ryan was the most articulate of the American Catholics asking for a fresh and less beleagured look at social questions, there were others whose concerns, insights, and work were also laying the foundations for a new Catholic approach to industrial problems. These men, like Ryan, were not averse to cooperating with the aims and methods of Protestant reformers in an effort to relieve the distress of the urban masses, many of whom were Roman Catholics.[89] In their reform proposals, they did not advocate radical changes in the social structure, but rather called for moderate changes in the functioning capitalistic system of America.

Catholic reformers had their reasons for calling for a fresh Catholic approach to social problems. The narrow American Catholic reading of *Rerum Novarum* had led the church to limit her social action ministry to combating socialism. As Edward Roddy points out, the fear of socialism had led to an embarrassing situation. Although Catholics in general and the Catholic press in particular recognized "the need for legislation to remedy or ameliorate the injustice of the economic and social order, the Catholic press was generally fearful that such action would lead to socialism, state paternalism or worse still, a monolithic state. This ambivalence toward the state is typical of the Catholic dilemma in these years." The spirit was willing but terribly confused. It soon became apparent, however, that the church's strident campaign against socialism was backfiring. The general public got the impression that the church stood on the side of the status quo. As Mary H. Fox notes, however, the most serious damage that this campaign inflicted was to the church's image

89. Betten, *Catholic Activism*, pp. 3–4.

in the eyes of the workers—especially Catholic workers: "This negative approach did not impress the Catholic workingmen; it gave point in fact to the Socialist contention that the Church was indifferent to their material welfare." As a result of this impression, Catholic workers began to abandon the church and to seek solace in the socialist camp.[90]

In the face of these defections, Catholic leaders began to question the adequacy of a totally negative and fearful approach to social problems. Thus in 1910, Msgr. William White of Brooklyn advised the church to examine its attitude: "It is time for us to awake to the fact that if we wish to keep our workingmen practical Catholics, we must give them some tangible proof that the Church is alive to the struggle they are making to better their material conditions." The following year, Peter Muldoon, the bishop of Rockford, issued a similar challenge: "We are ready with our condemnation of this and that dangerous tendency of the hour, but unless we go out into the open and do something practical for the solution of our pressing problems, our condemnations will react upon us."[91]

The reactions to these challenges were quick and diverse, although by no means universal. The hierarchy remained strangely quiet and refused to address social questions and thus implicitly denied official national sanction to the works undertaken after 1910.[92] Their silence stood in stark contrast to the activities of individual reformers and groups. Settlement houses modeled after Hull House sprang up throughout the country. The Jesuits founded the Loyola (Chicago) School of Sociology in 1912 and the Fordham (New York) School of Philanthropy and Social Services in 1917 to further the study of social problems and the application of Catholic social thought to these prob-

90. Roddy, "Catholic Newspaper Press," pp. 188, 47, 76; Fox, *Peter E. Dietz*, p. 27; Abell, "Reception of Leo XIII's Labor Encyclical," p. 482. In 1909, the *Catholic Fortnightly* observed that it was no wonder that socialism was making inroads among the faithful because the compassion the socialists showed to the working poor won their hearts: "Sympathy for the downtrodden masses, suffering from the undeniable abuses of our capitalist economic system, are driving not a few Catholics out of the Church" (Carl Reeve and Ann Barton Reeve, *James Connolly and the United States* [Atlantic Highlands: Humanities Press, 1978], p. 247).

91. Fox, *Peter E. Dietz*, pp. 35–36.

92. Roddy, "Catholic Newspaper Press," p. 56.

lems. In 1909, the German Roman Catholic Central Verein committed its energies to the pursuit of social justice, which led it to favor the work of the unions and some of the Progressive measures and to advocate the eventual restructuring of society along medieval lines.[93] The greatest advances in Catholic social action were made, however, in the realm of traditional charity. As Donald P. Gavin notes, Catholic involvement in social relief work before 1910 had been isolated from the developments that were occurring in other agencies in the field: "There was a defensive attitude on the part of many Catholics toward the developments in the field of charity. Some objected to the humanitarian approach of the 1890s, others to the growing professional approach to social work. Much of this opposition was probably colored by previous differences of opinion with the non-sectarian agencies, which were largely Protestant in origin." To bring order to the chaotic world of Catholic charitable work, the National Conference of Catholic Charities was founded in 1910. Through this agency, the social leaders of the American church were able to bring some degree of coordination to American Catholic welfare work and to foster professionalism among American Catholic social workers. In addition, the conference shifted the Catholic attitude toward a more environmental understanding of poverty and thus toward a greater appreciation of the need to fight social ills through institutional change rather than by individual relief work.[94] This new attitude coincided with the Progressives' understanding of the environmental causes of poverty and with their preference for far-ranging institutional responses to social distress.

During the years from 1906 to 1919, definite advances were made in American Catholic social thought that showed a new openness to collaboration with the American reform tradition. Progressive sympathies were at work within the church. One major problem, however, still stood in the way of the articulation of an official Catholic program for social reform: disunity. As late as 1916, the Reverend Peter Dietz bemoaned the absence

93. Philip Gleason, *The Conservative Reformers: German-American Catholics and the Social Order* (Notre Dame: University of Notre Dame Press, 1968), pp. 126, 102.

94. Gavin, *National Conference of Catholic Charities*, pp. 3, 185.

of an "American Catholic Social movement in any national sense of the term"; and the *True Voice* of Omaha pinpointed the culprit for this shocking state of affairs when it said that "our leaders have not been over anxious to point the way for us to go."[95] The hierarchy was neither unified enough nor brave enough to lead the church in her search for social justice. In a hierarchical institution like the Roman Catholic Church, this caution and disarray, this lack of leadership and unity, doomed the social liberals to failure. Even though there was evidence of an intellectual basis for a reform program, as well as genuine passion and urgency for the task, hierarchical timidity and factionalism remained a barrier to the articulation of an American Catholic strategy for dealing with social problems.

95. Quotes from Fox, *Peter E. Dietz,* p. 41, and Roddy, "Catholic Newspaper Press," p. 84.

Chapter 11

Unity Comes to the Bishops

The one barrier to Catholic social action which Ryan and his colleagues who were interested in a strong Catholic approach to social justice could not breach was the chronic fragmentation among the various elements of the American church. To be sure, personal opinions and judgments on social problems and the solutions to these problems were not lacking in the Catholic community. Unfortunately, however, as Father Peter Dietz pointed out in 1916, Catholics suffered from a serious social malaise as a result of that lack of unity which was the unfortunate and perhaps inevitable product of the cosmopolitan nature of the American church. This diversity among American Catholics unleashed a number of centrifugal forces within the church: competing national groups contended for influence within the church; and ideological differences and deep personal enmity set members of the hierarchy and the laity at odds with one another in battles that raged on both sides of the Atlantic, spilled over into the Catholic and secular presses, and confused and scandalized the faithful.

Although it is undeniable that nearly irreconcilable ethnic differences hurt the church as she struggled to find a social voice and a social message, the real stumbling block to the formulation of a unified and coherent Catholic social policy was the hierarchy itself.[1] As a result of the ethnic and ideological fights that marked the latter part of the nineteenth century, members of the different factions of the hierarchy viewed one another with suspicion; and many members of the hierarchy, ever sensitive to the threat of Nativist outbursts, felt that a unified and highly visible Catholic bureaucratic apparatus was a dangerous luxury the church could ill afford. They continued to

1. McKeown, "War and Welfare," p. 16.

believe that a low profile was the best way to defuse Nativist anger. Hence mutual suspicion and fear prevented the church from achieving that degree of institutional unity that would have enabled her authoritatively and realistically to address social problems.

At the turn of the century, some members of the American hierarchy expressed a desire for American Catholic unity. In 1900, James McFaul, the bishop of Trenton, was moved to forge an instrument of Catholic unity by his annoyance at the relegation of Catholics to second-class citizenship in the United States. In calling for the formation of the American Federation of Catholic Societies, he said, "American citizens, because they are Catholics, are discriminated against, and we are determined to unite for the purpose of defending ourselves. . . . My experience leads me to the conclusion that a policy of silence has been very detrimental to our interests."[2] The defensive—even bellicose—aspect of McFaul's founding vision for the federation accounted for both the successes and the failures the group met. As negative and reactive as the founding impulse behind the federation was, McFaul's action was significant because, as Elizabeth McKeown recounts, "The Federation made Catholics more conscious of themselves as a national organization with some ability to influence the course of national policy."[3]

Guided by his belief that the church "had been overlooked by the larger society because it had remained silent and had not united to advocate measures that would be to its benefit,"[4] Bishop McFaul called together representatives from all the independent Catholic societies operating in America and members of the Catholic press to found the federation, which he hoped would give the church a voice in American affairs com-

2. Quoted in Benjamin J. Bleid, *Three Archbishops of Milwaukee* (Milwaukee: N.p., 1955), p. 104; Bleid also notes that a fear of socialism was a motivating factor in McFaul's decision to found the AFCS. An alumnus of Seton Hall University in Newark, McFaul had come under the influence of Michael Corrigan, the archbishop of New York, and Bernard McQuaid, the bishop of Rochester, both of whom had begun their ecclesiastical careers at Seton Hall. This conservative connection may account, at least in part, for the negative response McFaul's plan received from James Cardinal Gibbons and Archbishop John Ireland.

3. McKeown, "War and Welfare," p. 21.

4. Ibid., p. 14.

mensurate with Catholic numerical strength. From its foundation, the federation showed a keen interest in social issues, although this interest was motivated by the fear of socialism that blighted American Catholic social thought in general in the opening years of the twentieth century. One of its leading lights, Archbishop Sebastian Messmer of Milwaukee, made the common nineteenth-century Catholic mistake of confusing the work of the labor unions with socialist intrigue.[5] Since Messmer was a towering figure in the founding of the federation, his fear of socialism and his muddled thinking on unions effectively short-circuited any fruitful reflection on social issues on the part of the federation, at least during its early years.[6] The later formation of the Social Service Commission of the federation, however, marked a change in both the leadership and the direction of the social thinking of the federation. Indeed, under the able and enlightened Bishop Peter J. Muldoon of Rockford, Illinois, the federation abandoned its purely negative antisocialist attitude and began to formulate positive Catholic strategies for dealing with social distress.[7] Upon the foundation of the Social Service Commission, the federation also formed a news service, which it entrusted to the Reverend Peter E. Dietz, who endeavored to bring some degree of national unity to the Catholic social outlook by supplying the member societies of the federation and American Catholics in general with up-to-date

5. Messmer said: "No Catholic can ever accept the principles of socialism, and there is no dispute over it any more and no doubt. . . . In most of the labor unions, and those being started today, there is the socialistic principle. . . . The fact is simply this, that if the labor unions will adopt these principles of socialism, no Catholic can belong to them" (Bleid, *Three Archbishops,* p. 106).

6. The failure of the American Federation was especially unfortunate in the light of Messmer's genuine conviction that the church had to concern herself with social issues. In this regard, Bleid says, "Despite his interest in the past, Messmer realized the necessity of influencing public opinion and of providing enlightened leadership in the new field of sociology. For that reason, he pushed the American Federation of Catholic Societies. . . . Although the Federation had recommended the study of *Rerum Novarum* at its very first convention, it shied away from endorsing labor unions. The leaders thought the Church could help the working class without the aid of unions" (ibid., p. 112).

7. Peter Muldoon's leadership of the Social Service Commission served as his apprenticeship in social action concerns. With this background, he was well-equipped to lead or foster social action at the National Council War (Welfare) Council (Conference).

information on social problems and suggestions as to how Catholics could respond to these issues.

Although the vision behind the federation marked a significant advance in the development of a national Catholic consciousness, the dream of full-fledged unity was never realized. The federation faltered, for the very fear that prompted its formation also led to its failure. Bishop McFaul had conceived of the federation as a means of overcoming the church's silence as the best strategy against the hostility of American Nativists. As Elizabeth McKeown points out, fear of Nativist outbursts caused many Catholics to shy away from the federation: "At its inception, the Federation ran into strong opposition from within the American Church. Many Catholics feared that the organization would become overtly political in its attempts to influence national policy and there was a corresponding chance that any political effort by American Catholics would alienate public opinion and make the problems of Catholic life in America even more difficult." Understandably, the liberal Americanizers among the hierarchy, who were still smarting from the rebuff received from Leo's *Testem Benevolentiae,* and who were ever sensitive to the climate of public opinion, led the criticism of the federation, which they saw as conservatively inspired and inopportune.[8]

Hierarchical opposition to the federation was not limited to the defeated liberals. As McKeown points out, some of the bishops "saw in the effort the possibility of lay interference in ecclesiastical affairs or the attempt to develop a national organization which would challenge the authority of the bishops in their own dioceses." Concern for episcopal privilege cut across ideological lines and united many bishops of different camps in common opposition to the federation. In addition, the willingness of the German Catholic Central Verein to cooperate with the federation's plans and activities roused suspicions among liberals and members of non-German ethnic groups. Finally, the internal structure of the federation, with its stress on maintaining the autonomy of the member societies, was too chaotic to

8. McKeown, "War and Welfare," p. 14. Bleid notes that "churchmen such as Ireland carped that the Federation would grow into a political party like the Center in Germany" (*Three Archbishops,* p. 105).

sustain the group. The federation thus seemed doomed from the start. A weak and ineffectual structure combined with hierarchical opposition to thwart Bishop McFaul's dreams.[9]

Despite its failure, the federation marked an important turning point in the development of a national American Catholic consciousness. Although the reasons for its formation were framed in defensive terms, the founders of the federation showed a perceptive awareness that unity was the most effective way of dealing with American pluralism. In time, the same bishops who opposed the federation would embrace another agency that was founded on this same insight. Furthermore, the wise realization on the part of the leaders (especially the later leaders) of the federation that the future of the church in America depended upon the formulation of a positive and unified national Catholic reform platform represented a decided advance over the defensive and fragmented approaches of the past.

The first two decades of the twentieth century witnessed other attempts to bring unity and order to a number of Catholic endeavors. Professional societies proliferated among Catholics. The most important advance toward Catholic organizational unity, and one with particular importance for social action, was the formation of the National Conference of Catholic Charities in 1910 at the instigation and under the leadership of the Reverend William Kerby, a professor of sociology at the Catholic University. This organization sought to convince the church of the need to respond positively and with modern methods to the problems wrought by industrialization. Further, the conference tried to persuade the church to coordinate her efforts on a national scale on the basis of a unified vision and to join with nonsectarian and non-Catholic denominational agencies in the fight against industrial problems. In all of these undertakings, Kerby and the conference were in essence moving the church closer to a Progressive approach to social ills.[10]

All these movements betokened a growing Catholic awareness of how to deal with the reality of American pluralism. All

9. McKeown, "War and Welfare," pp. 16, 21; McAvoy, "Catholic Minority," 63.

10. McKeown, "War and Welfare," pp. 25–26. The Catholic Educational Association was founded in 1904, the Catholic Press Association in 1911, and the Catholic Hospital Association in 1915.

demonstrated an appreciation of the power and direction that would flow from unity and thus enable the church effectively to compete for a place in American life. In addition, the charities conference shared with the federation a key insight that had great importance for the church's social ministry: the realization that the future of the church in industrial America was inextricably bound to the church's creative response to social problems. Nevertheless, the professional societies suffered from the same inadequacies that had restricted the Federation of Catholic Societies. They were not able to break down old hierarchical jealousies and fears. Once again, the timidity and fragmentation of the hierarchy stood out as the overwhelming obstacle to American Catholic social action.

As lamentable as it was, the fear of the bishops is understandable. The reappearance of Nativist activity (heralded and fanned by the publication of the virulently anti-Catholic *Menace* during the second decade of the twentieth century) convinced them that Catholic unity, which would raise the American Catholic presence to glaring and hence dangerously vulnerable visibility, could and indeed should never be achieved. Consequently, fear and prudence seemed to argue for the continuation of Gibbons's policy of masterful inactivity with regard to all issues, including those related to social justice. This timidity angered Catholic union men and saddened Catholic social liberals. It seemed that only a miracle or a catastrophe could galvanize the Catholic population and the hierarchy into action.

As McKeown notes, America's entrance into World War I "forced those leaders to overcome their earlier hesitations with regard to national cooperation and to achieve . . . a form of supra-diocesan organization."[11] Furthermore, in a providential switch, during the war emergency, Catholic unification was construed by the nation as a patriotic undertaking and not as a heavy-handed papist attempt to seize power. The war, then, was the midwife of American Catholic unity.

The outbreak of the war found the church in an unenviable situation. At least since the 1840s she had not been a part of the American mainstream. Her immigrant composition alien-

11. Ibid., p. 97.

ated many Americans. Further, as the church of immigrants, she had within her fold at least two major and highly visible groups, the Irish and the Germans, who could be counted upon to oppose any American support for the British war effort. Therefore, as John Sheerin notes, "as at the beginnings of other wars, American Catholics were standing trial, the issue being Catholic loyalty to the American Government." In response, the overriding "aim of the bishops was to demonstrate in a very public way that Catholics could be good Americans. In service of this aim, the hierarchy diligently supported American war aims and American political ideals."[12] Both the rhetoric that was used to sell the war to the American public and the needs of the government were aids to the bishops in their task of mobilizing American Catholic support for the war.

The war and America's involvement in it were presented to the American public as more than a mere conflict among nations. Indeed, Woodrow Wilson spoke of the war as a conflict between contrasting—even contradictory—ideologies. Moreover, to Wilson and his fellow Progressives, America's involvement was unmarred by the understandable but not fully laudable mixture of motives of the European belligerents. The European Allies fought against the terrible "Huns" for national self-survival and for democracy, but America would fight for democracy alone. World War I was thus for Americans a wonderfully idealistic and thoroughly Progressive war. Of course, this ideological basis presupposed the righteousness of the American cause. McKeown points out that "the conviction of the righteousness of the American cause led naturally to the effort to identify the war aims of the United States with the purposes of Christianity, so that . . . America seemed quite literally designated by divine authority to re-establish Christian virtue on earth through an Allied victory."[13]

To buttress the righteous underpinnings of the American war crusade, the government zealously enlisted the aid and blessing

12. Elizabeth McKeown, "The National Bishops' Conference: An Analysis of Its Origins," *Catholic Historical Review* 66 (1980): 567; John B. Sheerin, *Never Look Back: The Career and Concerns of John J. Burke* (New York: Paulist, 1975), p. 36. See also Shanabruch, "Catholic Church's Role," 2:5.

13. McKeown, "War and Welfare," pp. 173–74, 78.

of the churches. As Ray Abrams points out, all of the churches responded to the nation's call and were "flattered that the government took them into partnership." Charles Williams notes that in their war work, the churches and their respective clergies "were forward in patriotic zeal. They did much to crystallize the conscience and fire the spirit of the country. They interpreted the war rightly as a holy crusade."[14] In so doing, the churches performed an important morale-boosting service for the nation.

If the government gained a great deal from the churches' aid, the reverse was also true. The churches undertook to convince the populace of the righteousness of the nation's cause by their vigorous vindication of the equation between Christianity and the American way of life, and this work and the government's acceptance of it implied that the Christian way of life was thoroughly and essentially American. Although such an equation was something of a cliché with regard to Americanism and Protestant Christianity, if the equation were stated in terms of Catholic Christianity, it had new, clear, and important implications for the self-consciousness of American Catholics. The acceptance of the task of selling the war as a Christian crusade presaged a new American acceptance of Catholics as fellow citizens.

There was a practical as well as an ideological reason for increased government dependence on the churches during America's involvement in the Great War. The American government was unprepared for the vast work of mobilizing the nation for the glorious moral crusade called for by Wilson; no bureaucratic apparatus existed for dealing with the details involved in getting the nation on a wartime footing. Therefore, as Robert Cuff notes, the generosity and efficiency of voluntary agencies were needed to meet the crisis. Indeed, Cuff maintains that "the theme of voluntarism pervaded the literature on national mobilization during the Great War. The Wilson administration, ac-

14. For an analysis of the propaganda benefits the government reaped from this alliance, see Ray H. Abrams, *Preachers Present Arms: A Study of the War Time Attitudes and Activities of the Churches and the Clergy in the United States, 1914–1918* (Philadelphia: Round Table Press, 1933), p. 79; "Great Episcopal Bishop Flays Organized Greed and American Militarists," *Reconstruction*, March 1919, p. 70.

cording to this canon, achieved planning without bureaucracy, regulation without coercion, cooperation without dictation."[15]

The government called upon the churches to function as voluntary agencies in service to the nation and entrusted to them such practical tasks as the selling of liberty bonds and the encouragement of food conservation.[16] Both the government and the churches benefited from the alliance, and no church more than the Catholic church. The boon to the government was obvious. The work of church agencies enabled the administration to deal with problems for which it was ill-prepared. The churches in return basked in the approval of both their works and of their very existence implicit in the government's dependence upon them. This benefit was both crucial and startling for the American Catholic Church: the administration's recognition of the dependence on the church as a voluntary association charged with a patriotic mission legitimated the Catholic Church's existence in America. The church derived, albeit unknowingly at first, a further benefit from this mission. The voluntary system was a reflection of both the nineteenth-century Protestant crusade for America and the daughter of that crusade, Progressivism. Thus by cooperating in the war mobilization, the church was drawing near to an ideology from which she had shrunk in the past. War created strange allies indeed.

Catholic leaders were blind neither to the challenges nor the opportunities and potential benefits afforded them by the war. On the negative side, because they knew that Nativism was never far from the surface of American life, the bishops were aware "that anything less than full support of the war could lead to reprisals against American Catholics, by zealous patriots."[17] Consequently, they seized upon the war as a providential opportunity to enter into the mainstream of American life with such persuasive patriotic force as to leave behind forever the Nativist

15. Robert D. Cuff, "Herbert Hoover, The Ideology of Voluntarism and War Organization during the Great War," in *Herbert Hoover: The Great War and Its Aftermath, 1914–1933,* ed. Lawrence E. Gelfand (Iowa City: University of Iowa Press, 1979), p. 23. Cuff's article is helpful for understanding how voluntarism enabled the nation to achieve ideological unity at the same time that it met the practical challenges of mobilization.

16. Abrams, *Preachers Present Arms,* p. 79.

17. McKeown, "National Bishops' Conference," p. 567.

suspicions that had dogged the church's American history. As a result, the bishops gave themselves over entirely to the works of blessing and supporting the war effort.

James Cardinal Gibbons, the unofficial primate of the American church, spearheaded the Catholic response to the challenge of America's entrance into the war. On 28 October 1917, the national day of prayer for victory, while preaching in his cathedral, Gibbons advised his flock to support the war effort and to refrain from criticizing the government in any way.[18] In addition, in the name of the hierarchy, he composed a letter to the American church which carried his message beyond the borders of his own diocese. In the first draft of his letter, Gibbons voiced the common Progressive belief in the virtuous nature of America's war aims: "The mission of our country, so ably expressed by our President, is above all else a spiritual one. Our President has clearly stated the high principles upon which that sacred course rests—they are as universal as they are unselfish. We battle for the welfare of men of every nation, asking no special indemnities for our sacrifice other than those for which all free men always seek. Surely this raises our aims and purposes up to the noblest standards of action; and sets the soul of the nation above the meanness and pettiness of selfish conquest or unchristian hate." In the final form of the letter, Gibbons went so far as to identify the aims of the nation with those of the universal Catholic Church: "In the world today the strongest response to this new internationalism must come from the Church of the ages. The Catholic Church cannot remain an isolated factor in the nation. . . . Today, as never before, the Catholic Church in the United States has an opportunity for doing a nation-wide work. No one honestly doubts Catholic loyalty to the principles of the American nation."[19]

On the basis of this identification, Gibbons, and the archbishops in whose name he wrote, pledged, "Our people, now as ever, will rise as one man to serve the nation. Our priests and consecrated women will once again, as in every former trial of our

18. John T. Ellis, *The Life of James Cardinal Gibbons, Archbishop of Baltimore, 1834–1921*, 2 vols. (Milwaukee: Bruce, 1952), 2:247.

19. James Gibbons to the American Church, 18 June 1918, O'Connell Papers, NCWC file M-1035, AAB; *National Catholic War Council Handbook* (Washington: National Catholic War Council, 1918), p. 1.

country, win by their bravery, their heroism and their service new admiration and approval." Support for the American war effort among the hierarchy was not limited to Gibbons or the board of archbishops. Indeed, it would appear that there was general agreement among all the American bishops "on the justice of the American cause, the need to actively embrace the principal virtues of Catholicism in order to win American goals, and the practical identification of Americanism and Catholicism." Significantly, the bishops also identified themselves with the Progressive moralizing on the meaning of the war by making it clear in their addresses "that the war was necessary as a purifier to clean out the corruption and materialism of the modern age."[20]

The bishops thus fairly fell over themselves in their scramble to respond creditably to the call of the nation and to perform the rhetorical ministry entrusted to them by the government.[21] In addition, without reservation they promised that they would marshal all the energies of the Catholic community to provide material assistance for the moral crusade to make the world safe for democracy. These were, however, fairly empty words and vain promises. The bishops' lack of unity and the absence of a national Catholic bureaucracy were embarrassing barriers to effective Catholic action. The rhetoric employed by the bishops, however, located them firmly in the ideological camp of the Progressive idealists, who were leading and interpreting the American war effort. This was a signal advance in the Catholic reconciliation with American life in general and the American reform tradition in particular. A crisis with clear, practical challenges had begun to accomplish what Ryan's principled reasoning had not been able to effect. Practical challenges would cement the bond between Catholicism and American nationalism, and the challenge of the war would force the unity that would enable the church to deal with domestic problems which the Progressives had addressed in the decades before the war.

Because the bishops lacked both practical experience in directing wartime activities and a national board for funding and

20. Sheerin, *Never Look Back,* p. 36; McKeown, "War and Welfare," pp. 80, 86.

21. McKeown, "War and Welfare," pp. 96–97.

coordinating Catholic action, Catholic leadership in the war effort initially fell by default to a lay group that enjoyed both these advantages: the Knights of Columbus. In June 1917, the Knights launched a fund-raising drive to support their endeavors and petitioned Raymond Fosdick, the chairman of the War Camps Commission, for official status as an accredited war agency. On 21 June 1917, Fosdick answered their request by inviting them to work in an official capacity with the War Department's Commission on Training Camp Activities (CTCA). Following the model of their work during the Pancho Villa campaign, the Knights concentrated their efforts on improving conditions in the military training camps. The record of their accomplishments was staggering. As John Sheerin writes, "Before the war ended, the Knights had opened three hundred sixty recreational centers in camps at home, and an equal number abroad, staffed by about two thousand secretaries, assisted by twenty-seven thousand volunteer workers." The Knights advertised their accomplishments to the world through a publicity campaign and reaped a harvest of positive headlines for themselves and the church. Their success in garnering favorable publicity for what was essentially lay work variously embarrassed, piqued, and encouraged the hierarchy and those members of the church who had long advocated the formation of a truly national Catholic organization.[22] In this case at least, embarrassment was to prove to be the mother of invention and action.

Because the Knights seemed so visibly to have usurped the hierarchy's leadership role, some bishops began to see them as an embarrassing problem.[23] This, however, was not the only problem the Catholic war effort faced. In the first heady days of mobilization, many Catholic groups sprang forward to answer the nation's call. The rampant enthusiasm displayed by these groups unfortunately caused a great deal of duplication of effort

22. For a treatment of the work of the Knights, see Christopher J. Kauffman, *Faith and Fraternalism: The History of the Knights of Columbus, 1882–1982* (New York: Harper & Row, 1982), pp. 190–227. On their war effort, see McKeown, "War and Welfare," pp. 96–97, 101–3; Abell, *American Catholicism and Social Action*, p. 191; and Sheerin, *Never Look Back*, p. 37.

23. For a discussion of the suspicion with which some leading Catholics viewed the Knights' work, see Kauffman, *Faith and Fraternalism*, pp. 201ff.

which lessened the effectiveness of the Catholic involvement in the war effort. Finally, serious flaws attendant upon leaving the only national Catholic coordination to the Knights of Columbus soon became apparent. Although the Knights were engaged in noble and important work, it was of a largely recreational nature. There were also spiritual needs such as the effective assignment of chaplains, which were beyond the competence of even the most well-intentioned group of laymen to supply. As Michael Williams notes, all of these problems were aspects of one larger problem: "It was a problem of management, or organization; a question of the best practical methods of concentrating and applying swiftly and effectively the mighty resources which it [the Church] possessed."[24]

A group began to meet and consider these problems and their possible solutions. The members of this visionary group were the Reverend William J. Kerby of the Catholic University and the National Conference of Catholic Charities, the Reverend John J. Burke, C.S.P., of the *Catholic World,* the Reverend Lewis J. O'Hern, C.S.P., who was in charge of the assignment of Catholic chaplains during the war, and Charles O'Neill, a layman and former secretary of labor. These men shared a common sense of urgency, a unified vision of the way to deal with the war's challenges to the church, and a concern for the missionary work of the church in America. Moreover, at least two of them perceived the non-war-related benefits that would flow to the church if she had a unified national bureaucracy.

The titan of the group was John J. Burke, a Paulist priest who shared something of his founder's missionary zeal for America. There was, however, a difference in their thinking. Whereas Isaac Hecker had entertained fond hopes for the total conversion of Protestant America to Catholicism, Burke's more modest goal was to make Catholics the moral leaven of American life. According to Sheerin, he believed that the church could realize this mission only if it were internally unified. Therefore, even before the war, he "occupied himself with a scheme of organization for some sort of ecclesiastical agency through

24. Michael Williams, *American Catholics in the War: National Catholic War Council, 1917–1921* (New York: Macmillan, 1921), pp. 92, 88–89.

which Catholic action might be provided."[25] Conditions before the outbreak of the war were not propitious for the realization of his dreams. The war, however, afforded Burke ample reason to hope that his goal might be fulfilled as a result of the pressure the church felt to contribute to the American war effort. Therefore, "Burke saw the war as a most serious challenge to the American Church, precisely because the war demanded concerted public effort on the part of Catholics in the spiritual and social realms. If the majority of Catholics were unconcerned or forced into inactivity through inadequate organization, the Church would lose the place it claimed for itself in national life." Moreover, Burke perceived that the attainment of unity would have an importance and benefits for the church following the war. Despite his generally benign estimation of American life, Burke was practical enough to realize that recurring threats to Catholic interests in America's pluralistic environment "could in no wise be solved unless there was a recognized, authoritative Catholic center of representation and of action."[26] Thus he keenly perceived the defensive postwar potential of a national Catholic organization.

The Reverend William J. Kerby was also a visionary with a firm grasp on reality and an understanding of power. He too believed that since the American system was based on pluralism, which in turn was based on a realistic appreciation of power, the church would have to forge an instrument of unity that would provide her with a focus of power if she were to compete in and contribute to this pluralistic environment. Thus Kerby saw the formation of a unified and unifying wartime agency as a first step toward realistically inserting the church into the center of American life. In addition, as a man with Progressive and social action leanings, Kerby "saw the conflict pushing Catholics into the fields of social service and Americanization, a situation which would benefit the immigrant Catholics in the American Church."[27] As the founder of

25. McKeown, "National Bishops' Conference," p. 568; Sheerin, *Never Look Back*, p. 39.

26. McKeown, "War and Welfare," pp. 111–12; Williams, *American Catholics in the War*, p. 105.

27. McKeown, "War and Welfare," p. 87.

the National Conference of Catholic Charities, he appreciated the enormous help a national organization would be for such work.

The third cleric in the group, Lewis O'Hern, C.S.P., approached the question of forming a unified agency for the coordination of the Catholic war effort from a practical point of view: he was charged with the supradiocesan task of recruiting, training, and assigning chaplains for the American armed forces and thus was forced to think nationally.

In June 1917, the four men came to the conclusion that some action had to be taken to rescue the Catholic war effort from chaos. Although it is clear that the decision of Burke and his colleagues was important for shaping the American Catholic contribution to the war effort, it was also a decision of enormous consequence for American Catholic social action, for the formation of a unified central agency would allow the church to speak authoritatively, forcefully, and with one voice on social issues. In June 1917, however, eliminating disunity was as yet a fond hope. It would take some time before the hierarchy could be taught to "think nationally."

Delegated by the group and armed with his own plans, John J. Burke met with Cardinal Gibbons in the summer of 1917. Gibbons listened and pledged his heartfelt support to Burke's endeavors, but he advised Burke to follow the politic procedure of presenting his plans to the two other American cardinals, William O'Connell of Boston and John Farley of New York, for their approval. Once all the cardinals had been consulted and their approval secured, a national Catholic convention was called for 11–12 August 1917 at the Catholic University of America. The convention brought together a group of delegates from fifty-eight dioceses, twenty of the larger Catholic societies, including the Knights of Columbus and the Federation of Catholic Societies, and "virtually all the members of the Catholic Press Association." Michael Williams describes the atmosphere of the convention as being "heavily charged with elements for which the term discordant is too strong, but which may perhaps be described as elements of misunderstanding, of contending corporate ambitions, of cross-purposes, and, in particular, a confused and in some instances an erroneous consciousness of the purposes of the convention and of the necessities of the situation."[28]

To this unpromising audience, Burke preached the gospel of unity with great persuasive force: "It is a national problem that confronts us. We, in consequence, must learn to think nationally. The individual, the parish, the society, the diocese must emphasize and sacrifice itself to that larger Catholic unity of which each is a reflection." Spurred on by the urgency of the situation and swayed by Burke's words, the convention "endorsed the Knights of Columbus' war work and created the National Catholic War Council [NCWC] 'to study, coordinate, unify and put in operation all Catholic activities incidental to the war.'" It was an auspicious beginning, but it was a false start for the War Council. In the rush to form the council, the convention delegates saddled the new organization with an almost totally unworkable executive board and a chaotic lower structure.[29] Therefore, although the original War Council held great promise for advancing the work of the church in America, its organizational problems seriously limited its effectiveness.

Burke was sensitive to the shortcomings of the original NCWC. He realized that a hierarchical church could never function at optimal efficiency if it continued to think and act as a congeries of voluntary associations, which was precisely the way in which the original NCWC operated. A hierarchical church required true hierarchical leadership. Williams recounts, "Episcopal authority and direction supplied the only possible and permanent basis for unified Catholic war activities, and the recognition of this fact pointed the way to the solution of the conflicting claims and natural rivalries of powerful societies and individuals." Accordingly, Burke and his colleagues pressed the hierarchy to assume real and effective control of the NCWC. In presenting his arguments, Burke called attention to the problems the church faced as a result of the continuing division and lack of direction displayed by the various agencies nominally answerable to the NCWC. He was aided in his task of persua-

28. McKeown, "National Bishops' Conference," p. 569; Sheerin, *Never Look Back*, pp. 40–41; McKeown, "War and Welfare," p. 107; Williams, *American Catholics in the War*, p. 113.

29. McKeown, "War and Welfare," p. 103; Abell, *American Catholicism and Social Action*, p. 192.

sion by the bishops' fear of appearing to surrender power and leadership to the Knights of Columbus, whose work was daily more visible.[30]

By the end of 1917, Burke and his confreres had succeeded in convincing the bishops of the advisability of assuming more direct control of the NCWC. At their November 1917 meeting, the archbishops reorganized the War Council, putting themselves at its head as the coordinators of the Catholic war effort. As a result of this organizational shift, the Knights of Columbus were forced to accept a clearly subordinate role in the life and work of the NCWC.[31] The bishops would thereafter direct the Catholic war effort and, coincidentally, enjoy the benefits of positive publicity.

Following the November meeting of the archbishops, Gibbons wrote to all the members of the American hierarchy to apprise them of the archepiscopal decision and to ask for their reactions. In his letter, Gibbons made it clear that the organizational shake-up at the NCWC amounted to the creation of a wholly new agency under the direct and effective control of the bishops of the country. Although the action of the archbishops placed the NCWC under their own control, the archbishops felt that it was impossible for them to oversee the work of the NCWC because their duties were too heavy to allow them to perform this additional task effectively. Hence they entrusted the supervision of the NCWC to an administrative committee of four bishops: Peter J. Muldoon[32] of Rockford, Joseph

30. Williams, *American Catholics in the War,* p. 115; McKeown, "War and Welfare," p. 113; Sheerin, *Never Look Back,* p. 43; Kauffman, *Faith and Fraternalism,*.pp. 201ff.

31. McKeown, "War and Welfare," pp. 114–15.

32. Peter James Muldoon was born of Irish parents in Columbia, California, on 10 October 1863. He received his education at Saint Mary's College, Kentucky, and Saint Mary's Seminary, Baltimore. He was ordained in Baltimore on 18 December 1886 for the diocese of Chicago. In 1901, he was consecrated auxiliary bishop of Chicago, over the strenuous objections of a faction of Irish priests in the diocese of Chicago. Because of this Irish opposition to his appointment, he could not succeed Archbishop Feehan as archbishop of Chicago. In 1908, he was named the first bishop of Rockford, Illinois, where he remained until his death, turning down an offered appointment to the Archdiocese of Monterey-Los Angeles. Muldoon was an influential member of the Social Service Commission of the American Federation of Catholic Societies. Also, in the words of his biographer, he "in a sense became at least a semiofficial voice of an articulate Catholic position with regard to the social question in general and the

Schrembs of Toledo, William Russell of Charleston, South Carolina, and Patrick Hayes, auxiliary of New York. On 28 December 1917, Gibbons wrote to Muldoon advising him of the board's action and summoning him and the three other members of the committee to meet with him at the Catholic University on 9 January 1918 to discuss plans for the formation of the new National Catholic War Council. Subsequently, in a letter written on 12 January 1918, Gibbons stated the administrative committee's mandate:

> Permit me, first of all, to state clearly your position and authority. By its recent action, the Hierarchy has created a Catholic War Council, consisting of the Board of Archbishops, but as the Archbishops cannot meet at present to organize the work of the council and cannot give it the necessary time and labor, they desired to delegate their authority to Your Lordships, as a committee to act in their name. . . . As you will have the responsibility for its success, so, of course, you will have full liberty to take such means as you judge necessary or advisable. . . . Your task will be to direct and control, with the aid of the ordinaries, all Catholic activities in the war.[33]

Although the organizational structure of the new NCWC was complex and the membership of its various boards, committees, and agencies diverse, it avoided the chaos that had plagued the original organization because a clear division of labor and lines of responsibility were outlined from the start: the Knights of Columbus were to control only recreational centers; the Advisory Finance Committee was to oversee only fund-raising; and the farflung members of the general committee were to be merely the local agents of the council, charged with reflecting the mind and doing the will of the NCWC in Washington. All the committees were answerable to the NCWC's Committee on Special War Activities, which was in turn answerable to the bishops. The bishops had finally taken control of the Catholic war effort.

As a result of the archepiscopal actions of the period extending from November 1917 through January 1918, the germ of

---

labor problem in particular." Throughout his life, he remained a strong supporter of labor unions and their demands. See Francis J. McManamin, "Peter J. Muldoon, First Bishop of Rockford, 1862–1927," *Catholic Historical Review* 58 (October 1962): 375.

33. Williams, *American Catholics in the War*, p. 149.

Catholic unity was formed. It was not, however, until the 11 April 1918 meeting of the Administrative Committee that the Committee on Special War Activities (CSWA), the umbrella agency charged with the day-to-day coordination of war work, was created. As a result of this meeting, the NCWC's organizational scheme was completed, and John Burke's release for the chairmanship of the Committee on Special War Activities was secured from his Paulist superiors. Burke took on the work energetically, and NCWC-CSWA progressed. Its work, however, met with several problems. As an organization charged with the task of coordinating all Catholic war activities, but with a dubious canonical status (Gibbons was on shaky canonical grounds in forming the council and giving its administrative committee sweeping supradiocesan powers), the NCWC was in an anomalous position: for its continued existence and effectiveness, it was dependent upon the goodwill and support of the American bishops. This was the NCWC's most apparent weakness. Although the powerful and influential Cardinals Gibbons of Baltimore and Farley of New York were supportive in both word and deed of the council's efforts, as McKeown notes, the other metropolitans merely "gave strong vocal approval of these efforts but withdrew quickly to their own archdiocesan affairs."[34] This episcopal reticence to become too involved in the work of the War Council was not limited to the archbishops, nor was overwork the only reason for the conspicuous tepidity of the bishops' support. Indeed, there were many understandable reasons for the episcopal reserve. First, the bishops were jealous of their prerogatives and wary of any new umbrella agency that might undermine their privileges. Second, some bishops sincerely believed that the nation's cause could be better served through the work of their diocesan war offices.[35] Third, because the lack of bureaucratic machinery meant that

34. McKeown, "War and Welfare," pp. 122, 131–33.

35. Sheerin, *Never Look Back*, p. 44. Bishop John J. Nilan of Hartford wrote: "I am opposed to a standing committee to either declare the policy or shape the policy of the Church or to commit the Church publicly to any policy: as the method of dealing efficiently with all questions must depend on local conditions . . . and should be left in the hands of local Catholic authority" (letter to William Cardinal O'Connell, 25 March 1918, O'Connell Papers, NCWC file, M-1035, AAB).

all segments of the population had to unite in giving voluntary support and mutual cooperation, Catholics had to cooperate with non-Catholic agencies. For a church that had been a favorite target for attack by these same groups and agencies during peacetime, the prospect of ecumenical cooperation was a stumbling block. As a result, Catholics, both clerical and lay, grumbled about these new and unaccustomed ties with their former antagonists.

Against these odds and objections, the CSWA operated to fulfill the ambitious threefold mission entrusted to it by the hierarchy, "of arousing Catholic interest and educating Catholics in the demands of national war work, on the one hand, and of guarding Catholic national interests on the other,"[36] as well as demonstrating to the nation the consistency between Catholic and American ideals, which the bishops hoped would be proven by the war contributions of American Catholics.

In August 1918, the CSWA was finally recognized by the government as an accredited war agency, thus winning for the church new recognition in American life.[37] The agency cooperated with others in the great war fund drive and was eagerly courted by the nation's leaders. As McKeown notes, this governmental recognition of the CSWA was a real accomplishment: "The recognition won by the CSWA for the Catholic presence in America as a 'capable agency' in promoting both Catholic interests and the national welfare marks its real achievement. For the first time in its American sojourn the Catholic Church mustered the necessary strength to establish itself at the seat of national government as a special interest group, determined to make its influence felt in the shaping of the national consensus." This momentous achievement was largely the result of the work of the Committee for National Catholic Interests, which kept track of war legislation to protect Catholic interests. This committee was formed largely for defensive purposes. The Catholics feared that the Federal Council of Churches of Christ and its Washington lobby were gaining untoward influence in the legislative sphere. Thus the committee was formed to create

36. McKeown, "War and Welfare," p. 146.

37. Aaron I. Abell saw the irony in the NCWC's recognition as a war agency (*American Catholicism and Social Action*, p. 194).

a counter lobby dedicated to the promotion of Catholic interests. In a most pragmatic and decidedly un-Progressive way, the formation of the NCWC, CSWA and Committee for National Catholic Interests indicates a profound new Catholic understanding of the exigencies of power in American life. In the past, Catholic leaders had believed that the surest way for the church to win acceptance in American life was through the pursuit of a quiet, inoffensive profile. During the war, the bishops and the leaders of the NCWC began to realize that incorporation into the American scene demanded not the surrender of power but a realistic use of moral, political, and spiritual power by special interest groups. Thus the formation of the NCWC and its agencies betokened a new and sophisticated appreciation of American mores and demonstrated the existence and operation of a new American Catholic maturity.[38]

The formation of the NCWC was a momentous event with far-reaching implications for American Catholic life. It was also an event marked by certain ironies. First, in forming the council, Gibbons and his archepiscopal colleagues were stepping into an area not covered by the strictures of canon law. There were neither any positive canonical statements against such action nor any warrant or justification for it. Therefore, the formation of the council was of dubious legality, although, strangely enough, it did not initially excite any opposition from the normally jealous bishops. In searching for an explanation for this episcopal acquiescence, McKeown suggests that the bishops' jealousy of the publicity the Knights of Columbus had garnered for their war work may have been partly responsible. Internecine hierarchical jealousies were not dead but merely directed at a common foe. They would rise again and plague the NCWC when the national emergency of the war had passed. Second, the very bishops who had vigorously opposed the formation of the American Federation of Catholic Societies because they feared that its power-based conception and high visibility would draw hostile fire from American Nativists were in 1917 instrumental in pushing for the formation of the NCWC. It is clear from a study of the motives behind the episcopal support for the war that to some extent at least the same fear that

38. McKeown, "War and Welfare," pp. 147, 157, 162, 171.

had led them to withhold support from the federation led them to encourage the formation of the War Council: the war emergency and the government's lack of preparedness demanded that all segments of the population do their utmost for the nation if they did not want their loyalty to be questioned. A unified central agency was essential for the church to answer the nation's call effectively and thus escape charges that her people were unpatriotic. Thus in the war emergency, episcopal fears of Nativist reprisals forced the bishops to form an association which, because it was representative of Catholic unity and power, would almost certainly have caused an uproar among American Protestants at any other time. Third, although the NCWC was a special interest group, it did not draw criticism from the Progressives to whom such groups were anathema. Once again, the supercharged mood of the war emergency explains why it escaped criticism. During the war effort, the Progressives began to view special interest groups as voluntary associations dedicated to a common goal. They seemed to believe that ends justified means. Thus, because the bishops were doing work that advanced their cause, the Progressives did not condemn the bishops. Indeed, they praised them.[39]

A final irony involved in the formation of the NCWC has particular bearing on the church's ministry for the cause of social justice. Before the war, the American church had been extraordinarily wary of the Progressives and had resolutely refused to become involved in their crusades. In joining the war effort, even for defensive rather than truly enthusiastic reasons, the church identified her purposes with those of the nation. During the war years, however, American nationalism was particularly identified with Progressivism. Thus by contributing to America's national need, the church was also identifying herself with a Progressive crusade. Moreover, as the war continued, the church became more infected by Progressivism and more committed to the ideals, idealism, and crusades, both international and domestic, of the reformers.[40] National need had accomplished what Ryan had attempted: an almost complete identification of the church with the nation and its reformers and the

39. Ibid., pp. 122, 116.
40. Halsey, *Survival of American Innocence*, pp. 45, 8.

formation of an agency that would allow the church to contribute substantially and positively to other Progressive crusades. Thus the church joined the war effort to prove her Americanism, and she emerged from the war with the government's recognition that she was truly American and the reformers' acknowledgment that she was Progressive.

During the Civil War and the Spanish-American War, Catholics had labored mightily to convince their countrymen that they were loyal and truly American. In the end, they had convinced only themselves; the nation had remained largely skeptical. The problem was that before World War I, the church had passively accepted the verdict of major secular newspapers concerning her role in American life. This situation was challenged by two developments during the Great War: the formation of NCWC's Historical Records Committee and the mounting of a sophisticated publicity campaign to enhance the church's image in the public eye. The Historical Records Committee was formed as a direct result of Burke's desire that "Catholic efforts receive adequate recognition as an 'effective answer to the charge that American Catholics are not patriotic.'"[41] The work of the committee was twofold. In Burke's words, its principal task was "to preserve a record of the names of all Catholics in the service of the United States and of all Catholic activity with regard to the war and its subsequent problems." Pursuant to this goal, the NCWC undertook to conduct a vast parish-by-parish census of the American church to compile an exhaustive list of all Catholic servicemen, defense workers, war volunteers, and gold star families. The information was forwarded to Washington, where it was to be used to support and validate Catholic claims of patriotism.[42] The committee's second task was to write and present to the nation the overall story of the Catholic contribution to the war effort. This task was entrusted to Michael Williams, who wrote *American Catholics in the War: The National Catholic War Council, 1917–21*.

The use of modern public relations methods to create a new

41. Ibid., p. 109.

42. John J. Burke, "Special Catholic Activities in War Service," *Annals of the American Academy of Political and Social Science* 89 (1918): 219; McKeown, "War and Welfare," pp. 166–68. The results of the survey were spotty and the record incomplete.

and positive image of the church was a startling and sophisticated move. During the course of the war, Francis P. Garvan, a prominent Catholic lawyer from New York City, also realized that the war offered the church an enormous opportunity to solidify her position in American life that would be lost if she depended on the secular media to report her activities to the nation. Anxious that the church seize the opportunity for publicity offered by the war and exploit that opportunity to the full, he wrote to Burke to present his case: "Four fifths of the people of the United States must gain or lose interest in this national service of the Catholic Church as they do or do not learn of its progress through the regular news channels, which form their only source of such information. If they fail to read or hear of the development of this work, they will unconsciously be impressed with the idea that it has come to nothing. . . . If they find accounts of its accomplishments regularly reported in the current war news, they will gather the fixed impression that it is succeeding in taking its place as a national force, of universal benefit to the country's cause." Garvan pointed out that "most of the splendid achievements of the men of our Church in the Civil War are today unknown and unappreciated by the American public, solely because the press records of that time did not chronicle them." Because the church's place in the American society in the future could be secured not merely by her contribution to the war effort but also by the nation's appreciation of that contribution, the bishops would have to take action to make sure that the Catholic achievements were kept before the public eye. Garvan suggested hiring a public relations firm to provide news of Catholic endeavors to the nation's newspapers and thus allow the church "to gain our proper place in the eyes of the world and in history."[43]

Apparently, Garvan's logic was persuasive. The treasurer of the original NCWC, John Agar, contacted Larkin Mead, a New York public relations specialist, and asked him what services he could provide for the council. On 22 December 1917, Mead responded that he was anxious to secure the NCWC account for his agency. To help the church achieve the goal of creating "in

43. Francis P. Garvan, "Report on Publicity, 1918," pp. 1–4, NCWC-CSWA (Burke), Box 14, folder 14, ACUA.

the minds of the entire American public a recurring and fixed impression of the patriotic, united and practically cooperative attitude of your Church toward the war," he said he could supply the wire services with Catholic news items, prepare editorial comments ready for publication in the fifty most influential dailies of the country, and arrange interviews between editors and the principals of the NCWC. Mead buttressed his request for the account by pointing out that the crush of war news made editors less likely to publish Catholic stories unless a professional publicist brought such news to their attention consistently and forcefully and in forms that could be used quickly and with little alteration.[44] The obvious conclusion to Mead's presentation was that the bishops needed him—badly. Mead's arguments were persuasive. Unfortunately, any positive action on his suggestions was stalled because at the very time that he, Garvan, and Agar were engaged in their negotiations, the NCWC was undergoing radical reorganization.

Thus it was not until May of 1918 that Msgr. Michael J. Splaine once again raised the question of publicity at an executive committee meeting of the CSWA. Thereafter, matters moved quickly. On 4 June 1918, Mead wrote to Walter Hooke, the executive secretary of the NCWC, announcing that Garvan had arranged for him to meet with Burke to discuss publicity for the council. Following their meeting, Mead wrote to Burke and outlined the services he had mentioned to Agar in December of 1917 and detailed the costs involved in the program he proposed.[45] For the annual sum of fifteen thousand dollars, Mead promised to upgrade the image of the church in America and thereby secure her a place in the American future.

Mead proposed an attractive package, but money stood in the way. Fifteen thousand dollars a year may have been a small price to pay for the attainment of security in America, but to Burke and the bishops, it was a princely sum beyond their means. Ac-

44. Garvan's report indicates that he already had Larkin Mead in mind as a candidate for the job he was encouraging the bishops to create. See also Mead to John Agar, 22 December 1917, pp. 1–3, Appendix, p. 2, NCWC-CSWA (Ex. Sec.) Box 10, folder 13, ACUA.

45. CSWA minutes, 13 May 1918, NCWC-CSWA, minutes; Mead to Walter Hooke, 4 June 1918, NCWC-CSWA (Ex. Sec.), Box 10, folder 13; Mead to John J. Burke, 10 June 1918, NCWC-CSWA (Burke), Box 24, folder 14, all in ACUA.

cordingly, Burke wrote to Garvan of his enthusiasm for the plan and his misgivings: "I would engage him at once but the amount of money is more than I am at liberty to put into this part of the work. With the extensive plans made by the Knights of Columbus, the work of the Chaplains' Aid, the great expense of this office and its Seven Committees, the fund of money which we have collected is pretty well spent." Burke, however, was unwilling to let the idea drop. Therefore, he asked Garvan to take responsibility for seeing that Mead was paid. Garvan accepted the challenge. As the minutes of the June 1918 meeting of the CSWA reported: "The Reverend Chairman reported on the matter of publicity which had been referred to him at the previous meeting and stated that through the kindness of Mr. Francis P. Garvan, Mr. Larkin G. Mead has been placed at the disposal of the Committee to inaugurate a campaign of proper publicity." Following the July meeting of the executive committee, Burke issued Mead his press credentials, and Hooke informed Garvan that his dream had been realized.[46]

Following the completion of these negotiations, Burke wrote to Mead in September of 1918 to confirm the arrangement and urge Mead to "prepare big plans and follow them." Obviously, Burke and the bishops were anxious that the work of the church not be slighted again on the American scene. It is also clear that the NCWC saw the publicity work that was being undertaken both as an opportunity to compete with the agencies of other church bodies for the esteem and affection of the American people and to make it clear that the bishops and not the Knights of Columbus were in charge of the American Catholic war effort. From then on, as much as possible, the Catholic Church was to appear before the nation as the premier agent of wartime charity and thus as America's greatest benefactor, and the bishops alone were to reap the rewards of this portrayal.[47]

46. Burke to Garvan, 15 June 1918, p. 1, NCWC-CSWA (Burke), Box 24, folder 14; Garvan to Burke, 3 July 1918, p. 1 NCWC-CSWA (Burke), Box 24, folder 15; CSWA minutes, 6 June 1918; Hooke, press clearance for Larkin Mead, 30 August 1918, and Hooke to Garvan, 15 July 1918, NCWC-CSWA (Ex. Sec.), Box 10, folder 13, ACUA.

47. Burke, telegram to Mead, 12 September 1918, NCWC-CSWA (Burke), Box 24, folder 15; Mead to Hooke, 24 September 1918, NCWC-CSWA (Ex. Sec.), Box 10, folder 13, ACUA. Garvan, Mead, et al., were not the only ones concerned with the problems of creating a new, positive Catholic image. After Mead had

The activity of the NCWC in hiring Larkin Mead stands out as an important but unsung moment in American Catholic history. In hiring him in 1918, the church determined to become the mistress of her own destiny and the creator of her own image. This Catholic development coincided with a general American awakening to an appreciation of the power of the press and publicity. Big business, organized labor, the government, and other Christian churches began to court public opinion assiduously and with surprising sophistication.

On balance, the war was a watershed experience for the church. Indeed, some would go so far as to say that it was a turning point in American Catholic history.[48] Certainly the changes—both ideological and practical—which the war wrought in the life of the church were striking and had implications for her postwar experience. Although she joined the war effort largely out of fear that anything less than full participation would spark accusations of disloyalty, in the course of the war, she adopted the ideas and rhetoric of the nation. As a result, she emerged with a real sense of belonging in America and a real commitment to American ideals. William Halsey goes so far as to claim: "The war precipitated within Catholicism a new sense of identity, an enthusiasm for ideals, and a rather disconcerting confidence in their beliefs. This hardly coincided with the unsettling spiritual, cultural and intellectual effects others experienced in the war's wake." Following the war, when others

---

been on the job four months, Michael Slattery, a California layman, wrote to Archbishop Edward J. Hanna of San Francisco, lamenting the shoddy treatment the church received at the hands of the press. He said, in part, "It is admitted on all sides by those competent to judge, that our Catholic press is not up to the level of its opportunities, and that the Catholic action as expressed through the medium of the secular press is lamentably weak, spasmodic and without adequate influence upon public affairs." Slattery recommended that the church embark upon a campaign of publicity to present its works to the nation and the world in a proper light. Slattery saw such publicity as being, "truly an apostolic work." Slattery, however, suggested a different route than that proposed by Mead and Garvan. He urged the establishment of a permanent "Catholic Information Bureau" under the direct control of the bishops, which would oversee the publication of stories that would redound to the church's glory (Michael J. Slattery to Edward J. Hanna, 14 November 1918, NCWC-CSWA [Burke], Box 15, folder 3, ACUA). His plans were forwarded to the NCWC, and following the war they reached fruition in the formation of the NCWC News Bureau, which obviated the need for Mead's services.

48. McKeown, "National Bishops' Conference," p. 566.

were beginning to suffer disillusionment and to abandon Progressive idealism as a failed ideology, Catholics were quick to embrace and to further this idealism, fortified by the belief that their political and social philosophies enabled them to understand as no other group could or did the meaning of the concepts of freedom, democracy, and natural rights upon which the republic was founded and in whose name the Progressive campaign of the war had been prosecuted.[49] This new confidence in the congruence of American and Catholic traditions and the new Catholic commitment to Progressive ideals were to prove helpful to the postwar work of Catholic social activists.

The effects of the war on American Catholic consciousness were not limited to an embrace of Progressive ideology. The depth of the church's commitment to American mores can also be appreciated on that most American of all levels: the practical. In a society ultimately based on power and its effective use, the church had learned how to deal with the reality of power. The church learned a marvelously un-Progressive lesson (which the Progressives also learned in the course of the war): the heart of power lay in organization, and with the rise of powerful corporate structures across the American landscape, all of America raced toward centralization. Trusts, interlocking directorates, and organized capital became the hallmarks of business life. Labor likewise organized. The Federal Council of Churches provided a degree of unity and thus a power base for Protestant denominations, a power unavailable to individual and fragmented communions. In all of these developments, business provided the model.[50] The formation of the NCWC marked the entry of the Catholic church into this competitive and highly organized American mainstream.[51] Although the NCWC was a supremely practical answer to a particular crisis, Charles McMahon's appraisal of the NCWC and its work makes it clear that the council's formation and existence had an importance that transcended its ad hoc inspiration: "For the first time in their history the Catholic people of the United States had, in

49. Halsey, *Survival of American Innocence*, pp. 8, 2.

50. Ellis W. Hawley, *The Great War and the Search for a Modern Order: A History of the American People and Their Institutions, 1917–1933* (New York: St. Martin's Press, 1979), p. 147.

51. McKeown, "War and Welfare," pp. 119–20.

the War Council, a representative national organization, one that safeguarded their interests in the multifarious questions arising out of the conduct of the War; one that enabled their hitherto scattered and disorganized forces to assume a unity and a cohesiveness and because of these, a resultant efficiency that added immeasurably to their ability to serve the nation and to advance the prestige and the glory of the Catholic name."[52] The benefits of and need for organization were patent. Indeed, the benefits were so attractive that for the bishops, the war seemed to end too soon.

The National Catholic War Council did not achieve government recognition as an accredited war agency until late in August of 1918, a scant three months before the signing of the armistice. In these few months, however, the benefits accruing to national organization had become clear to the bishops. Accordingly, during the immediate postwar period, the council's leaders "began to receive requests to find some means of making their council permanent from Catholics aware of the wartime gains in Church prestige."[53] At the same time, however, that the cessation of hostilities brought adulation and a desire to continue the life of the council, it also brought problems. The War Council had been formed to answer a specific need—the mobilization of Catholic resources for the national war effort—and its creation had been largely justified within the church on the basis of arguments of national need and the desire to protect the church from criticism. There was thus a question as to whether, with the war over and the national emergency past, the NCWC could be justified. The focus of argumentation for its continued existence had to be shifted to other grounds and other goals. As Sheerin notes, Burke "feared that when the Catholic soldiers returned home, each diocese would soon be back to business as usual, back to antiseptic insulation from other units of the American Church."[54] The War Council leaders, encouraged by the requests they had received and spurred on by fears of a reemergence of prewar eccle-

52. Charles A. McMahon, "Bishop Muldoon's War and Reconstruction Services," *Illinois Catholic Historical Review* 10 (1928): 296–97.

53. McKeown, "War and Welfare," p. 219.

54. Sheerin, *Never Look Back*, pp. 56–57.

siastical fragmentation, sprang into action and "convinced a substantial part of the hierarchy to continue the national organization on a permanent basis."[55] The work of persuasion was, however, not accomplished without difficulty.

In a hierarchical church, and especially in light of the tenuous canonical standing of the National Catholic War Council, the council leaders did not have to sell the Catholic population on the idea of keeping the NCWC in existence. They merely had to convince the bishops of the desirability of retaining the council. This was to prove a difficult task.

In their arguments, they stressed that because the life of the nation was increasingly dominated by large interest groups, it was necessary for the church to form such a group "to take common action for Catholic welfare, and to provide representation for their concerns at the federal level."[56] At the request of James Cardinal Gibbons, on 12 December 1918 William T. Russell, the bishop of Charleston, wrote a confidential letter to the members of the hierarchy outlining the arguments for continuing the council: "Events in recent years especially have painfully demonstrated, that, whereas the Catholic body by reason of its numbers and its prominent men is one that ought to be taken into account by the national government, we have been in relation to the forces that stand in opposition to us somewhat like China at the mercy of Japan. Unless some definite program be initiated, we have reason to fear that our condition will become analogous to that of the Church of France."[57] Therefore, and because other faiths already had committees operating in Washington to influence the legislative process, Russell strongly urged the erection of a permanent Catholic agency in the national capital. Not surprisingly, Gibbons staunchly supported Russell's proposal and his belief that the church needed an agency to protect Catholic interests. In his advocacy for the reorganization of the NCWC on a permanent basis, however, Gibbons made it clear that he did not wish to encourage the formation of a specifically Catholic political

55. McKeown, "War and Welfare," p. 4.

56. Ibid., p. 244.

57. William T. Russell, confidential communication to the archbishops, n.d., NCWC-CSWA (Burke), Box 21, folder 22, ACUA.

party like the Centre party in Germany. Rather he "drew a previously neglected distinction between Catholics who would act as political partisans in the American system, a course traditionally viewed with disfavor by most Catholic leaders, who feared reprisals from a public that readily believed in stories of Catholic political plotting; and Catholics who would act as representatives of a special interest group and look after Catholic welfare on a national level."[58]

Gibbons envisioned the formation of a Catholic lobby that could work effectively and nonthreateningly within the context of American pluralism. John Burke also favored the council's retention as a lobbying group, and he added urgency to his arguments by iterating Bishop Russell's point that other faiths, notably the Federal Council of Churches, had already established themselves as forces to be reckoned with in the capital.[59] Clearly, denominational competitiveness was being embraced by the Catholic leadership, and the ways of religious pluralism were being followed. The advocates for the retention of the War Council thus mustered their arguments and marshaled their supporters. At a plenary meeting of the hierarchy in September of 1919, over the strenuous objections of some of their number who pointed out the dubious canonical nature of the body, the bishops decided to form a permanent council that could coordinate Catholic postwar activities: the National Catholic Welfare Council.

The war thus had two extraordinarily important effects on the American church: it forced the church to form a unified central agency, and it fostered a heightened sense of Catholic identification with American ideals. Both of these—indeed the combination of the two—had important implications for the church's social ministry. Before the war, the fragmentation of the church and her distrust of the Progressives, their dreams, and their programs had seriously hampered the church's work for social justice. Indeed, although a few stalwart activists such as Ryan and Kerby had joined the Progressive fold, they had been unsuccessful in convincing the church at large to embrace Progressivism. The war had forced the church to unify so that she could con-

58. McKeown, "National Bishops' Conference," pp. 577, 570.
59. McKeown, "War and Welfare," p. 222.

tribute to what was essentially a Progressive crusade, and in the course of the war, the church began to appropriate more and more of the rhetoric and idealism of the reformers. The social activists within the church, who had previously worked without portfolio, were able to capitalize on the church's new war-born unity with the reformist spirit. In addition, the unity achieved by the formation of the NCWC magnified the words of the Progressive churchmen such as John A. Ryan who were employed by the NCWC's central office. This amplification of the voice of the Progressive wing of the church was further assisted because the bishops both during and after the war had assiduously courted public opinion and sought, through the sophisticated use of the media, to project a highly visible image of the church to the nation. The church's prestige and the glare of the press lights lent weight to what Ryan and his colleagues said and created an impression of unity and strength on social matters that was somewhat shy of the truth.

Hence, with the war, internal fragmentation and distrust of American reformers, the last great barriers to Catholic social action, were breached—and in a spectacular way. Social crusading was now safe and possible for American Catholics. The war, however, did not merely make the church more Progressive. It also made her vulnerable. Because of her high visibility during the war, the eyes of the American public were on her. As a result, the church could no longer play the ostrich on social issues, for during the postwar period the nation shifted its attention away from the challenges of war mobilization to those questions of domestic economic and social justice that the war had relegated to the back burner.

Chapter III

1919, The Acceptable Year of Favor: Social Dreams and Rhetorical Struggles

The bishops' unification and their courting of the media in the course of the war had made them and the church newly visible and vulnerable on the American scene. In the months immediately following the signing of the armistice, the church's usual masterful inactivity in the social sphere would have proven untenable. The climate demanded that the bishops take sides in what proved to be a pitched battle to determine the future social direction of the nation.

Touched—indeed almost maddened—by the exhilaration of its wartime experience, the entire nation entered the postwar period with a chorus of praise for America's achievement and her new prominence in the world.[1] Confronted by the enormous changes the war had wrought in the world order, fortified by a wartime legacy of idealistic fervor, and using the rhetoric that had been employed to muster support for the war during its prosecution, Americans rushed to offer their interpretations of the war's meaning. For most, the war was clearly a turning point in human history and the American experience. Flushed with pride at the vindication which victory bestowed on the American war effort, Sherwood Eddy, the international secretary of the Young Men's Christian Association (YMCA), offered his appraisal: "The World War seems to have gathered up in one final climax all the suffering and horror, all the cost and destruction of previous wars; and, on the other hand, all the idealism and

1. Donald B. Meyer, *The Protestant Search for Political Realism, 1919–1941* (Berkeley and Los Angeles: University of California Press, 1960), p. 6.

heroism of all former wars combined in one."[2] Clearly, the war was a victory for idealism.

If the war represented an international victory for idealism, it also signaled a domestic triumph for Progressive idealism, for as William Leuchtenberg points out, it "offered an outlet for the messianic zeal of the Progressive era without jeopardizing the structure of American society. It gave a sense of national unity, partly real and partly imposed, to quiet the concerns about rifts of class and partly of race that haunted the last years of the era." The war thus seemed to offer a shortcut to the unified, classless, and pacific society for which the reformers had yearned since the turn of the century. Strangely enough, then, the war seemed, to the idealistic Progressives, to be providential. Charles Evans Hughes gave voice to this estimate of its domestic benefits when he said: "We emerge from the war with a new national consciousness; with a consciousness of power stimulated by extraordinary effort; with a consciousness of the possibility and potency of cooperation and endeavor to an extent previously undreamed of." This Progressive vision of its meaning and purpose continued, at least initially, to inform not only all evaluations of the war's domestic results (dare one say benefits) but also all estimates of its effects on the international scene. Thus Harry Wheeler, the president of the United States Chamber of Commerce (and no Progressive), interpreted the war as the definitive victory of democracy over autocracy: "War swept down the world like a withering flame, bringing in its train barbarity, devastation and unutterable sorrow. Justice, like an avenging Angel, has scattered to the four winds the boastful hoards of Central Europe. Peace stands upon the threshold of a new day, bidding us lift the curtain upon a world from which the menace of military autocracy has been forever removed."[3] Virtue was triumphant. It was also triumphalistic.

2. Sherwood Eddy, *Everybody's World* (New York: Doran, 1920), p. 5.

3. William E. Leuchtenberg, *The Perils of Prosperity, 1914–1932* (Chicago: University of Chicago Press, 1958), p. 45. As Leuchtenberg points out, in retrospect there was a great deal of irony involved in calling the war a religious crusade. Charles E. Hughes, "Economic Aspects of Peace Readjustments," in *Reconstructing America: Our Next Big Job*, ed. Edwin Wildman (Boston: Page, 1919), pp. 37–38; Wheeler quoted in Thomas H. Uzzell, "An Industrial Pentecost," *Nation's Business*, January 1919, p. 10.

Everyone seemed to acknowledge the exceptional scope of the war's devastation. Drunk on the heady wine of idealism, however, most Americans took the destruction in stride and made allowance for it by recalling that the war was, after all, a mighty conflict between opposing ideologies. When considered in this light, most Americans believed that it was not to be wondered at that virtue's victory was won at so great a price. Following this logic, Herbert Quick blessed the awful war and justified its cost: "The immediate future of the world must be its greatest period of fruition, or the death of its hope in inescapable destruction. For the first time in history, a world war has been fought. . . . This war beginning in dimness and confusion of ideas emerged as not only the first world war, but the trial by battle of the very principle of self-government among the peoples. So far from being a contest in which peoples were given no more than a choice of tyrannies, it became a crusade on the part of the free peoples of the world against all tyranny." Quick's remarks reveal the extent to which the Progressive idealism that had ushered America into the war continued to inform American interpretations of it and its legacy for the nation and the world. Revisionism was as yet a thing of the future. When America finally did begin to question the received wisdom concerning the war's meaning, there was, as Henry May asserts, a realization that "a profound change had taken place in American civilization, a change that affected all the contenders in the prewar cultural strife. This was the end of American innocence. . . . Many had glimpsed a world whose central meaning was neither clear nor cheerful, but very few had come to live in such a world as a matter of course."[4] This awakening to the harsher realities of the war and its effects would usher in an age of self-doubt and disillusionment. In the opening days of 1919, however, the nation had no time for questions and doubts.

4. Herbert Quick, *From War to Peace: A Plea for a Definite Policy of Reconstruction* (Indianapolis: Bobbs-Merrill, 1919), p. 3; Henry F. May, *The End of American Innocence: A Study of the First Years of Our Own Time, 1912–1917* (New York, Alfred A. Knopf, 1959), p. 393. For a discussion of the growth of a revisionist school of interpretation concerning the war and America's involvement in it, see Warren I. Cohen, *The American Revisionists: The Lessons of Intervention in World War I* (Chicago: University of Chicago Press, 1967). In the immediate postwar era, any questioning of the meaning of the war seemed unpatriotic.

America entered the postwar era with the same idealistic hopes and schemes that had made her war effort a signal success.

Given the heady climate of the age, the unquestioning enthusiasm of the war experience, and the uncommon unity of idealistic rhetoric, it is not surprising that many wished to offer blueprints for restructuring the social order following the war. Reconstruction became the rallying cry of 1919. The moral fervor of the war spilled over, reconstruction was deemed a crusade or the moral equivalent of war, and men and women tumbled over one another to rush their ideas on the subject into print for scrutiny and eventual adoption by the nation. From every quarter of American society came calls for the development of a carefully supervised national scheme for reconstructing America that would answer the two great challenges of the postwar period: the readjustment and resettlement of returning soldiers and the realignment of industrial life.[5] Although there was a general consensus that the nation should undertake the work of reconstruction (or, in the parlance of the industrialists, the work of readjustment), there was no corresponding agreement on how the task should be engineered or what that new social creation should look like.[6] It soon became apparent that America's much vaunted postwar unity was shallow indeed; it was a unity of rhetorical terms, and it was merely word deep. A vision of an almost miraculously unified America depended upon and reflected the use of a common vocabulary of idealism and high emotional fervor. In the period following the armistice, however, it soon became clear that the war had changed America and that emotional and rhetorical unity had blinded Americans both to the changes the war had brought to the nation's way of

5. Estella Weeks, *Reconstruction Programs: A Comparative Study of Their Content and of the Viewpoints of the Issuing Organizations* (New York: Women's Press, 1919), p. 11; Burl Noggle, *Into the Twenties: The United States from Armistice to Normalcy* (Urbana: University of Illinois Press, 1974), p. 44. Glenn Frank lamented, "We are in many ways a nation of improvisors. Our social and political thinking is too often done under the spell of the immediate" Thus, he warned, "We have come near to missing an appointment of readjustment left in the wake of the war. We learned in a costly school what it means to become a nation unprepared for war; we are now in the equally embarrassing position of a peaceful nation unprepared for peace" (*The Politics of Industry: A Foot Note to the Social Unrest* [New York: Century, 1919], p. 5, 3).

6. Noggle, *Into the Twenties*, p. 43.

dealing with problems and to the divisions beneath the veneer of unity. It soon became apparent that the rhetoric of patriotic idealism was not univocal and that different groups used the same vocabulary with vastly different understandings.

In the immediate postwar era, confusion reigned as groups struggled to claim credit for the American war victory, to lay claim to American ideals, and to prove that they alone possessed the right interpretation of these ideals. Indeed, the period of reconstruction, and 1919 in particular, was dominated by the struggle between two groups that tried desperately to define the meaning and bases of American democracy. Proponents of substantive social changes argued that the internal logic of the democracy for which the nation had fought in the Great War and the evolutionary nature of humanity made such changes both inevitable and desirable. The general appropriation of the Progressives' vocabulary of righteousness laid the groundwork for the creation of a broadly based reform alliance and raised the stakes of the postwar debate that developed concerning the meaning of American values and their connection to social reforms. Opponents of this course contended that such hopes and arguments were based on a flawed understanding of the traditional bases of American greatness, a utopian vision of democracy, and a foolish desire to redefine the terms of the American social contract on the basis of socialistic wartime experiments in the industrial sector. Tempers flared and charges flew as worthies on both sides of this ideological struggle argued their cases. The signing of the armistice did not bring peace to America. It merely shifted the war to the American theater.

In these rhetorical struggles, the American experience of the war was subjected to minute scrutiny by both camps. The meanings and importance, first of the war, then of the American industrial experiments it fostered, and finally, and perhaps most important, democracy as the rallying cry of the war crusade were exegeted and debated. In a certain sense, then, the war became the subject of a new war concerning the nation's prospects for domestic peace. Because both sides believed that the spoils that would fall to the victor in this war of words would be tremendous, it is necessary to examine their logic and positions.

Whereas the general public believed that the war represented a victory for traditional American values and beliefs and a turning point in world history, the Progressives, who believed that America's war victory was attributable in large part to their efforts, rushed to offer more detailed and sophisticated explanations of the meaning of the war, its battle cry, and its experiments, which they hoped would create a groundswell of support for postwar domestic reforms. Confident that they alone could correctly interpret the meaning of the war, the reformers announced that it marked the end of a decadent order of civilization, which had been a product of the Old World. Correspondingly, they were quick to point out that the war, seen in the light of progress and the crusading zeal of American ideals, was the continuation of the peculiarly American reform quest for an ever purer democracy buttressed by an increasingly purified religious observance. Thus the reformers and their allies developed a curiously positive vision: the war was an important point along an evolutionary continuum. Otto Kahn gave voice to this view: "Even before the war a great stirring and ferment was going on in the land. The people were grasping, seeking for a new and better condition of things. The war has intensified that movement. It has torn great fissures in the ancient structure of our civilization."[7]

Because they viewed it in this evolutionary light, the Progressives ardently believed that the war offered a hint as to both the overall meaning and direction of history and the shape of the future. Such speculation led them logically to believe that the war victory represented an international, God-blessed, and American-fostered triumph for the forward march of democracy. Hence they felt that the war and its aftermath must be viewed as a vast opportunity to advance the cause of democracy and human rights on every front.[8] Significantly, this line of thinking (at least to the reformers) served to link the war crusade with other, more domestically oriented Progressive causes. On the practical level, the reformers understood that if this link could

7. Otto H. Kahn, "Capital and Labor: A Fair Deal," in *Vital Forces in Current Events,* ed. Morris E. Speare and Walter B. Norris (New York: Ginn, 1920), p. 130.

8. Noggle, *Into the Twenties,* p. 31.

be substantiated, they would be able to tap into the vast reservoir of patriotic feeling and religio-political fervor that had been generated by the war to advance their postwar programs.[9] As a result, the perception that the war was not an end in itself but part of an evolutionary spiral formed the basis of the reformers' postwar rhetoric as they sought to convince the nation to join in a domestic crusade that would replicate America's war victory on the home front.[10]

A brief survey of the American industrial scene at the time of the armistice and shortly thereafter will reveal why the Progressives believed that it was urgent to channel the idealistic fervor of the war crusade toward the consideration of domestic social concerns and the alleviation of domestic social ills.

Despite the high spirits and rich hopes evident in America following the armistice, the nation's industrial relations mocked the general optimism of the age and were viewed by the

9. The Progressives endowed the war with great religious significance. They regularly borrowed biblical images, especially images connected with the atoning sacrifice of Christ, to explain the war to the American public. See Harry F. Ward, *The New Social Order: Principles and Programs* (New York: Macmillan, 1919); Samuel Z. Batten, "The Churches and Social Reconstruction," *Biblical World* 53 (1919):594–617; and Eddy, *Everybody's World,* for the extravagant religious meanings that were attached to the war.

10. Glenn Frank gave voice to the Progressive connection of the war crusade and other issues: "The fact is that the war is only one of many factors that have made this a transition day in history. The war did not of itself make this a time of transition; the war merely dramatized and gave added urgency to processes of readjustment and revolution that were already under way and of which we as a people were but indifferently aware" (*Politics of Industry,* p. 19). See also Ward, *New Social Order,* pp. 11–12. This line of reasoning did not so much diminish the importance of the war in the eyes of the Progressives as it served to make the connections between the war lessons, which were evident to everyone, and peacetime tasks more evident. The war demanded that the world's attention be focused on those glaring inequities on the international scene that were the products of a decadent and aristocratic view of life. By interpreting the social unrest in the domestic economic sphere in terms of the war, the Progressives wished to raise these problems and their underlying causes to the same degree of clarity as the war issues enjoyed. It must not, however, be imagined that the Progressives were opportunistic or duplistic in making this connection. They truly believed that the two conflicts, the one international and the other domestic, were reactions to the same human need for fuller human rights. They were merely grateful that the war allowed them to make their point more forcefully. Further, such a view invited others who had joined the war crusade to join domestic Progressive crusades and provided an ideological basis for doing so.

reformers as the major area in which the battle for the war's ideals had yet to be fought. Insightful social commentators such as Robert MacIver realized that since the war had upset all social relations, social upheaval was bound to be evident, especially in the relations between labor and capital: "In the flux of all things, of ideas and systems which the war has hastened rather than created, it was not to be supposed that so unstable an equilibrium as that of 'capital and labor' would remain as it was before." MacIver pointed out that the war had only exacerbated traditional tensions in the economic sphere: "The war has destroyed many things; it has not destroyed but rather nourished the roots of industrial strife. For its material legacy is debt, a vast array of claims on future production, which will increase the consciousness of power in the interest-receiving class and increase the consciousness of burden in the wage-earning class."[11]

Confronted by the reality of industrial unrest and the inequities that underlaid it, but buoyed up by the idealistic victory for democracy which the war represented and informed by their own belief in the evolutionary nature of history, the Progressives undertook to advertise the continuity they saw between the war crusade and the work to alleviate domestic social distress. In this endeavor, their reasons were both strategic (and hence practical) and idealistic. The strategic logic for their actions is clear. For all their idealism, even the most optimistic Progressive prophets fully realized that the moment for creative social action would be brief and dependent on the maintenance of the electric and idealistic wartime mood of the nation. The *World's Work* voiced this belief as well as the Progressive spirit when it said, "If we keep our ideals as high as they have been, we shall not only conquer easily our own perplexities of peace, but be one of the greatest of the servants of humanity for all the world." Glenn Frank shared this opinion: "The end of the war has given us the chance to do many unprecedented things that will set us forward for a generation in political and social organization if we act while the flush of the creative moment is on, while the spirit of readjustment is still in the air, and before the

11. Robert M. MacIver, *Labor in the Changing World* (New York: E. P. Dutton, 1919), pp. 27, 36.

old social inertia and our every day spirit take possession of us once more."[12]

To maintain the wartime level of idealistic fervor, the Progressives directed their energies to establishing and substantiating a connection between the two crusades that would ensure the maintenance of a pure heart and a clear and common reforming vision among all Americans. Sherwood Eddy invited the nation to think of the postwar era as a "permanent and moral equivalent of the war; in a task infinitely harder and grander, the winning of a new world." These were grand words well suited to the grand task proposed by Eddy and the other reformers. To buttress such calls to creative action, writers added a note of religious and patriotic urgency to their pleas by recalling the sacred memory of the men who had sacrificed their lives to bring about the international victory of the ideals whose domestic realization the reformers now envisioned: "The new era is upon us, the new world for which millions of men suffered and died; and new problems have come with it. Things can never be as they were. Human thoughts have undergone change; democracy has taken on new meaning; old solutions are valueless; reconstruction is the watchword; more than that, it is the task." Thus it was that the reformers tried to bless the postwar era and call the nation to a continuation of the idealistic crusade of the war through emotional rhetorical appeals to religious belief, patriotic duty, and traditional American values.Their rhetoric had moved a nation to war. They hoped it would continue to muster up human spirits in peacetime as well.[13]

The reformers' insistence upon connecting the causes of the war and industrial reform was based on their understanding of the end for which the war had been fought—the advance of democracy. The war was the starting point for the Progressives' arguments. Because the war had been accepted by Americans as an ideological battle, it became a powerful symbolic expression of the longing of the human heart for greater freedom which was understood by all Americans. That the war had achieved

12. "The End of the War and the Dawn of Peace," *World's Work*, December 1918, p. 128; Frank, *Politics of Industry*; p. 15.

13. Eddy, *Everybody's World*, p. 10; Annie M. MacLean, *Some Problems of Reconstruction* (Chicago: A. C. McClurg, 1921), pp. 1–2.

the desired goal of advancing humanity toward a luminously American form of democratic political footing was not open to debate. All Americans fairly glowed with pride because America had made the world safe for democracy. Therefore, a connection between the war crusade and the drive for industrial rights would lay the groundwork for a national reform movement.

The reformers were not content with the establishment of political democracy on foreign shores. Since America had fully and publicly committed her resources to the cause of democracy and since modern life was largely dominated by economic concerns, the next logical and crucial step was to extend the benefits of the democratic process to the industrial sphere so that, as Paul Drake put it, "those who wished that all the world might be made safe for Democracy shall never again go naked, hungry and without proper shelter in a land of wealth and plenty." Estella Weeks was even more blunt: "At this time there comes a particular challenge to Americans . . . to face squarely the facts of the industrial world of yesterday and today, and to face them in the broadest possible way, realizing that in the days to come America must not only stand before the world for the declaration of democratic ideals and practices among the nations in their political activities, but must call for their adherence to democratic ideals in industry as well as government." Algie Simons, the Socialist-turned-Progressive author, used shame and logic to move the nation: "Unless all of our talk about a death-grapple between autocracy and democracy was but sounding brass to rally the tribe to battle, then the war is not won until we have firmly established democracy upon the ruins of autocracy throughout every social institution. The knowledge that we can, within quite broad lines, now make of our society what we wish is the biggest lesson of the war."[14]

For the reformers, then, the challenge was clear, and the internal logic of a belief in democracy was persuasive of the need for action. Although the Progressives applauded American democracy's belief in natural rights, they pointed out that natural

14. Paul H. Drake, *Democracy Made Safe* (Boston: LeRoy Phillips, 1918), p. 96. Labor leaders shared the same outlook as the reformers. "Democracy in Industry," *Railroad Trainman*, February 1919, p. 78. See also, Weeks, *Reconstruction Programs*, p. 70; Algie Simons, *The Vision for Which We Fought: A Study in Reconstruction* (New York: Macmillan, 1919), p. 184.

rights "will do him [man] little or no good unless they are social rights at the same time . . . it is evident that the aim of all social progress and reform is to take up natural rights one after another, and make them social rights."[15] Such talk conjured up the founding ideals and fundamental, normative texts of the republic and added both urgency and an almost sacred warrant to the task at hand. In a sense, the Progressives wanted to place American society in a position from which it could not retreat. The sacredness of the war dead, the Declaration of Independence and the urgency of the hour seemed to demand the extension of democracy to the economic order.

On the basis of their perception of a necessary and demonstrable connection between the war crusade for political democracy and the domestic crusade for industrial rights, the Progressives used the concept of democracy to criticize American industrial practices, to point the way to the future, and to invite the nation to join a reform alliance in the postwar era. Consequently, in their analyses of current industrial problems the Progressives continued to point out that both struggles were concerned with the issue of human rights. The reformers believed that the denial of the human rights of workers by industrialists led to the creation of an adversary relationship that resulted in a heightened sense of warfare, or a struggle of contending interests, that threatened the common good and led each to heap abuse, both verbal and physical, on the other. Hence reformers called for an overhaul of the wage system, which Paul Drake saw as "another form of slavery" (and a denial of human rights) that treated labor as a commodity and thus served to widen the gulf between classes and heighten class hatred.[16]

Such a class-conscious situation was anathema to the reformers, who hoped for the eventual erection of a classless society which alone could protect America from upheaval such as had visited class-conscious Europe. They buttressed their appeals for the nation to join in the fight for industrial rights by hinting ominously that if America did not face the challenge squarely

15. Ross L. Finney, *Causes and Cures for the Social Unrest* (New York: Macmillan, 1922), p. 16.

16. Drake, *Democracy Made Safe*, p. 63; MacIver, *Labor in the Changing World*, p. 42.

and cooperate with the march of democracy, she would face a domestic war like that which had ravaged Europe. Strife was the reward of those who stood in the way of progress. Thus their arguments, based on their belief in the irrepressible nature of evolution, took on an air of dogmatism and urgency. Herbert Quick gave voice to these sentiments: "Unless we have a better country in which to live in myriads of ways, unless that deep dissatisfaction with his lot which has been for so long taking possession of the common man is removed by removing its causes so far as they are curable, and making plain to him the extent to which they cannot be ameliorated, this war [the industrial war] will be ruinous to America."[17]

On the basis of this analysis of the root causes of industrial unrest, the reformers launched their attack upon American capitalists. They lambasted the forces of autocracy, who now wore the garb of the businessman rather than the uniform of militarism,[18] and called for a total restructuring of economic society along more humane lines. In short, the Progressives persisted in linking the fight for industrial rights to the fight for democracy for which the Great War had been fought and linking both to their earlier campaign for American social reform. From the war they borrowed the strong and persuasive emotional vocabulary that had brought victory to a reform impulse. From their initial prewar reform efforts they derived a belief in evolutionary change and a conviction that since poverty was environmental rather than purely personal, its amelioration had likewise to be systemic. The war's successful prosecution was the firm rock upon which they anchored their plans, for they saw the war as a moment when the old order was changed as a result of a universal longing for democratic, Progressive idealism on a worldwide scale.

Thus to the Progressives the concept of democracy to which the nation had committed itself in the Great War both stood in judgment on the contemporary American industrial scene and

17. Quick, *From War to Peace,* p. 164.

18. As MacIver wrote, "The present system is in its very nature an autocracy. Those who own determine essentially the lot of those who work, for the management represents the interest of those who own. It is in that interest that wage-rates are fixed and beyond certain minimal determinations, the conditions of work appointed" (*Labor in the Changing World,* pp. 52–53).

logically demanded that the nation commit itself to a domestic crusade to extend democracy to the social and industrial spheres. Buoyed by the resounding victory of political democracy in the Great War and convinced of the righteousness and persuasive logic of their position, the reformers presented an expectant nation with the idea of industrial democracy. They clothed this new concept with the same crusading idealism that had marked the American war effort and their previous reform drives. Hailed variously as the harbinger of a second Industrial Revolution, an earnest of the reign of full social justice, and the final and definitive articulation of American ideals, the concept of industrial democracy was seen as the final rejection of "the assumption of the old liberalism that unrestricted pursuit of selfish interests and unrestricted greed will automatically safeguard the welfare of all people and bring about a regime of social justice."[19] Drawing once again upon the experience and rhetoric of the war, the Progressives believed that the extension of democratic ideals to industrial life would make industry "a form of service" in the interest of the common good.[20]

Of course, the ideal of industrial democracy called for the introduction of radical changes in the American economic system. The Progressives did not shrink from contemplating such alterations. Indeed, they rushed to offer suggestions as to how democracy should transform American industry. Since the concept was developed as a response to the desire to reject the old economic liberalism, which seemed, almost necessarily, to degrade the worker and perpetuate class inequality, advocates of industrial democracy strove mightily to suggest practical systemic changes that would promote equality and minimize class distinctions. In general, for the advocates of industrial democracy, the extension of democratic processes to the economic sphere meant that rational collaboration, discussion, and arbitration for the common good would replace the selfish power-based maneuvering that had produced the bellicose feelings that had previously characterized the relationship between labor and

19. John A. Ryan, "The New Industrial Revolution," in his *Seven Troubled Years, 1930–1936: A Collection of Papers on the Depression and on the Problems of Recovery and Reform* (Ann Arbor: Edwards Bros., 1937), p. 129.

20. F. Ernest Johnson, *The New Spirit in Industry* (New York: Association Press, 1919), p.20.

capital. To achieve these goals, the reformers favored the establishment of a copartnership in industry,[21] which called for profit sharing and the ownership of the tools of production by the laboring classes, the establishment of cooperative industrial undertakings to reduce interference by middlemen, the sharing by both labor and capital in the determination of working conditions and wages, and the recognition of the right of labor to organize and bargain collectively to secure such a share of power. In sum, the advocates of industrial democracy called for an increased share in industrial management on the part of labor. F. Ernest Johnson of the Federal Council of Churches assured the nation that such plans did not mean a radical takeover of America. They were, rather, "the industrial counterpart of the demand for political democracy that is sweeping the world."[22]

The reformers believed that the benefits of industrial democracy were many and praiseworthy. The democratization of the industrial process would reduce class friction, ennoble the worker, continue the war crusade on a domestic scale, and save America from the fate that had befallen a decadent Europe. In short, the Progressives believed that the introduction of industrial democracy would hasten the establishment of a classless society. This desire for the narrowing of the gaps among classes gave rise to adverse reaction among the business classes and accusations that the reformers were preparing the way for the erection of a socialistic state. Nothing could have been further from the truth, or, at least, further from the reformers' minds. The reformers feared socialism as much as big business did.

21. Mackenzie-King defines copartnership as meaning that "after Labor and Capital in a business have each received a return in accordance with the accepted or prevailing rates, and other items of the cost of production have been duly cared for, an additional sum is paid out of the excess of profits to Capital on a percentage basis in accordance with the amount invested, and to Labor also on a percentage basis, usually of equal rate, on wages earned" (*Industry and Humanity*, p. 297).

22. George F. Perkins, "The America of Tomorrow," in Friedman, ed., *American Problems of Reconstruction*, p. 48; Claude W. Warren, "The Call of a New Day," *Reconstruction*, October 1918, p. 317; John Graham Brooks, *Labor's Challenge to the Social Order: Democracy Its Own Critic and Educator* (New York: Macmillan, 1920), pp. 279–80; Johnson, *Spirit in Industry*, p. 2.

They believed that the introduction of industrial democracy would not hasten but retard or even render impossible the growth of socialism in America. They hoped through their schemes to extend the middle class—to homogenize the American population. Hence they believed that they were not abolishing private property but extending it. Correspondingly, they did not wish to banish the profit motive from industrial life; rather, they wished to distribute profits both more broadly and more equitably.

With the announcement of the discovery of a connection between the war crusade and the crusade for the promotion of domestic reform and the enunciation of the concept of industrial democracy that grew out of this perceived connection, the structure of the Progressive rhetoric was nearly complete. Indeed, even if the Progressive postwar position had been couched solely in such patently idealistic terms, the reformers would have had every right to believe that their logic and rhetoric would have been persuasive. After all, the Great War had amply demonstrated the power of idealism. The Progressives, however, were wise enough to perceive that the war had also disclosed the possibility of harnessing the nation's high emotional fervor to effect practical changes in the social order.

The war had realized the Progressives' fondest hopes of creating a unified cooperative national society dedicated to the pursuit of a democratic ideal.[23] Moreover, in prosecuting a perilous foreign war under an idealistic banner, the nation had created a domestic social apparatus that incorporated, through various government boards charged with the supervision of industrial life, many of the regulatory features for which the Progressives had worked so long.

References to these wartime industrial experiments figured prominently in the Progressives' postwar rhetoric because their adoption and the changes they wrought seemed to indicate that America was moving in an evolutionary fashion away from unbridled capitalism that trampled human rights toward a regulated economic system in which government boards, acting as

23. Otis L. Graham, *The Great Campaigns: Reform and War in America, 1900–1928* (Englewood Cliffs, N.J.: Prentice-Hall, 1971), p. 98.

umpires mediating the claims of labor and capital, could ensure protection of the rights of all.[24] As much as this movement cheered the reformers, they were even more heartened that under government supervision the American economy had thrived and industrial strife had been minimized. Therefore, ever sensitive to charges that they were utopian dreamers, the reformers called attention to the success of the measures and insisted that they indicated the direction the nation should follow in ordering industrial life in the future. This argument gave a verifiable, practical cast to their crusade. In addition the proven practical benefits of these measures shifted the burden of proof concerning the feasibility and desirability of social change to the standpatters in the business community who were enraged by the changes in industrial life wrought by the war. Appeals for the adoption of similar alterations formed the capstone of the Progressive rhetoric following the war. The war was a watershed experience, providing grist for the Progressives' ideological mills. The same wartime measures that provided aid and comfort to the reform position, however, caused alarm to advocates of the status quo ante bellum.

Clearly, in developing and presenting their case for the continuation of the war's crusade on a domestic plane, the reformers structured their arguments around three central ideas, all of which were integral to their position, enormously useful to their task of persuasion, and informed by their characteristic belief in the evolutionary nature of human life: a belief that the Great War represented a triumph of idealism over autocracy; the understanding that a commitment to the extension of democracy in any sphere of human endeavor logically demanded a commitment to the extension of that same ideal to all areas of human endeavor; and an adamant insistence that the nation's war experience showed the practical ways in which the reign of democracy could be extended to embrace and govern all human activities. The combination of these three ideas convinced the

24. J. A. Hobson warned against a precipitous return to the old ways: "It is self-evident that any sudden lapse from the State Socialism of wartime, with its enormous control of engineering, agriculture, transport and other vital industries, and its correspondingly enlarged expenditures, into the pre-war conditions, would spell disorder and disaster" (*Democracy after the War* [London: George Allen & Unwin, 1919], p. 164).

Progressives both that their domestic postwar crusade was realistic and that they possessed the ideological means with which to answer reactionary critics and to spur America on to the creation of a more equitable social order.

The war campaign had effected a widespread appropriation of the idealistic rhetoric of the Progressives by large segments of the American population, and it explains in large part how the creation of a postwar reform alliance came about. By tying their reform schemes to both the patriotic crusade of the Great War and the practical measures fostered and vindicated by the national war campaign, the reformers provided an attractive and broad platform on which various groups could easily reach agreement and for whose enactment they could easily make common cause. The articulation of this rhetorical system, however, does not fully explain either the need the reformers and their allies felt or the willingness they displayed to cooperate with other groups for the attainment of social justice. This need and willingness are important for understanding the eventual reconciliation of the Progressives and the American Catholic Church.

While the Progressives were busily preparing their plans for reordering American industrial life and protesting constantly that their intentions were honorable and their dreams essentially conservative, American industrialists were becoming increasingly nervous. They rightly perceived that they were the victims of a new, united, and evangelically fervent attack. However lamely or insistently the reformers might protest their innocence of radical intentions, it was undeniable that the war had not diminished their cordial hatred of big business. In addition, the fervor of their new attacks, carried out under the war-hallowed standard of democracy, seemed to legitimate labor's demands and offer a righteous cover for radical protests. It was no wonder that business began to take action to deflate this crusade. To their credit, the industrialists realized that they were not engaging merely in a war of words, although both sides did engage in a war of rhetorical usages, and both realized that the victor would emerge with the power to shape the future. Therefore, both sides sought to buttress their arguments by hearkening back to the values, ideals, and practical traditions that undergirded American life.

In a sense, then, businessmen, labor, and reformers fought to secure their respective rights to shape the future of American life by establishing themselves as the true heirs to and custodians of America's past and her values. As Robert Moats Miller notes, the battle was anything but genteel, and the war over words led to the firing of real bullets and the shedding of real blood: "If the Western Front was now quiet, the industrial front in America erupted in a succession of strikes so numerous, so vast in scope and so bitter in their conduct as to dangerously threaten the whole process of national reconversion to peace. The fact is, the Armistice brought war, not peace, to the American labor scene. Labor was determined to maintain its wartime wages, particularly since the cost of living continued to soar. Management, on the other hand, naturally wanted to retreat to 'normalcy,' that is, 1914 wages." The reformers realized that they needed allies to confront, combat, and turn back the power of big business. Thus the reality of postwar warfare explains the reformers' need for an alliance with other groups in America.[25]

Before the Great War the reformers had cherished a belief that since their plans were directed to the good of the people, they would attract the goodwill and agreement of the population. Their failures, however, taught them that they could not presume that the benevolence of their plans would create a groundswell of popular support, and the war campaign taught them the importance of public opinion. They began to realize, as Edward Hayes sagely put it, that "the triumph of democracy depends ultimately on the development of public opinion that is adequately intelligent and public sentiment that is adequately

25. Robert Moats Miller, *American Protestantism and Social Issues, 1919–1933* (Chapel Hill: University of North Carolina Press, 1958), p. 256. Clarke Chambers says of the Progressives' postwar plans: "The program of specifics that followed read like an updating of the social justice planks of the old Progressive Party, which welfare leaders had helped to compose in 1912. It [the new platform] called for permanent compensation and insurance for war veterans; federal aid to elementary, secondary and higher education; the restoration of civil liberties . . . a system of probation in federal courts, a separate cabinet department of public health; and acceleration of federal-state extension work in rural areas; a comprehensive program to conserve natural resources; in industrial life, preservation of the wartime federal employment service" (*Paul U. Kellogg and the Survey: Voices for Social Welfare and Social Justice* [Minneapolis: University of Minnesota Press, 1971], p. 70).

socialized."[26] As a result, the reformers realized that if they wished their postwar schemes to succeed, they would have to court the public and create a favorable climate of opinion. The press was ready at hand and powerful. Therefore, the reformers fairly fell over one another in the rush to keep their ideas before the public, hammering away at the emotionally charged issues of democracy, values, the war, and Americanism in their endeavors to clothe their ideas with the legitimacy of the past and the urgency of the war crusade.

The war brought other epiphanies of reality to the Progressives. Before America had entered the war, the reformers had consistently praised the disinterested benevolence of the middle class as the bulwark of the reform movement and had just as consistently denounced any group whose interest in social reform was tainted by the slightest trace of self-interest. The successful prosecution of the war eroded the reformers' fear of special interest groups as they began to realize that successful reform crusades resulted more from the exploitation of a community of interest among a diversity of groups than from the operation of disinterested benevolence. With this realistic grasp of the meaning and use of power, the reformers consciously attempted to create alliances with different centers of power in American society in hopes of advancing the cause of reform.

As a result of this new attitude, the relationship between organized labor and the reformers underwent significant and surprising alteration. Previously, the relationship between these two camps had been tentative at best. The war eroded much of the distrust that separated the camps as both groups realized that they shared a common dream (the extension of the reign of democracy) and a common rhetoric (the call for industrial democracy). In addition, as Stanley Shapiro notes, both sides appreciated that they shared a common foe. Perhaps most important, during the war, the Progressives shifted leftward, gaining a new appreciation of a positive aspect to class division, and "class consciousness now suffused progressives' writings, dom-

26. Edward C. Hayes, "Democratization of Institutions for Social Betterment," in *Democracy in Reconstruction,* ed. Frederick A. Cleveland and Joseph Schafer (Boston: Houghton Mifflin, 1919), p. 116.

inated their thinking and animated their hopes." This positive evaluation of class-consciousness was founded on a realization among reformers that "liberalism . . . had proven itself to be an inadequate half-hearted faith, one that had been powerless to reform long-standing abuses and to prevent world catastrophe." Thus they moved away from a dogged belief in the efficacy of disinterested benevolence to an appreciation of the need for power to effect change. The reformers could now embrace formerly anathematized groups as potentially potent allies in the quest for social justice. As a result, the formerly despised unions were rehabilitated in the eyes of the reformers. Indeed, as Shapiro notes, "Progressives, therefore, looked to the newly-strengthened labor unions for the creation of industrial democracy and the adoption of such reforms as a national minimum wage and social insurance."[27]

These seismic shifts on the American reform scene did not remain at the level of ideology. Postwar Progressives began to demonstrate a surprisingly cordial advocacy for the demands of labor. For example, Benjamin Rosenthal gave an approving nod to labor's most precious demand, the right to bargain collectively: "They should also have the right of collective bargaining and the employer who is unwilling to concede that right is an enemy to both labor and capital, the latter of which he grossly misrepresents."[28] The Progressive entente with labor went beyond the piecemeal endorsement of specifics in the list of labor's demands. The reformers heartily endorsed and campaigned for the establishment of industrial democracy that would usher in a wider reign of the ideals of democracy and coincidentally recognize, bless, and advance radical changes in the social order. To be sure, some Progressives embraced the union cause merely for expedient reasons, allying themselves with labor because they believed that power politics based on union strength was a convenient means to advance their own cause. They continued to believe that unions and the need for them would vanish once industrial democracy was functional.

27. Stanley Shapiro, "The Great War and Reform: Liberals and Labor, 1917–19," *Labor History* 12 (1971):332, 338, 340; Shapiro, "The Twilight of Reform: Advanced Progressives after the Armistice," *Historian* 33 (1971):355.

28. Benjamin J. Rosenthal, *Reconstructing America Sociologically and Economically* (Chicago: Arcadia, 1919), p. 45.

Their ultimate goal was the erection of a classless society, a social Zion. These long-term dreams, however, do not diminish the importance of the shift in Progressive thinking brought about by the war. The war experience and especially the actions of the War Labor Board revealed the need and the desirability of a realistic balance of powers, through which both special interests and the common good could be served.

The leftward shift of the reformers was met by a complementary shift among organized labor's membership, also effected by the experience of the war, which brought labor many benefits and a surprising new cordiality toward reformist ideologies. During the war, the unions experienced a dramatic rise in membership.[29] Labor gained confidence and public esteem. In addition, the labor movement adopted reformist beliefs in democracy, progress, and moderate evolutionary change and showed a new sympathy for the reformers' vision of a regulatory and welfare state. Labor's new openness to Progressive dreams was largely the result of its experience at the hands of the War Labor Board. This federal agency, established in March of 1918, enunciated four principles by which industrial life was to be ordered for the duration of the war:

> First: "The right of workers to organize in trade unions and to bargain collectively through chosen representatives is recognized and affirmed"; . . . Second: "The right of employers to organize in associations of groups and to bargain collectively through chosen representatives is recognized and affirmed"; . . . Third: "Employers should not discharge workers for membership in trade unions, nor for legitimate trade union activities." Fourth: "The workers, in the exercise of their right to organize, shall not use coercive measures of any kind to induce persons to join their organizations, nor to induce employers to bargain or deal therewith."[30]

Through the articulation of these four guiding principles, the War Labor Board effected a revolution in American industrial life by forcing the acceptance of labor's previously disputed claim for the right to organize and to bargain collectively. It soon became clear that these principles were not to remain a

29. Hawley, *Great War*, p. 27.

30. Isaac Lippincott, *Problems of Reconstruction* (New York: Macmillan, 1919), p. 124.

dead letter. Indeed, their use by the War Labor Board in the mediation of industrial disputes advanced the cause of labor beyond anything that the unions had believed possible before the war. The War Labor Board forced employers to welcome union officials into a share in the work of management.[31] With government approval, labor leaders joined with management not only to determine wages but also to discuss and decide upon hours, benefits, and working conditions. Labor was ecstatic, and the unions warmed to the prospect of government aid in the pursuit of their goals.

At the end of the war, union officials were determined to solidify their gains. They emulated the reformers by appealing to the wartime actions and principles of the War Labor Board to justify their demands. In so doing, they were arguing that they had the weight of legal precedent on their side. As even the probusiness Isaac Lippincott noted, such reasoning had potentially far-reaching implications: "It is hardly possible to grasp the significance of these new departures in the labor policy of the country. These are announced as war measures, and they are voluntary with respect to the fact that they are usually reached by agreement among the parties concerned. But there freedom ends. Once principles are established and once a method of procedure is agreed upon, the various federal agencies cooperating with the Department of Labor bring varying degrees of pressure to bear upon employers to obey the restrictions."[32] If labor could successfully argue that the temporary measures fostered by the war emergency amounted to legal precedents, labor would have a great advantage in its dealings with big business. Management would now know the deadening force of inertia. Thus, realizing that the wartime experiments added legitimacy to their claims and demands, the laborers, like the Progressives, entered the postwar era with a reverence for the war and a desire to make the industrial expedients of wartime the pattern upon which to model the industrial future.

Labor shared more than a reverence for the war and its benefits with the Progressives. The conflict had provided both groups with a moral vocabulary well suited to postwar domestic

31. Hawley, *Great War*, pp. 26–27.
32. Lippincott, *Problems of Reconstruction*, pp. 136–37.

reform campaigns. This rhetoric allowed the two groups to enter into an alliance just as labor was entering the American mainstream. Labor rightly perceived that because, as Algie Simons put it, "this war is fought in the mines and factories as well as in the trenches," labor was largely responsible for the American victory. Indeed, laborers saw themselves as the great defenders of democracy, who could take credit for making the world safe. Matthew Woll of the photoengravers union and a protégé of Samuel Gompers used the moral vocabulary of the war to plead labor's cause before the American people: "We have gone through this war impregnating the hearts of our people here to everything to promote democratic freedom and justice, and unless we now respond to those things which we preached during the period of war, rest assured industrial strife will follow, and so we must bring into our industrial life democracy, freedom and justice."[33]

Woll's remarks bear all the hallmarks of a dyed-in-the-wool Progressive. The adoption of this righteous vocabulary marked a serious departure from the nonideological outlook of American labor before the war, when labor leaders had avoided emotional idealism and fuzzy ideology, preferring to concentrate on bread-and-butter demands that were attainable through the use of raw power. As the war had convinced the Progressives that power resided in sheer numbers, it taught the unions the opposite lesson: that power resided in ideals. There was, however, an additional startling, and strategic benefit to labor's appropriation of this rhetoric. Through the use of the blood-blessed vocabulary of the war and their identification with the noble cause of democracy, laborers attempted, as did the Progressives, to lay claim to traditional American values. In addition, using these same value-laden terms, labor leaders went out of their way to draw a clear distinction between labor and radicalism.[34]

33. Simons, *Vision for Which We Fought*, pp. 12, 38; Matthew Woll, "Industrial Democracy," in Society of Industrial Engineers, *Industrial Reconstruction Problems* (New York: Society of Industrial Engineers, 1919), p. 90.

34. Robert K. Murray, *The Red Scare: A Study in National Hysteria, 1919–1920* (Minneapolis: University of Minnesota Press, 1955), p. 106. John Frey displayed this tendency on the part of labor to use American values and Progressive rhetoric to distance the cause of labor from radicalism: "The American workers . . . have not developed the same revolutionary tendencies which have been and are manifesting themselves across the Atlantic; instead of this, the democratic

They pursued this potentially powerful rhetorical strategy because they believed it would have the positive effect of endearing labor's cause to the hitherto suspicious American public and the corresponding negative effect of poisoning public opinion toward big business. In the hands of a skillful writer, the possession of the American heritage became a powerful weapon.[35] Thus labor drew closer to the idealism of the reformers and used their rhetoric to identify its cause with the war-hallowed search for pure democracy. Hence the two camps learned to respect each other's strengths and sought to consolidate them on the basis of a community of interest which each called the drive for industrial democracy. The existence of a shared rhetoric explains the ease with which laborers were able to make common cause with the reformers. It does not account for the laborers' willingness or need to enter an alliance.

The experience of the war had created a favorable impression of labor among the American population. At the war's end, however, many Americans were still suspicious of labor and big business was still a formidable adversary. The rhetoric of righteousness and the internal logic of democracy may have been helpful to the cause of labor, but perceptive union men realized that allies would be more helpful.

The leaders of the labor movement sought to advance both their program for social amelioration and their standing in America by forging alliances with respected and responsible in-

---

principles upon which our nation was founded have profoundly influenced their viewpoint and have played no small part in shaping the policies and methods which they have adopted in their efforts to find a solution for industrial, social and legislative problems" ("What American Labor Wants," *Nation's Business*, April 1919, p. 23).

35. The *Machinists' Monthly Magazine* used the internal logic of democracy to drive home the demands of labor: "During the past few months our Association, in common with other trade unions, has found itself confronted with the cold and unmistakable fact that, notwithstanding all that has been said concerning a world made safe for democracy—of the dawn of a new era wherein a new and better relationship between employer and employee would be established, which would insure the wage earners of the country a square deal—many employers who during the period of active hostilities shouted their patriotism from the housetops while filling their coffers with dollars, are imbued with the idea that industry can be operated on the same old basis which prevailed in pre-war times" ("Our Opportunity," *Machinists' Monthly Magazine*, November 1919, p. 1027).

stitutions in American life. Samuel Gompers declared, "The American labor movement will cooperate with all other agencies to help in this reconstruction time. Our movement is not to destroy but to construct." Realizing that they shared a common rhetoric, which bespoke a new community of interests and a common foe, and a common belief that the wartime readjustments of American economic life should be a pattern for the future, the laborers extended the hand of fellowship to the Progressives in an alliance that was beneficial to both parties. Together, they believed they had the power to shape the future.[36]

In their search for allies in the work of social reform, both labor and the reformers turned to the churches. Both groups realized, as had the government in wartime, that their chances of getting national approval for their schemes would be enhanced if the national arbiters of morality were on their side. Speaking for the reform camp, Claude Warren issued a ringing call to the churches to take a more active role in the work of social reconstruction: "If the Church is honest, she will not deceive herself by thinking she has done her full duty. If she is dishonest, she cannot deceive others, who think she has failed. The real friends of the Church realize that this is no time to enter a plea of defense. It is no time to talk about the glory of the past. The Church finds her glory today in the duty of the present hour. Her message, in the face of such a challenge, must be a constructive program of social betterment." To make their arguments or invitations more persuasive, postwar Progressives told the clergy that because of traditional Christianity's stress on personal salvation and the works of charity, the churches had provided the foundation of the decadent system on which economic life in America was built. Against this background of past failure, the Progressives advised the churches to abandon their classbound attitudes and to step into "a new world, born

36. Samuel Gompers, "The Demands of Labor," in Speare and Norris, eds., *Vital Forces in Current Events,* p. 110.

In spite of his expression of willingness to cooperate with all groups in America, Gompers reacted negatively to the Progressives' overtures. He viewed them as fair-weather friends whose plans smacked of socialism. He preferred to follow his own lights and concentrated on bread-and-butter issues and pragmatic methods for attaining advances for labor.

amidst bloodshed and suffering, filled with the spirit of sacrifice, fraught with infinite possibilities."[37]

Labor too turned to the churches for assistance in reconstructing the social order: "Labor expects the Church to help him realize this new thought [of equality], this new impulse, this new inspiration, and I speak with the knowledge of association with laboring people today. If the Church will do this, it will come in the appearance of having a new life and new garments to the eyes of labor. . . . We believe the world is ready to give us our just dues, and we expect the Church to help us in maintaining our industrial liberty."[38]

At least one camp in the Christian churches, the Social Gospellers, responded favorably to the challenges articulated by the Progressives and labor. Since the Social Gospel was one of the sources of Progressive ideology,[39] it is not surprising that its adherents were open to a union with the reforming forces of the Progressive movement. The Social Gospellers shared with the reformers a common belief in the environmental causes of poverty[40] and throughout their history had called attention to the roots of poverty and the need for systemic change. Perfectionist in inspiration, evolutionary and progressive in expectation and outlook, they hoped to bring gospel urgency to the alleviation of social evils, and their preferred method of bringing about the establishment of the Kingdom of God was through the conversion of Christians whose actions in the world would morally transform society.[41] Their early crusades, however, had

37. Warren, "Call of a New Day," pp. 317–18.

38. "What Labor Expects of the Church," *Railway Conductor,* June 1919, p. 270.

39. May, *End of American Innocence,* p. 22.

40. T. Howland Sanks, "Liberation Theology and the Social Gospel: Variations on a Theme," *Theological Studies* 41 (1980):674. Paul Boase says of the Social Gospellers' view of the world and the work of religion: "In every stage of competence and from nearly all denominations, the prophets of the Social Gospel set forth on their crusade with less concern for the sweet bye and bye and more for the sour here and now. Their God was immanent—not off in the clouds, but in the world, working out His purposes through men. Sin was no longer limited to persons but infected society and therefore, had to be attacked directly on the social and industrial level and swept from the economic and political systems" (*The Rhetoric of Christian Socialism* [New York: Random House, 1969], p. 20).

41. Charles Hopkins, *The Rise of the Social Gospel in American Protestantism, 1865–1915* (New Haven: Yale University Press, 1940), p. 89.

not produced the desired results, for, although the Social Gospellers had enjoyed success in gaining control of the denominational hierarchies of the mainline Protestant churches and the Federal Council of Churches, the appeal of the Social Gospel message was limited to a select middle-class audience. The message never penetrated the ranks of American Protestantism to any great degree, and a privatized conservatism continued to dominate in many congregations. The narrowness of its appeal and the small size of its audience were not, however, the only factors that limited the effectiveness of the Social Gospel. As Henry May implies, the Social Gospellers' confidence in the power of preaching to effect social change through personal conversions was idealistic and misplaced: "Many of its hopeful leaders had believed, for instance, that an appeal for social reform on Christian grounds might disarm the opposition, leading conservatives to a change of heart and persuading believers in 'selfish' economics to adopt more kindly principles. Such hopes proved illusory to a large extent." In the early twentieth century, the optimism of the Social Gospellers ran up against the reality of hardened hearts impervious to their best efforts to foster conversion.[42] Against all odds, these social Christians continued to preach their message. In the halcyon days following the armistice, their faith seemed to be redeemed and their hopes seemed realizable.

In the aftermath of the war, the Social Gospellers had good reason to hope and better reason to exult. The war had, as Eldon Ernst makes clear, brought the churches to a position of great prominence: "The wartime experience seemed to demonstrate that the churches' programs remained essential to the health of the nation, that the well-being of mankind continued to depend upon the Christian influence of America. . . . To Americans the war had presented a supreme challenge to Christian civiliza-

42. Henry F. May, *Protestant Churches and Industrial America* (New York: Harper and Bros., 1949), p. 213. May exposes the roots of this optimism: "The most obvious and persuasive weakness of the Social Gospel, its tendency toward facile optimism, was partly an inevitable consequence of its position in the history of Christian thought. The ideas of the Enlightenment, with their exalted view of the nature and possibilities of man, had long since dominated American political thought and finally, having penetrated religion through the Unitarian salient, were overcoming their last adversary in Protestant theology" (ibid., pp. 231–32).

tion, and, the military conflict won, it remained for a full cultural thrust . . . to seal the overall moral victory." Indeed, the crusading aspect of the war both validated and advanced the Social Gospellers' evangelistic identification of Christianity with American values and the American way of life. The Social Gospellers did not stop at such a neutral stance. They insisted that the war crusade had established the validity not of American Christianity in general but of social Christianity. As Reinhold Niebuhr said: "The war has greatly encouraged the interest of the Churches in and the advocacy of the Social Gospel. The agonies of the past years have proved human happiness to be dependent upon conditions of life as well as upon personal attitudes and have taught us the error of the ancient religious confidence that individual happiness can be achieved in defiance of every unfavorable circumstance of life or that an individual could be completely saved in a lost world."[43]

Conscious that the hour of their deliverance from the retarding forces of conservative inertia had arrived, the Social Gospellers rushed to secure their position in the churches and to move them into the reforming camp. They used the heady rhetoric of the postwar era, which connected the war with the struggle for social justice. Harry Ward, a radical Methodist, announced in boldly Pauline tones: "It is the hour of travail of mankind. A new world is struggling to come forth and the old order is holding it back. It is an hour of torturing uncertainty, but also the hour of a great hope." The Federal Council of Churches followed Ward's lead in words that showed gratification that the day of vindication for social Christianity was at hand: "The industrial unrest and uncertainty of the period following the World War bring to the Christian Church an imperative summons and a boundless opportunity. If it be true that chaotic conditions exist and the whole earth seems at times 'without form and void,' it is also true that again 'the Spirit of God' moves on the face of the waters. That Spirit . . . summons

43. Eldon G. Ernst, *Moment of Truth for Protestant America: Interchurch Campaigns following World War I* (Missoula: American Academy of Religion and Scholars' Press, AAR Dissertation Series, 3, 1974), pp. 70, 12; Reinhold Niebuhr, "The Church and the Industrial Crisis," *Biblical World* 54 (1920):588.

the Church to reconsider its own Gospel, to redefine its attitude toward the present social order and to interpret for all time the way of life involved in Christian discipleship."[44]

Everywhere, the Social Gospellers announced the emergence of a socialized religion that sought social justice in the belief "that the world is the subject of redemption."[45] Moreover, with the Progressives, they believed that the war's struggle for democracy on the international political scene must be continued in the domestic industrial sphere. Using the rhetoric of the reformers, an anonymous clergyman invited the clergy to "come on in! Humanity's fine! Fine even under its heavy bondage. Come, help us break that bondage and set men and women and little children free." The flamboyant Ward called upon the churches to share in a "mighty struggle to determine what kind of a world and in what manner humanity shall live for a long time to come." With perhaps more enthusiasm than the situation warranted, Samuel Zane Batten, director of the Northern Baptists' Division of Social Education, announced that socially active Christianity had nearly captured the churches, implying that privatized religion was dead: "The churches are fairly committed to the interpretation of the social gospel and the work of social reconstruction. They recognize that Christianity is here not alone to save individuals but to become the constitutive power of a new social order."[46]

Filled with confidence, the Social Gospellers felt they could mold the future to their specifications.[47] As Niebuhr pointed out, the social mission of the church envisioned by the activists demanded its involvement in secular affairs. Neither he nor the churches shrank from such involvement: "The whole church now freely avows its ambition to exert a direct influence upon

44. Harry F. Ward, *The Opportunity for Religion in the Present World Situation* (New York: Women's Press, 1919), pp. 19–20; Committee on the War and the Religious Outlook, *The Church and Industrial Reconstruction* (New York: Association Press, 1920), p. 1.

45. Commission on Church and Social Service, "The Church and Social Reconstruction," *Federal Council Bulletin* 2 (1919):126.

46. "A Clergyman's Confession," *Reconstruction*, July 1919, p. 212; Ward, *Opportunity*, p. 8; Batten, "Churches and Social Reconstruction," p. 616.

47. For a summary of the reconstruction schemes advanced by the various churches, see ibid.

world affairs and manifests an eager interest in the moral problems involved in political issues."[48] Such an assertion marked an advance over the previous Social Gospel reliance upon indirect influence through the actions of converted stewards for effecting social change. Indeed, Niebuhr's words show a bold new advocacy of overt political action. Donald Meyer argues that this radical departure from past methods was dictated by a new realism in the thinking of the activists: "Shaping the vision of a new social order, then, was a mixture of motives. Behind the exalted sense of possibility lay much more than pure vision alone—anxiety, prudence and temporary defeat." The pastors were terrified that if the churches did not adopt a crusading social program, they would be crippled by indifference and defections on the part of workers. Fear thus explains their advocacy for social action. It does not explain the choice of a specifically political mission. Quite simply, the socially active pastors came to appreciate power and its uses. They realized that in the industrial world the power of big business was overwhelming.[49] To counter that power they had to support all forces in American life that could deal with business on an equal or superior footing. Logically and practically this meant that the churches had to support legislative reform and enter into power-bestowing alliances with reformers and laborers. Thus, like their Progressive colleagues, the Social Gospellers confronted the problems of postwar America armed with the righteous idealism of Christian-American democracy, a new appreciation of power, and a belief in the normative nature of the wartime industrial practices.

The churches' uniting with the Progressives was easily achieved and easily understood: they shared a common rhetoric

48. Niebuhr, "Church and the Industrial Crisis," p. 588.

49. Meyer, *Protestant Search for Political Realism*, pp. 32, 56. On the change in the Social Gospellers' outlook, Meyer writes: "Seeking closer and more stable relations with capital and labor, Social Gospel pastors were going beyond mere proclamations of the ideal, into the realm of means. They were becoming political, in the larger sense of the word. They had many inhibitions to overcome in their search, so, seeking both righteousness and power in the same agent, they found it difficult to accept compromises, partial measures, short-run expediencies. This was to be seen more explicitly in their judgments upon politics in the narrow, more conventional sense, the politics of parties and state action" (ibid., p. 118).

and had learned similar lessons in the war. Their alliance with labor, however, was more startling. Although from the time of Washington Gladden's Columbus ministry, Social Gospellers had been concerned with the problems of labor, Gladden's sympathy for the cause of labor was not the norm for the social prophets, much less for the churches as a whole. There were, of course, reasons for Protestantism's tepid support for labor. First, the laborers who suffered most from industrial inequities were for the most part Catholics, whom Protestants viewed with disdain and whose difficulties they regarded with indifference. Second, the Social Gospel idea of stewardship tended to canonize social division, for though it encouraged charity, it never really challenged church members to examine the root causes of social evils. These attitudinal problems created a barrier between labor and the Protestant—and even the Social Gospel—churches.[50] As the reconstruction era dawned, the Social Gospellers recognized this division as a potent barrier to the social reform they wished to effect.

The social activists rushed to analyze the roots of the division in the hope that a frank admission of past failures would provide a fruitful basis on which to found a new relationship for the future. Harry Ward decided that the deplorable divorce of labor from the churches had occurred because as conservative institutions with an interest in the status quo, the churches had allowed themselves to "be more or less controlled directly and indirectly, by property interests." As a result, the churches were held hostage to wealth. In a stinging indictment, Harry Sloane Coffin accused the churches of sacrificing social advocacy for comfort: "And far too many of them think of maintaining themselves as organizations and keeping their existing machinery in motion rather than of giving life to the society in and for which they exist. Our churches are class-bound in their outlook and sympathies." James Coale suggested that the pastors were quiet on social issues because breeding and ambition were uppermost in their minds: "In some of the strongest churches it is not good form to allude to the pressing problems of the day. It is a sign of poor breeding to bring before the congregations of

50. Boase, *Rhetoric of Christian Socialism*, p. 12; Miller, *American Protestantism*, p. 206; Meyer, *Protestant Search for Political Realism*, p. 79.

the strongest churches the point of view of the industrial masses, much more to defend them and the pastor who has ambitions simply does not do it." The judgment of the Social Gospellers was harsh and unrelenting: the churches not only participated in but were largely responsible for the class division that marred the American scene. The socialist churchwoman Vida Scudder pointed out the exquisite irony of the situation and admitted the understandable nature both of labor's dissatisfaction with the churches and its willingness to seek comfort elsewhere: "The people who most loudly glorify submission and renunciation belong to the class least called upon to practice these virtues; those who extol a homeless Lord command fair homes where their children gather in peace around them, while the landless and homeless have wandered far from Him and are seeking strange new guides." Niebuhr begged the church to redeem itself by rejecting "some of its complacent confidence in its divinely appointed destiny and trying more sincerely to achieve the moral leadership to which it lays claim."[51]

As a result of their reflections on the churches' past failures and the current urgency, Social Gospel churchmen made a concerted effort to effect a rapprochment with labor. The *American Church Monthly* of the Episcopal church advised clergymen "to familiarize themselves with the program that has just been set forth by the American Federation of Labor," assuring its readers that "the demands set forth are reasonable and moderate and deserving of hearty support." While advising its readers to draw nearer to labor, the journal lambasted entrenched capital: "The only answer is that our whole business and industrial system is controlled by the few; and operated primarily in their interests. One need not be a Socialist or a Bolshevist to see that this sit-

51. Ward, *New Social Order,* pp. 300–301; Henry Sloane Coffin, *In a Day of Social Rebuilding: Lectures on the Ministry of the Church* (New Haven: Yale University Press, 1918), p. 9; James A. Coale, "The Church and Labor," *Biblical World* 54 (1920):360. William H. Morgan said, "There is a growing consciousness of the unrighteous conditions in our social system, also an increasing consciousness of the responsibility of the Christian Church for the existence of these conditions" ("The Church and Labor Reconstruction," *Methodist Review* 102 [1919]:199). Vida D. Scudder, *The Church and the Hour: Reflections of a Socialist Churchwoman* (New York: E. P. Dutton, 1917), pp. 80–81; Reinhold Niebuhr, "Religion's Limitations," *World Tomorrow,* March 1920, p. 79.

uation is all wrong. One need only be a Christian." William Morgan went so far as to identify the goals of labor with those of the churches: "The mission of Christianity is to raise the quality of human life, to purify, elevate and dignify human existence. It is occupied with the problems of social well-being because these problems lie at the root of all our moral and spiritual progress. The labor movement in the midst of the turmoil and conflict of life seeks the same noble end."[52] The Federal Council of Churches endorsed the views of the Social Gospellers and in its updated social creed and its pronouncements on reconstruction approved the legitimate demands of labor to organize, to bargain collectively, and to earn a living wage.[53] It is therefore not surprising that the socially concerned churches and clergymen embraced the idea of industrial democracy that was so close to the hearts of the reformers and the laborers.

With the Progressives and labor, the Social Gospellers saw the introduction of industrial democracy both as the ultimate antidote for social unrest and the continuation of the struggle against autocracy for which the war had been fought. The churchmen, however, added yet another endorsement to an ideal already sanctified by close association with the tradition of American values and the blood of American soldiers and thus enhanced its appeal. As early as 1914, Harry F. Ward identified the struggle with Christianity: "This principle of democracy is a Christian product. It is the application in the social order of the great teaching of Jesus concerning the worth and value of individual life. . . . When men once believe that every human life has eternal value, then they must begin to give the downmost man the chance to realize that value. Hence, the struggle for political and religious freedom has been pre-eminently a Christian struggle."[54] Fired with the holy zeal that the war generated and spurred on by the gospel urgency which Ward articulated, the Social Gospellers joined with reformers and laborers to bring about Christian democracy in industry. The Social Gospellers meant to marshal the righteous elements of the nation

52. Editorial comment, *American Church Monthly,* March 1919, p. 588; ibid., February 1920, p. 517; Morgan, "Church and Labor Reconstruction," p. 193.

53. Miller, *American Protestantism,* p. 221.

54. Harry F. Ward, *The Social Creed of the Churches* (New York: Abingdon Press, 1914), p. 129.

so that their consolidated economic and political power would be equal to the power held by capital. The struggle for democracy would end in an ultimate triumph of Christian virtue.

The Social Gospellers hoped that they could convince the churches to assume a major role in the reforming alliance's work of ushering in the reign of full industrial democracy. Thus they called upon the churches to abandon their prewar caution about social issues. Vida Scudder exhorted the churches to teach their members the Christian foundations of the struggle for social justice and advised the clergy to defend the rights of the poor in the class struggle that was wracking America. Others went beyond the advocacy of a merely educational role for the churches. Bernard Iddings Bell, cofounder of the Church Socialist League (Episcopal), contemplated a gadfly role of critic whereby the church was to measure and judge all social orders and all social plans by her own eternal lights: "The true function of the Church of Jesus Christ is not to make or remake social orders, to devise social panaceas or to glorify forms of government, either political or industrial. Her sole interest, if she is to follow the example of her Lord, is to insist that in any social order, according to whatever may be the economic system under trial, under all forms of government, the welfare of human beings be placed ahead of that of mere property."[55]

The advocacy of a critical role for the church of course demanded the enunciation of criteria of judgment. At the urging of the Social Gospellers, the Federal Council of Churches provided these criteria in its programmatic *Church and Industrial Reconstruction:* "The worth of personality, brotherhood, the duty of service which we are now to discuss are principles which other than Christians have held. The distinctive contribution which Jesus makes to their interpretation is in always viewing them as grounded in reality and destined to be realized because they have their foundation in the very character of God." Using these three principles, which were also the bases of Progressive thought, the Federal Council of Churches submitted American economic life to scrutiny and found it scandalously wanting: "In our present industrial order we have

55. Scudder, *Church and the Hour,* p. 26; Bernard I. Bell, "Church's Chief Function to Talk Straight to Democracy," *Reconstruction,* June 1919, p. 183.

found much in which, as Christians, we cannot acquiesce. Our vision of the social order that ought to be will not allow us to be content with our social order as it is. Impelled by Christian motives, we seek to change existing conditions wherever they are incompatible with the Christian ideal."[56] The council did not stop with criticism. It found the measures advocated by Progressives and labor aimed at the establishment of industrial democracy worthy of active support, both because they conformed to Christian teaching and were feasible. Their feasibility was confidently argued, in true Progressive fashion, by an appeal to the wartime experiments in industrial management. Thus, the council heartily endorsed a living wage, social insurance, child labor laws, collective bargaining, cooperative industry, profit sharing, and indeed the complete establishment of industrial democracy. The council's pronouncements signaled a willingness on the part of the churches to enter the political arena. In addition, they bear eloquent testimony to the existence of an emerging reform consensus following the war that united labor, church, and reformers. This alliance was fired by Progressive idealism, which provided a common rhetorical idiom for all three parties to the coalition and pointed the way to the attainment of an idealistic goal: the establishment of democracy and full justice in the industrial sphere. In addition, all three elements believed that their plans were redeemed from utopianism because their feasibility had been proven by the industrial measures enacted during wartime. This reform coalition entered the reconstruction era with confidence that the future was plastic to its touch.

Obviously, there was neither complete nor perfect harmony in America following the war. While the reform forces pressed their advantage in the social sphere, other groups came forward with radically different ideas on the course American life should follow in the postwar era.

The Social gospellers were challenged in their belief that the future of religion in America belonged to them alone by more conservative evangelical churchmen in all of the churches. For these conservatives, the work of the church in the reconstruc-

56. Committee on the War and the Religious Outlook, *Church and Industrial Reconstruction*, pp. 11–12, 108.

tion era was to be circumscribed by and subordinated to the primary task of teaching the gospel message of saving faith to individual souls. Henry May notes that "the conservative social Christians looked at current social unrest with fear and horror; they devoted a major part of their energies to pointing out the evils of socialism. Usually they were at least skeptical of trade unions and some of them were overtly hostile."[57] They thought the activists' environmental analysis of poverty smacked of socialism and argued, as did one conservative Methodist, that "the rights of the laboring man will be protected and cared for—not by labor agitators, but by the Christian men to whom God in his infinite wisdom has given the control of the property interests of the country."[58] In short, the conservative Christians believed in Christian stewardship, which transferred responsibility for effecting social change not only from the hands of the clergy to the laity but ultimately from a human to a divine agent. Although such reasoning pleaded for a properly reverential deference to the workings of God's Word, it could be used to justify an irresponsible church and an unchanging status quo. Therefore, it was a favorite argument used by laymen who opposed church interference in the economic sphere.[59]

The idea that the church should avoid social concerns was not, however, voiced only by a few lay businessmen who desired an ethical holiday. Some churchmen were appalled by the activism shown by their colleagues. In answer to the Social Gospellers' challenges and their confident expectation of the immanent establishment of the Kingdom, Edgar Daugherty said, "The Church's mission is purely inspirational, regenerative, and on that basic fact there will never be on earth a consummated reform." Surprisingly, in light of the advanced social teaching of the Anglican communion, the Episcopal *American Church Monthly* shared Daugherty's view: "My conception of the relation of the Church to these problems of Reconstruction is that

57. May, *Protestant Churches,* p. 162.

58. Quoted in Walter G. Muelder, "Methodism and Society in the Twentieth Century," in *The Methodist Church in Social Thought and Action,* ed. Georgia Harkness (New York: Abingdon Press, 1964), p. 53.

59. Paul A. Carter, *The Decline and Revival of the Social Gospel: Social and Political Liberalism in American Protestant Churches, 1920–1940* (Ithaca: Cornell University Press, 1954), p. 62.

in the direct sense it has none. The Church is primarily . . . the organ and medium of religion, the channel of communication between God and man. She has one great task—to minister the religion of Jesus Christ. The mission of Jesus Christ was not to reform the world; but to save the world." When the *New York World* took the *Monthly* to task for shirking the responsibility of sharing in the work of reform, the editor of the journal snapped back, "When will our modern philosophers learn that the Church was founded primarily to make people religious and to bring them into union with God, and not to do a thousand other things which can be done far better by other agencies?" In essence, the *Monthly* was arguing for a clear, complete, and distinct separation of realms. This was the basic position of all the conservatives. They did not oppose reform so much as they believed that the church had no business becoming embroiled in the secular processes that effected reform.[60] Thus as the reformers were trying to make the world safe for democracy, conservative churchmen were trying with equal might to save the churches from a worldliness that would make a mockery of religion. The central issue in the conflict was one of ecclesiology. There was no resolution of the conflict in 1919, but the opening volleys in a battle that was to last through the following decade were fired. For the moment, the liberal reformers were confident that they would win. Their optimism would be mocked during the 1920s.

The most serious challenge to the dreams of the emerging reform alliance, however, came not from the forces of conservative Protestantism but from members of the business community. As the reconstruction period dawned, businessmen made it clear that they wanted nothing to do with the schemes of the reformers. Although businessmen were a powerful force

60. Edgar Daugherty, "The Church's Message and Method in the Period of Reconstruction," *Christian Century,* 17 April 1919, pp. 9–10; Latta Griswold, "The Church and Reconstruction," *American Church Monthly,* August 1919, pp. 1036–37; editorial comment, ibid., November 1919, p.234.

The *American Church Monthly* thus cautioned its readers: "We need to be on our guard lest the American Church should be led to make itself ridiculous by advocating any temporary or doubtful expedients for the solution of our present industrial difficulties. . . . The duty of the Church is to teach religion, to provide for the worship of God, and to administer the sacraments" (editorial comment, ibid., April 1919, p. 636).

on the American scene, the crusading zeal of the reformers and the radical changes in the American economic system wrought by the war put them on the defensive. Nevertheless, it would be wrong to assume that business harbored no dreams for the future. Businessmen did have such hopes, which were shaped by the war experience, albeit in a negative way. They too saw 1919 as a year of splendid opportunity: the opportunity to dismantle rather than to extend the cumbersome wartime machinery that governed economic life.

At first, the business community shared in the general national rejoicing at the scope of the American war victory. There was even a feeling that the efficiency of American business was largely responsible for that triumph. At the 1919 convention of the United States Chamber of Commerce, Harry Wheeler, the president of that body, announced that business would leave the past behind and take the lead in forging the future: "Businessmen are not competent in matters of diplomacy, but, by the same token, diplomats are not wholly competent advisers in matters of business. . . . And a message for the world . . . American business knows a cleaner and a fairer way to conduct the affairs of mankind and, if necessity requires, will take a hand to see that these better ways are tried." Business had had enough of idealistic crusades. Without wishing to appear unpatriotic, the business community wanted to put the war behind. There was to be no more foolish talk of continuing the war crusade on a domestic battlefield. Wheeler bravely announced that the business at hand was to "restore business as usual . . . in order to insure the maintenance of peaceful conditions at a time when anarchy and socialism and misguided efforts and unsound theories are clamoring for an opportunity to try out experiments which . . . must result only in misery and ruin if put into practice."[61] Business longed for a return to normal conditions and expressed annoyance at the attacks it suffered from the reformers: "American business is sound and sweet at the core. It is becoming overtired of submitting to the hectoring of hireling lawyers who assume an attitude as to say, 'I know that you are guilty, but you are too smart to be tricked into making danger-

61. Wheeler quoted in Uzzell, "Industrial Pentecost," p. 63; Harry A. Wheeler, "Foundations for the Future," *Nation's Business*, June 1919, p. 17.

ous admissions.' The only hope of recovery from the dreadful conditions caused by the war lies in stimulating work and business in the United States."[62] Confronted by the animosity of the reform alliance and fervently believing in the wisdom of its own plans for the future, the business community struck back at its attackers. The business community examined, denied, and discarded the Progressives' positions and rhetoric. Business leaders ridiculed the reformers' analyses of the war, the "necessary connection" between the war crusade and the need for industrial change, the wartime industrial changes, and the drive for industrial democracy.

The first reaction of capital to the bright plans offered by labor, church, and reform was withering ridicule for what it took to be a foolish utopianism emanating from the reform camp, which was based on an unfounded belief that the war had somehow transformed humanity. Samuel Crowther mocked the fair dreams of business' nemeses: "Everywhere is the notion that the war somehow changed the world in an elemental way. A lot of very high authorities said that it was going to and not a few were quite specific about it. The common difficulty of all these milleniums is that while they point out the various ways in which we should all like to have the world bettered, none of them gives a clue as to how Mother Nature may be made more generous. In fact, the more you examine this old world the less you can discover in the ways of improvement wrought by several years of war." By refusing to recognize the salvific meaning of the war, the business community refused to see the vital (and necessary) link which the reformers insisted existed between the war's struggle for democracy and the domestic social unrest that continued that struggle for human rights. In this way, businessmen denied the fundamental basis upon which the reform rhetoric of the postwar period rested. Therefore, while the reformers could perceive a salutary yearning of the human spirit for democratic rights behind the social unrest of 1918–19, Crowther believed such talk to be mindless prattle. Having denied the link between the war and the crusade for industrial change, he offered a different explanation of the roots of the

62. "Honest Business and Sinister Investigation," *Manufacturer's Record,* 28 August 1919, p. 90.

problem: "It is this aesthetic divorce of Labor from work that is behind much of what we may call 'industrial unrest.' There is a great clatter about rights and only a few whisperings about work."[63] In the view of capital, the cause of all social unrest was the intransigent attitude of the labor unions, which glorified inefficiency and exasperated employers.

Since the reform rhetoric appealed to the wartime industrial measures to justify the reformers' schemes, these measures also came in for scrutiny by American capitalists. For the business community, the return to normal and the creation of a stimulating economic climate were conditional upon the removal of those very wartime measures which the reformers so heartily hailed, for, as Robert Murray points out, the normalcy of the businessman was "a special kind. It was the normalcy of the pre-Spanish American War era. Normalcy to him meant freedom from government regulation, from labor unions, from public responsibility—the freedom of laissez-faire." Isaac Lippincott spoke for many businessmen when he pointed out "that the war organization is regarded as temporary" and not the pattern upon which to construct a new economic order in peacetime. The National Industrial Conference Board iterated Lippincott's statement and pointed out that the continuation of the war apparatus would be a step toward socialism: "The relinquishing of personal (i.e., economic) liberty as a patriotic duty in the stress of a great national emergency is, however, not to be construed as a voluntary movement toward socialism and a demand for Government control of private enterprise in time of peace." Conjuring up the fearful images of radical socialism was part of the businessmen's strategy to discount reform schemes by throwing a red pall over them. Such talk was a potent and emotional weapon against which the reformers had little defense. When occasion demanded, the business community shrewdly borrowed concepts from the Progressive ideology. Turning the Progressive belief in evolution to his own purpose, Samuel Dunn argued that laissez-faire was the product of an evolutionary development and the use of governmental restraints would betray a law of nature: "The fundamental trouble

63. Samuel Crowther, "Some ABC's for Capital and Labor," *World's Work*, January 1920, p. 232.

with government ownership is that it reverses a tendency which has marked the progress of modern civilization and has contributed greatly toward promoting it—the tendency toward differentiation of political and economic functions." The ultimate argument, however, which business used to move the nation toward a disavowal of the war measures was advanced by the National Industrial Conference Board: "The policy of looking to Congress or to Governmental agencies to definitely control the details of business is a radical departure from the nation's traditions."[64] Clearly, business wished to leave no stone unturned, no argument unmet, in its attempts to discredit reform and to move the nation back to its own kind of normalcy.

Business found the ultimate reform dream of industrial democracy dangerous and foolish: "It is assumed that industrial democracy will eliminate strikes and agitation, will make for satisfaction and contentment. The least thought will indicate the utter absurdity of such a proposition. There will simply be greater agitation and greater trouble because those who may be given representation in the management may utilize their position to force concessions which the owners of the property know would, if carried into effect, result in eventual bankruptcy."[65] The business community registered disapproval of every element of or term in the reformers' arguments and offered a radically different plan for the shaping of America's industrial future.

Business also still possessed an adversary spirit toward labor. During this period, business became increasingly—even stridently—hostile to the unions and their demands for the rights to organize, bargain collectively, and earn a living wage, and business leaders sought to convince the American public to share their distrust of labor. Part of their strategy was a campaign of innuendo in which they associated union activity with dangerous red radicalism. *Law and Labor,* a journal with strong

64. Murray, *Red Scare,* p. 9; Lippincott, *Problems of Reconstruction,* p. 5; National Industrial Conference Board, *Problems for Industrial Readjustment in the United States: Research Report #15* (Boston: National Industrial Conference Board, 1919), pp. 56, 64 (see also Alfred Keet, "Big Thinkers on Reconstruction," *Forum,* January 1919, p. 102); Samuel O. Dunn, "Government Ownership vs. Private Control," in *Vital Forces,* ed. Speare and Norris, p. 84.

65. "Industrial Democracy," editorial comment, *Industry,* 15 June 1919, p. 7.

ties to the National Association of Manufacturers, cautioned the nation on the dangerous tendencies of the unions: "Trade Unions oppose legal responsibility and they dismiss their moral responsibility whenever they precipitate a calamity by the quaint statement that if the employers had done as they demanded the calamity would not have occurred. Local unions encourage lawlessness and the national organizations are indifferent to it." Even the moderate Gompers, who eschewed ideology of all kinds and who was nervous about Progressive dreams, did not escape censure. *Law and Labor* questioned his leadership and found it wanting: "He reviews the contribution of American labor to the success of the overthrow of political autocracy in Europe and acts of labor's loyalty to American ideas and ideals. . . . What guarantee will Mr. Gompers give that labor will meet its share of responsibility to uphold our laws and to produce its utmost in order to create the wealth with which to satisfy its hopes and demands?" Taking a leaf from the rhetorical manual of the reformers, the *Manufacturers' Record* even went so far as to say that it was the unions, not big business, that reduced men to slavery, thus deftly turning the reformers' talk of rights against them: "Radical unionism is today slavery. It enforces slavery upon its members. It compels the intelligent men among its members to do things against which their patriotism, their hearts and their brains protest." Indeed, if *Law and Labor* could be believed, the unions were not only harmful to workers, they were also nonrepresentative of the desires of workers: "Labor unions promote strikes. The proportion of strikes conducted by unions as against those in non-union establishments, where strikes represent the spontaneous will of the actual workers, shows that the liability for strikes between unionism and non-unionism is about 30 to 1." In this effort to convince the nation and laborers that unions were counterproductive and dangerously radical, businessmen did not hesitate to use the most powerful weapon in America's postwar rhetorical arsenal. The *Manufacturers' Record* told its readers that the unions were dominated by foreigners and hence un-American: "We are permitting these aliens, these men of foreign birth and foreign language and foreign morals, men foreign to everything America holds dear, to do all in their power to stir up throughout this country the Bolshevistic spirit. . . . Is it not time for the people of America to wake up and stand for Americanism over and above everything else?" *Law and Labor* took the *Record's* position one step further and argued that the American Federation of Labor's reconstruction program aimed to destroy the Constitution.[66] Thus it was that business attempted to discredit labor in the eyes of the nation in its efforts to stem the tide of reform.

Vilification of labor and ridicule of the plans of the reformers, however, were only parts of business' postwar strategy. To discount the claims of labor and to deflect or derail the drive toward the establishment of industrial democracy, business embarked on a campaign to establish itself in the eyes of the public as the true defender of American values. *Law and Labor* proudly proclaimed that capitalism was the foundation of America's greatness: "We have established the power and strength of the American nation by adherence to a political, economic and social system which rewards the individual according to his energy and capacity and we will desert that principle for the schemes of trade unions which level all men to the ranks of the mediocre." *Industry* pointed out that capitalism, not industrial democracy, had legal—even constitutional—warrant in the American system, and *Law and Labor* justified the union-busting tactics of big business on the thoroughly Progressive-sounding grounds that such activities protected both the rights of workers who did not favor unions and the public interest.[67] The *Mining Congress Journal* used the notion of human

66. "The Issue in Industrial Strife as Mr. Gompers Has Drawn It," *Law and Labor*, November 1919, p. 6; "Mr. Gompers in the April McClure's," ibid., May 1919, p. 12; "The Open Shop and Free Labor against the Radically Closed Shop and Slave Labor," *Manufacturers' Record*, 9 October 1919, p. 95; "Seeking to Destroy America," ibid., 14 August 1919, p. 74. "Destroying the Constitution: For a number of years the AF of L has been endeavoring to devise methods whereby the Courts would be deprived of their power to declare laws unconstitutional and one bill which it backed provided that any judge who attempted to exercise such authority would automatically forfeit his Judgeship. In keeping with this idea, the most dangerous proposal in the Federation's program of reconstruction which would impair the rights of minorities by destroying constitutional restrictions, is the demand that an act of the legislature, if twice enacted, should override the constitution, whether State or Federal" ("Program of the American Federation of Labor," *Law and Labor*, April 1919, p.2).

67. "The Issue in Industrial Strife," p. 7; "Industrial Democracy," *Industry*, 15 June 1919, p. 6. "The way into the field of light and life is not by laws that will aid the AF of L to compel everybody to seek admission to it, or failing to

rights which the Progressives employed to criticize capital to defend the plans of business and attack what it perceived to be the rights-eroding tactics of labor: "Organized labor cannot hope to include all working men in its ranks nor command entire public confidence until it not only repudiates all lawlessness but strives by every effort within its power to prevent it. Organized labor will never reach its highest efficiency by asking for itself liberties entirely subversive to the rights of others."[68] In its thrust to claim the American spirit as its own—and partly as its own creation—American business frankly called its all-out offensive for the open shop "the American Plan." The American business community thus employed the same rhetoric that was used by the reform alliance. Talk of human rights, American values, and democratic ideals filled the air. Although businessmen used the same vocabulary as did their opponents, they were not willing to accept either the premises or the supposedly univocal definitions assigned these terms by the members of the reform alliance. Indeed, the business community insisted that it had as much right to define the terms of the postwar social debates as did the reformers and their colleagues. History would prove the capitalists the better and more persuasive debaters.

Some businessmen, of course, such as John D. Rockefeller, Jr., advocated moderation and even granted some measure of industrial democracy to the workers. Such proposals were rare, however, and the vogue for moderation was short in duration. During the reconstruction era, capital became increasingly hostile toward labor. Labor returned the feelings in kind. During 1919, strikes erupted with alarming frequency and resulted in bloodshed and bitterness. The strikes only served to strengthen capital's resolve to break the power of the unions. This resolve gave birth to two complementary campaigns: the open-shop drive and the drive to develop a system of welfare capitalism that

---

be admitted, starve to death. We need a law which will compel workmen who have made a contract to regard it as better than a scrap of paper, to regard a strike—an interference with the orderly progress of industry—as incompatible with the public interest unless it be the last possible resort for securing individual's rights" ("Mr. Gompers in the May McClure's," *Law and Labor,* June 1919, p. 14).

68. "The Road to Industrial Slavery," *Mining Congress Journal* 5 (1919):330.

would make the unions less attractive by providing all the benefits the workers could possibly ask.

In its struggle against both labor and government, the business community recognized the importance of public opinion[69] and forming alliances with the centers of power in the nation. Hence businessmen sought to mold public opinion through advertisements and public relations. In its public relations work, business was remarkably successful in winning the approval of the American people. In searching for partners in its task, however, it was remarkably unsuccessful. Viewing the reformers and labor as enemies, it could turn only to the churches for help. The *Manufacturers' Record* tried to forge a union with the churches on the grounds that both shared a deep distrust of socialism: "One of the most hopeful signs of the awakening conscience of America and the realization of what the anarchistic campaign of the hour will mean if not halted, is the way in which the ministers of all denominations, Protestant and Catholic alike, are calling upon their people to antagonize the socialistic element which now seeks to rule and ruin." Business journals gave wide exposure to the statements of clerics who denounced unions as socialist in inspiration. This talk of the red bogey, however, was merely a camouflage. Business did not truly want the aid of the churches to fight socialism; it expected them to help it in crippling the unions. Further, capital wanted the churches to produce docile workers who were more tractable than unionists were. Thus the *Record* called for "a religion that will make the laboring man, who by threats or actual violence against the non-union man, strives to keep him out of employment, realize that he is at heart a murderer and is murdering the individuality and the liberty of his fellow man." When it became clear in the course of 1919 that the churches wanted little part of such a sycophantic ministry and in fact threw in their lot with the reform alliance, capital's reaction

69. Thomas Uzzell reported that at a Chamber of Commerce convention in St. Louis, "'The greatest revelation of this conference,' another pilgrim to Saint Louis assured me, 'is that business has discovered a new asset—public opinion. Before the war, it was supposed that public opinion was the concern only of government; now businessmen see they too are dependent upon the same check and the same inspiration'" ("Looking Forward," *Nation's Business*, June 1919, p. 27).

was swift and bitter. The *Literary Digest* reported on one particularly vitriolic attack made by the *Wall Street Journal* in response to the churches' choice to side with the cause of reform: "The Church is infected with radicalism, retorts the *Wall Street Journal,* and all this talk of bribery, 'sounds like a certain protest of virtue from the gutter and carries about the same implications.'"[70] Business' disgust for the work of the churches became particularly strong as a result of the activities of the Inter-Church World Movement and the almost universal ecclesiastical censure of the open-shop drive. The attempt at creating a union with the churches failed.

In the reconstruction era, then, business stood virtually alone in its attempts to turn back the tide of change ushered in by the war. This did not mean, however, that it lacked resources. Business leaders shrewdly sought to win the nation's affection by claiming a share in the heritage of American values. Thus, like the Progressives, the laborers, and the churches, they too framed their arguments for the erection of a new postwar society in an idealistic and traditional rhetoric. Because of their lack of allies, their battle for the right to determine the future was fought on many fronts: against labor, against the new-old ideas of state control, against the reformers, and against the newly socially alive churches. As the distance from the armistice lengthened, business' attacks on its opponents grew both more vicious and more effective. The key to the effectiveness of capital's campaign for a return to "normal" prewar conditions was its use of public relations. In an age when emotions were high and rhetoric was a weapon, business succeeded in creating an image that represented the business community as the primary benevolent agent on the scene, an agent that could create, protect—indeed, embody—American ideals and values.

In summary, then, 1919 was a year of tremendous promise and great unrest. All elements of the population shared in the euphoria of victory, but it soon became clear that the unity and the high emotional mood of the nation were shallow and masked underlying problems. In those halcyon days, idealism

70. "Socialism a Denial of God," *Manufacturers' Record,* 23 October 1919, p. 77; "Am I My Brother's Keeper?" ibid., 28 August 1919, p. 73; "The Church and Social Revolution," *Literary Digest,* 18 June 1921, p. 30.

reached tidal proportions as different groups rushed to claim credit for the great crusade's success. Labor, reformers, churchmen, and business all claimed a share in the victory (voluntarism made all their claims valid) and on the basis of their participation and contributions claimed as well the right to plan the future of the nation. Each group agreed that the social question would dominate the postwar era, and each scrambled to present plans for the future. During the course of this reconstruction debate, a new reformist alliance emerged, embracing labor, the Progressives, and churchmen. These three parties were united by the bond of a shared rhetoric, looked to the establishment of the full reign of democracy, hearkened back to the wartime measures that governed industrial relations for hints as to the pattern to follow in the future, and justified their programs by appealing to the ideas of the Declaration of Independence. Business opposed the reformist coalition at every turn and appealed to the Constitution and statute law as the justification for this opposition. All groups vied for honor in the eyes of the public. More important, all vied for real power, for all realized that to the victor in the postwar battle of words and pasts belonged the ultimate prize: the right to shape the future. Thus, 1919 was Armaggedon and Parousia at the same time. It was a time of hope. It was a time of despair. It was a time of struggle. The bishops, fresh from the war and newly confident of an American identity for the church, would have to join the struggle and fight for the right to shape the future.

Chapter IV

The Genesis and Contents of the Bishops' Program of Social Reconstruction

Catholic conviction of the need for reconstruction antedated the heady days and dizzying proposals that followed the signing of the armistice in November 1918. Along with other segments of the population, Catholics recalled the Civil War and the tremendous challenges that had confronted the nation as a result of that catastrophic conflict. Hence they realized that the aftermath of the Great War would present the nation with serious problems as it tried to readjust to a peacetime economic and social footing. In addition, in common with almost all segments of the American population, Catholics, and especially the American Catholic leadership, realized that the "social problem," that complex of problems touching upon socialism, employment, social justice, and unionization, would clearly dominate the period and the process of readjustment. Thus there were clear and pressing external circumstances and considerations that seemed to challenge the church in 1919 to abandon her long-standing timidity with regard to social issues.

External pressures made Catholic social action desirable—indeed necessary—and internal changes in the church's understanding of her place in modern American society made such action possible and urgent. Fortunately, the experience of the war and the way the American church had responded to the challenges offered by war mobilization removed two of the major obstacles that had blocked all prior efforts to articulate a unified national Catholic response to America's industrial problems: internal fragmentation and isolation from the American reform tradition. The church's wartime activities thus equipped her to participate in the struggle for social justice in the postwar era: she was unified, and she was at home with the rhetoric, dreams, and idealism of the Progressives. Moreover, one aspect of the church's wartime strategy made her vulnerable to criticism. During the war the church had consciously chosen to advertise her loyalty to American ideas and idealism to the American public through the sophisticated use of the news media. The great praise in the form of positive headlines that she received was enjoyed and appreciated by the church's leadership. Yet this highly visible and widely publicized incorporation into the political and ideological mainstreams of American public life at a time when Progressive idealism fueled the American spirit presented problems for the church in the postwar era. Could she sustain the momentum of positive publicity built up during the war? Would she, or could she, remain truly at home in America? These questions in turn posed a further question: in the postwar era, when national attention was once again focused on social issues, would the church address herself to these issues on the basis of a coherent set of principles and ideals (which were at one with the bases of Progressive thought), or would she continue to address such issues on an expedient and ad hoc basis? The challenge she faced and the pressure she experienced were largely of her own making. She had consciously chosen to train the spotlight of publicity on her activities so as to magnify her American virtues, and she would have to live up to the expectations which her highly publicized wartime exploits had created.

Thus a combination of external circumstances and internal changes and pressures conspired to make the question of a Catholic response to the industrial problems highlighted by reconstruction quite momentous. In a real sense, the future of the American church hung in the balance. Hence, for the American church in general, the postwar period was, as it was for many groups in America, a time of both crisis and opportunity. For the Catholic social activists, this age was equally, if not more, momentous and equally critical. For men such as Ryan, Dietz, and Kerby, the last barriers to the articulation of a passionate, positive, and comprehensive Catholic social program seemed to have been demolished by the war: the church was internally unified, at home with her American environment, and finally, albeit initially expediently, open to the idealism of the reforming age, which they felt could be justified in purely Catholic terms. For these social activists, the mandate for action and the specifics of a program of reform came from two different, although in their minds essentially and even materially congruent, directions or sources: the American reform tradition and the Leonine vision of the mission of the church in an industrial society. Both strains of thought revered the dictates of natural law in their insistence on the inviolability of the dignity of the human person. Both supported industrial workers' rights. Both espoused the use of union activism and government intervention to further the cause of social justice. Indeed, the Catholic social activists believed that the reformers' schemes were merely the local means whereby Leo's dreams could be realized on the American scene. The participation of the church in the reformers' war seemed to them to open up the possibility that the church would finally recognize the congruence between the two traditions to which their own writings testified, and on this basis that the American church could make her peace with these two strains of her heritage and environment by coming to terms with the social questions facing the church and the nation following the war. Indeed, it seemed that 1919 was the year of favor, the acceptable year of the Lord.

The events that led to the publication of the Bishops' Program of Social Reconstruction of 1919 reveal how this complex interplay of forces, motives, circumstances, and internal pressures conspired to bring about a significant and highly public shift in the American church's attitude toward and strategy for dealing with social issues.

At the first meeting of the newly constituted Committee on Special War Activities on 13 April 1918, the members of the committee told the bishops that the church would have to face the national problems attendant upon industrialization during the reconstruction period that would follow the war and that the task of planning for and participating in this work should constitute an important part of the church's national war work.[1] Accordingly, the CSWA Committee on Reconstruction was established, and Msgr. Michael J. Splaine of Roxbury, Massachu-

1. Walter G. Hooke, Report of the Executive Secretary, February 1919, p. 4, NCWC-CSWA (Ex. Sec.), Box 1, folder 1, ACUA.

setts, the former chancellor of the Archdiocese of Boston and a protégé of William Cardinal O'Connell, was named its chairman.[2] In establishing this committee, the CSWA gave the group the mission of examining and coordinating Catholic interests in industrial matters and of planning for the future.[3] As perceptive and foresighted as this mandate was in April of 1918, seven months before the armistice, there was a deceptive simplicity about its statement of purpose. In April of 1918, Splaine was the only member of the Committee on Reconstruction. He was already overburdened by the diverse responsibilities of his other ecclesiastical posts. He was the pastor of Saint Joseph's Church in Roxbury, a trusted and heavily taxed lieutenant of the autocratic Cardinal O'Connell of Boston, and a member of the CSWA board, which necessitated his commuting from Boston to Washington for meetings. At this point, Splaine cut a quixotic figure. He was a committee of one with no budget, no concrete plans, and no colleagues with whom to face the awesome task of mapping the national church's postwar strategy. He was undeterred by these obstacles.

Splaine attacked the committee's problems systematically. First, he assembled his committee. He chose Charles P. Neill, the federal commissioner for railroad adjustments, M. P. Mooney, executive in the Saint Vincent de Paul Society in Cleveland, Charles G. Fenwick, professor of political science at Bryn Mawr College, the Reverend J. Elliott Ross, C.S.P., the Reverend Frederick Siedenberg, S.J., of Loyola University of Chicago, the

2. As events unfolded, there was a certain irony to this appointment. O'Connell, who was Splaine's friend and patron, became displeased with the NCWC's reconstruction work and was blunt and persistent in his criticisms of it.

3. CSWA minutes of 13 April 1918, NCWC-CSWA (Minutes), ACUA. With the passage of time, the duties of the committee became more complex as its area of concern became both more specific and more pressing. Michael Williams recounts that at the end of the war, the committee was concerned with a multiplicity of areas: "Immediately after the signing of the Armistice, the subcommittee proceeded to put its plans into effect. These included the organizing of Catholic groups for the reemployment of returning soldiers, sailors and marines; cooperation with the American Red Cross through the better equipment of local clinics to give medical care to soldiers and their families; cooperation with the Federal Board of Vocational Education in the rehabilitation of the wounded, a general program on reconstruction problems and a back to the land movement" (CSWA Report, 1 January 1919, NCWC-CSWA [Burke], Box 19, folder 19, ACUA).

Reverend Frank O'Hare, professor of economics at Catholic University, the Reverend Edward O'Hara of the State University of Portland, Oregon, and the Reverend Ignatius Smith, O.P., the national director of the Holy Name Society. The lay representation envisioned by Splaine was rounded out by the appointments of Robert Biggs, an attorney from Baltimore, and James E. Hagerty, a professor of economics at Ohio State University in Columbus. Splaine hoped that through the appointments of these men, the Committee on Reconstruction would reflect the best Catholic thought on the problems confronting the nation following the war.

In presenting these members of the committee to the CSWA leadership at its meeting on 19 October 1918, Splaine outlined the work of the committee as he saw it: "The Committee is first of all a Catholic Committee, which means that it will view the After the War Problems from the Church's standpoint and that it will endeavor in any material work that it undertakes to have it interwoven with spiritual help." Splaine therefore saw the work of the committee as partly catechetical and partly patriotic. He advised the bishops that these two goals could be served if the committee turned its attention to six areas: the improvement of the working conditions of workers in the war industries, the reabsorption of returning soldiers into a peacetime economy, the rehabilitation of the war wounded, the dissemination of data on reconstruction work, the securing of funds to reimburse Catholic institutions helping in the war work, and the willing and complete cooperation of church agencies with secular agencies engaged in reconstruction work.[4]

From Splaine's list of activities to be undertaken by the Committee on Reconstruction it is clear that he was animated by the same thinking that motivated the founders of the NCWC. He frankly believed that the war was a splendid opportunity for the church to advance her own interests while coincidentally proving her loyalty to America by advancing the welfare of the nation. Further, with his social activist colleagues, he believed that in the postwar period, the church could most effectively pursue her complementary catechetical and patriotic goals

4. Ibid., pp. 3–4.

through decisive action in the area of social concern. Splaine thus told the bishops: "A second important problem of Reconstruction will be the influencing of the political, industrial and economic leaders of the country so that they may all adopt measures of readjustment along lines that will be perfectly safe and beneficial from a moral and religious standpoint." After reminding the bishops that the war was the result of the lack of a correct and fully moral social philosophy, Splaine pointed out that to correct this glaring social immorality, "the public mind has to be educated on the matter and the leaders of thought have to be enlightened in regard to the correct understanding of the immutable laws of justice and rights. In this way the legislator will reach a public opinion so crystallized that the public at large will not be satisfied with any system that is not fundamentally sound and capable of affecting good for the whole people."[5]

Splaine thus envisioned the work of the committee to be largely persuasive and educational. Specifically, he wished to bring the moral principles contained in Leo XIII's writings to the attention of the entire nation, and particularly of legislators, in the hope that Catholic moral thought would inform America's reflections on the future. Thus, with the members of the reform alliance, the church, in the person of Splaine, was showing a shrewd appreciation of the drift of the nation toward federal control of national life through legislation. With the members of the reform alliance, the church desired to help shape that legislation. In addition, and again in common with the reform coalition, the church was showing both an awareness of the importance of public opinion and an eagerness to mold that public opinion. To bring her influence to bear upon that national scene and thus shape a future in conformity to or informed by the teachings of the church, Splaine announced that the members of the committee would write articles for the media which would expose and explain Catholic social teachings. Unfortunately, Splaine's plans were too modest. He modestly (or foolishly) refused to trouble the bishops for money and thus condemned the committee to ineffectiveness. A stronger hand

5. Ibid., p. 6.

and a clearer head would be needed to give the committee's work more focus and force.[6]

At its 19 October 1918 meeting, the CSWA approved of Splaine's work, but the members of the parent body had one practical reservation about his ability to accomplish what was necessary. Splaine had already anticipated this criticism and, with Burke, had entered into negotiations with John O'Grady to become secretary of the committee. Because Splaine had so many other responsibilities that he could not devote his full attention to the work of reconstruction, Burke advised that the reconstruction committee appoint a secretary who would reside in Washington and supervise its day-to-day activities. For this important post, Splaine nominated the Reverend John O'Grady, a young priest from the diocese of Columbus, Ohio, who had studied at Catholic University and the University of Chicago.[7] O'Grady was a wise choice for the post of secretary, for he possessed knowledge and sympathy for both the Leonine Catholic tradition of social thought and action, which he derived from his studies at Catholic University under William Kerby, and the American reform tradition, which he derived from his stay at the University of Chicago. O'Grady's appointment, however, was not accomplished until some delicate negotiations had taken place. Burke and Splaine had to convince both O'Grady and the bishop of Columbus that the need of the national church outweighed that of the local church. By September of 1918, Splaine, Burke, and O'Grady were discussing the contemplated appointment. On 30 September 1918, Splaine wrote to

6. Ibid., pp. 6–7. As the work of the committee grew, its functions multiplied as a result of its members' desire to offer a comprehensive Catholic response to postwar problems. As a result, seven departments evolved: the employment service department; hospital social service; vocational rehabilitation; educational research; land colonization; library; and motion pictures. All were enjoined to work with government agencies doing similar work. The Bishops' Program of Social Reconstruction was the product of the educational research department. See the Report of the Reconstruction Committee, n.d., NCWC-CSWA [Reconstruction Committee], Box 33, folder 5, ACUA.

7. CSWA minutes of 19 October 1918, NCWC-CSWA (Minutes), ACUA. At Chicago, O'Grady had studied under Albion Small and Richard Henderson and had met Jane Addams. At Catholic University, he had studied under William Kerby. See Thomas W. Tifft, "Toward a More Humane Social Policy: The Work and Influence of Msgr. John O'Grady" (Ph.D. dissertation, Catholic University of America, 1979), p. 12.

Burke announcing that O'Grady had agreed to serve as the committee's secretary and that the bishop of Columbus had released him from the diocese. It was with a sense of relief that, five months after the committee's establishment Splaine was able to write to Walter Hooke at NCWC headquarters and say, "I believe that we are on the high road to making distinct progress with our committee on Reconstruction."[8] Splaine was not mistaken. With the appointment of O'Grady as secretary of the committee, the work of reconstruction began in earnest and at a rapid pace.

Soon after his appointment, O'Grady shouldered a twofold task: much of the responsibility for completing the formation of the committee fell on him, and he had to give its work a more concrete focus and a practical sense of direction. Accordingly, on 9 October 1918, less than two weeks after he had agreed to accept the position and while he was still in Columbus, O'Grady wrote two letters to Splaine outlining the task of the committee as he saw it and suggesting the names of men whose appointment he favored. In presenting his plans, O'Grady made it clear that he agreed with Splaine that the social question would dominate American life in the postwar era and that the church's position would depend on her ability creditably to contribute to the solution of industrial problems. He felt, however, that the American church was unequal to this task because her past history of involvement in and understanding of social concerns had been so lackluster. Therefore, he agreed with Splaine that the first and most basic task of the committee was to educate the Catholic population about the roots of Catholic and contemporary American and European social thought and to persuade the faithful to become involved in the pressing work of alleviating industrial ills on the basis of the insights of those traditions. He offered a practical strategy for the committee. First, he outlined the eight specific areas to which it should turn its attention: land colonization, Americanization, health, rehabilitation of the wounded soldiers, industrial relations (to

8. John J. Burke to Michael J. Splaine, 26 September 1918, and Splaine to Burke, 30 September 1918, NCWC-CSWA (Burke), Box 19, folder 10, ACUA; Splaine to Hooke, 30 September 1918, NCWC-CSWA (Ex. Sec.), Box 9, folder 8, ACUA.

be considered under a number of subheadings: labor standards, minimum wage, industrial sickness, unemployment, superannuation of industrial workers, and social insurance), the nature and function of the government after the war, government ownership and regulation of industry, and problems of markets and marketing. He further proposed that the committee gather the best contemporary and traditional thought on these subjects so that its proposals for Catholic action might be both well-informed and acceptable to the people. Finally, he believed that the committee should seek to disseminate Catholic ideas on all of these problems, not merely through a random newspaper campaign, but through the publication of pamphlets that would be distributed widely among the Catholic population.[9]

O'Grady told Splaine that to advance the ambitious and Progressive educational work of the committee, ultraconservative businessmen should not be appointed.[10] Rather, the members of the committee "ought to represent different interests and different viewpoints. The various professions ought to be represented on the committee. Labor and capital ought also to be represented. The Catholic womanhood of the nation ought to have at least two members."[11] O'Grady provided Splaine with a list of names he thought should be considered.[12] Splaine responded favorably to O'Grady's suggestions concering the committee's work and membership and, chastened by O'Grady's mention of

9. John O'Grady to Splaine, 9 October 1918 (II), pp. 2–3, NCWC-CSWA (Ex. Sec.), Box 9, folder 8, ACUA.

10. O'Grady to Splaine, 9 October 1918 (I), ibid.

11. O'Grady to Splaine, 9 October 1918 (II), p. 1, ibid.

12. O'Grady's list of names shows the balance he hoped would mark the committee. From the clerical sphere, he suggested the Reverend Henry (sic.) Siedenberg, S.J., of Loyola (Chicago) School of Sociology and the Reverend Hubert LeBlonde, director of Cleveland's Catholic Charities; from the academic world, Carlton Hayes, the historian and political scientist from Columbia University, and James Hagerty, dean of the School of Social Sciences at Ohio State University; from the professional area, Dr. Harrington, a surgeon from Boston, and Walter Smith, a Philadelphia lawyer and the president of the American Bar Association; from the public sector, Arthur Mullen, a Nebraska member of the National Democratic Committee, and Robert Cuddihy of the *Literary Digest*; from the ranks of labor, Frank Duffy, of the executive council of the AFL, and an unnamed woman active in labor circles; and Senators Henry Ashurst of Arizona or James Phelan of California. He left the choice of one woman and two prominent Catholic businessmen up to Splaine. See ibid., pp. 1–2.

the need for money, promised to press the NCWC for any appropriations O'Grady deemed necessary. By return post, O'Grady told him to request an annual appropriation of $37,075, explaining, "It may not be necessary to expend the entire amount appropriated, and it may be necessary to ask for more before the end of the year. Give the Committee to understand that it is exceedingly difficult to make out an exact budget for our work on account of its newness." O'Grady would encounter the latter difficulty. His plans and the work of the committee would be costly, but the results achieved in "building up a Catholic literature of permanent value"[13] in the area of social concern, thereby creating a new and vital social tradition for the American church, show that it was money well spent. Together, O'Grady and Splaine began to guide the reconstruction committee and to make it a powerful tool for educating their fellow Catholics and non-Catholic countrymen in the Catholic principles of social action.

O'Grady had formulated his ideas on the direction and scope of the committee's work in consultation with Professor Hagerty while he was still in Columbus. He finished his work there at the beginning of November 1918 and moved to Washington to devote himself full time to the reconstruction committee's work. As Thomas Tifft points out, when he arrived in Washington, he had "only the most general ideas on what a reconstruction program should include." He realized, however, that the church was already at a disadvantage because, even before the signing of the armistice, several well-developed programs "had already been drawn up and published by prominent groups of persons both in Europe and the United States." Confronted with this challenge and fearful that the church would lose the momentum of positive publicity she had built up during the war, O'Grady's first thought was, according to Tifft, to assemble a team of fifteen Catholic scholars in Washington to compose a reconstruction statement that would compare favorably with

13. Splaine to O'Grady, 12 October 1918, NCWC-CSWA (Reconstruction Committee), Box 7, folder 4, ACUA. In addition, Splaine nominated Peter W. Collins of the Electrical Workers of America as a labor representative and James P. Phelan, a Boston banker as a business member. O'Grady to Splaine, 16 October 1918, NCWC-CSWA (Ex. Sec.), Box 9, folder 9, ACUA.

other reconstruction programs and thus enhance the church's image.[14] The swift pace of developments on the national and international scenes conspired to render O'Grady's leisurely plans unfeasible.

The signing of the armistice on 11 November 1918 introduced a new note of urgency to O'Grady's task. The CSWA pressured Splaine for results, which he promised would be forthcoming by the time of its meeting in New York on 26 November 1918.[15] In this swirl of events, the incomplete Committee on Reconstruction met and prepared a report to be presented at the CSWA executive committee meeting. The report once again outlined the work the committee felt it should do, and once again, O'Grady's guiding hand is evident: "The work of the Committee is primarily educational and directive. It will endeavor to supply information to Catholics on the various social and industrial problems arising during the reconstruction period and to develop social service programs for Catholic societies." The report also contained a distinctly new (for the committee) and old (for the American church) note of alarm in the statement of goals and rationale: The reason for studying industrial problems was that "many people are apprehensive of the spread of radical doctrines among the working classes in America." The committee noted with satisfaction that "it is the general feeling that no institution is better fitted to deal with the rising tide of radicalism than the Catholic Church."[16] It would appear that at this point the reconstruction committee was on the verge of committing the church to the same narrow and insensitive social thinking and action that had proved to be so sterile before the war. Such an approach would have seriously damaged the church's already shaky relationship with labor and undercut any possibility of rapprochement with the reform alliance that was advocating some measures which, because of their reliance on extensive government interference with the industrial processes, bore a slightly radical tinge. The commit-

14. Tifft, "Toward a More Humane Social Policy," p. 20.

15. Splaine to Hooke, 18 November 1918, NCWC-CSWA (Ex. Sec.), Box 9, folder 9, ACUA.

16. John O'Grady, Reconstruction Report, n.d., p. 1, NCWC (Historical Materials, XIV), ACUA.

tee, however, did not envision its actions as being out of step with national sentiment. Indeed, the members clearly saw the work they proposed as a continuation of the patriotic work the church had performed for the nation during the war. On the basis of this confidence that the church was fully American and indeed the greatest servant of the nation, the committee proposed that the church cooperate in every way with the government to ensure a stable social situation in peacetime.

The committee's articulation of its goals and its contemplated method of acting make it clear that its motivations were multifarious and that it hoped to impress and influence diverse groups. There were three motives behind the contemplated program of activities: the committee hoped to check radicalism, to secure the working classes for the church, and to solidify the church's position in the American mainstream through strenuous demonstrations of Catholic loyalty to the nation that would make the value of the church manifest to the American public. In this way, the church could serve her own interests at the same time that she served those of the nation. Therefore, the committee understood that its words and works were addressed to the American church as a whole, to Catholic workers, to the government, and finally to the American public. The proposals presented to the CSWA were ambitious. Because of the mixture of motives, the diversity of publics, and an unmistakable caution, however, these proposals lacked the unity of purpose and specificity of detail that marked other reconstruction programs already circulating in America. By the time Splaine presented them to the CSWA in late November 1918, the war was already over and the nation was awash in more focused and practical programs, and the committee's proposals were unacceptable. Accordingly, at the 26 November 1918 meeting of the CSWA, the American Catholic leadership sent the reconstruction committee back to work and set a deadline for the formulation of new plans: "On the motion of Bishop Russell, seconded by Msgr. Drumgoole, it was resolved: that a programme shall be presented for the approval of the Administrative Committee, within two weeks of this date [that is, by 8 December 1918], by the Chairman of the Committee on Reconstruction . . . to include . . . a definite outline of the work proposed, both for immediate application and progressive development, with particulars of the personnel required, together with an estimate of the work to be done within one month and within two months, and a statement of the maximum expense involved."[17] The bishops wanted action.

In early December, Splaine wrote to O'Grady to apprise him of the situation and ended his letter with a desperate appeal that O'Grady "kindly bend some of your thought and energy to making a specific detailed plan that we can present at the meeting and further send to the four bishops of the Administrative Committee." The pressure from the CSWA and the bishops was not the only goad to action which O'Grady and Splaine felt. On 10 December 1918, Larkin Mead wrote to Burke with an urgent request for a story about the church's plans for reconstruction. He made it clear that since the church had gone public with its war programs, the public expected some follow-up in the post-war era: "I am on the lookout for a good New Year story for national distribution. I want you to indicate your whole revised program for meeting after-war problems and convey to the American public a pretty clear idea of what you are going to do with the money they have turned over to you. You will remember that you promised me you would make a statement for me on this subject. . . . I should have material for it . . . within a week or ten days." Mead ended his note with a tantalizing reference to the Knights of Columbus "prattling about sending over footballs, overalls and plum pudding" and challenged the bishops to "come out with a big, brainy statement, analyzing the situation and announcing the plans of your organization for meeting it." Mead's words were well calculated to get a response from Burke and his associates at the NCWC. Any hint that the Knights of Columbus were grabbing all the headlines and thus giving the public a distorted (at least to the bishops' way of thinking) view of Catholic leadership was a sore point at the NCWC. Mead therefore insisted that the bishops place themselves once more before the American public as the truly reflective and responsible agents behind all Catholic work for the nation. Further, Mead reminded his episcopal clients that in the

17. NCWC Executive Committee minutes, 26 November 1918, NCWC (Rockford File), Box 1, folder 19, ACUA.

business of public relations, timing was of the essence.[18] If they wished to sustain the momentum of their wartime push, the bishops would have to act quickly. Burke passed Mead's letter on to Splaine and O'Grady.

The demands that were thrust upon O'Grady, first by CSWA and then by Mead, placed him under considerable pressure. He had been presented with two deadlines. He was to have a coherent program of specific recommendations ready for the bishops' perusal by 8 December, and the revised final version was to be ready for Mead's prepublication campaign by 20 December at the latest. In the face of these deadlines, his previously contemplated plan for producing a committee-authored statement had to be reevaluated. The committee could never be convened, much less produce a coherent statement, before the bishops' 8 December deadline. Nonetheless, O'Grady issued a hurried summons to the members of the committee asking them to appear in Washington for a meeting to develop a Catholic reconstruction plan. After he had wired the committee's members, he turned to his old mentor, Kerby, for advice. In an interview with Kerby, O'Grady outlined his plans to assemble his committee. Kerby advised him that the committee method was not a very efficient way of getting out such a statement so quickly.[19] He suggested instead that a statement written by a single author would have several advantages, chief among them being internal coherence and the speedy completion that bypassing committee meetings would ensure. Since O'Grady had already invited his committee of experts to assemble in Washington, he was torn. He could see the wisdom of Kerby's advice, but he realized that following it would mean insulting the members of his own committee. Necessity, however, finally forced him to follow the course suggested by Kerby. O'Grady would have to find a single author to plot the course the American Catholic Church would follow in addressing the postwar problems facing the nation and the church.

Fortunately, O'Grady was not the only Catholic reformer

18. Splaine to O'Grady, 5 December 1918, NCWC-CSWA (Reconstruction Committee), Box 7, folder 4, ACUA. Mead to Burke, 10 December 1918, pp. 1–2, NCWC-CSWA (Burke), Box 24, folder 16, ACUA.

19. Tifft, "Toward a More Humane Social Policy," p. 20.

whose thoughts were centering on reconstruction and the social and industrial problems confronting the nation. Ryan, the indefatigable Catholic Progressive, was also thinking about reconstruction and lecturing extensively on the industrial problems of the age. He had become an authority on the subject of reconstruction. To be sure, his ideas were not altogether—perhaps not at all—original. During 1918, he collected newspaper reports and press releases from a wide variety of sources and grouped them under eight headings: employment plans and opportunities; editorials, politics, and miscellaneous suggestions; land projects; state commissions, etc.; miscellaneous organizations and phases; United States government reconstruction plans, including the Federal Board for Vocational Training; training sites and methods of training; and foreign governments' plans.[20] He clipped, collected, and categorized every reconstruction plan that came along, and all the plans became grist for his ideological mill.

In his reaction to the challenges of reconstruction, Ryan showed himself to be a thorough Progressive. In typical reformist fashion, he heralded the idealistic climate of the times: "Idealism saw need and believed it could be met comprehensively." Because he shared in the high Progressive idealism of the postwar era, at the time of the armistice Ryan believed that though there was the possibility that the problems attendant upon industrialization would grow more severe following the war, there was reason to hope—indeed to expect—"that fairly radical reform will be attempted within the next few years." With his Progressive colleagues, Ryan believed that his hopes for postwar social changes were both well founded and realistic, for in common with the reformers, Ryan viewed the war as a watershed experience for American social action. That experience had demonstrated that the American people could unite in the pursuit of an ideal to accomplish great things. Ryan exulted in this triumph of idealism and believed that a continuation of the struggle for democratic rights on the domestic scene would bring about a transformation of society. In addition, with his reforming colleagues, Ryan looked to the wartime experiments

20. Ryan's personal papers at the Catholic University of America contain his press clippings collection and his notes on these stories.

in industrial relations to discern the pattern such relations should follow in the postwar period. He isolated two distinctive contributions which America's wartime experience made to the task of planning for the future, both of which were at one with reformers' prewar and postwar visions. Ryan noted that "during the War, the Government has exercised many and great new industrial functions." He welcomed this intervention and the success with which it regulated the economy as a practical vindication and embodiment of both Leonine and Progressive ideals. Therefore, he suggested that "certain governmental agencies which have done good work during the war period should be retained and strengthened; for example, the War Labor Board and the National Employment Service." In addition, he believed that the cooperation of labor and capital around a common task and goal and mediated by the decisions of the War Labor Board had taught both parties to the industrial process important lessons about the proper ways of dealing with one another. On the basis of the war experience, Ryan thought that capital had learned and would have to affirm in the future "that the rights and welfare of property are less important than the rights and welfare of the laborers." He also believed that labor had learned that it must "become more interested in the efficiency of industry and the increase of the social product. For the betterment of the condition of the masses is very largely a question of having a larger product to distribute."[21]

Because the war had taught each side to understand and appreciate the concerns of the other, Ryan hoped that an efficient and righteous social order could be built "through the industrial devices of cooperation and co-partnership. . . . These will enable the workers to become property owners as well as wage-earners and will gradually fit them to become owners, at least in part, of the instruments of production. This is the ultimate goal of our industrial system, and the only enduring remedy for our social unrest." In the desired end of this contemplated establishment of what amounted to industrial democracy, Ryan envisioned not the destruction of private property and the middle

21. John A. Ryan, "Some Problems of Social Reconstruction," class notes for Marygrove College Summer Session, 24 June–2 August 1929, p. 72, Ryan Papers, Socio-Politico, Box B2-35, ACUA.

class, but rather, in true Progressive fashion, the extension of the middle class, which he saw as the only basis for ensuring the stability of society. As he made clear in his autobiography, Ryan believed that this readjustment of the social order was a continuation of the war and that he "assumed that the war had made the world safe for political democracy and that the peoples of the world were now ready to establish a regime of economic democracy and social justice."[22] In the general tenor of his thinking on reconstruction then, Ryan betrayed a thoroughly Progressive turn of mind. With his reforming brethren, he believed in the righteous power of idealism to effect social change, and he insisted on viewing the struggle for domestic industrial rights as a continuation of the idealistic crusade of the war. Thus he demanded that the nation follow the logic inherent in the ideal upon which it was founded and to which it was devoted and support peacetime reform measures that would achieve a fuller victory for democracy. In addition, with the emerging reform alliance, Ryan protested that the wartime experiments in the regulation of industry redeemed the reform platform from utopianism by demonstrating both the feasibility and potential benefits of radical social and industrial change.

Armed with this general Progressive optimism and his own expedient approach to social questions, which led him to favor the adoption of any and all measures that would, through incremental changes, produce conditions conducive to or reflective of a closer approximation of social justice, Ryan surveyed the reconstruction scene. As he later related in his autobiography, Ryan was particularly impressed (although he insisted on maintaining that it was the bishops who were impressed) by the program outlined by the British Labour party: "Several months before the end of the Great War, the British Labor Party published a 'Social Reconstruction Program,' which presumably was written by Mr. Sidney Webb. On the industrial phase of reconstruction, it is very comprehensive, setting forth at considerable length the implications of its four 'pillars' of the new social order: 1. legal enforcement of a national minimum of leisure, health and subsistence; 2. nationalization of all monopolistic industries; 3. taxation to compel capital to pay for the war; 4.

22. Ibid.; Ryan, *Social Doctrine*, p. 143.

use of the surplus wealth of the nation for the common good." Although Ryan found the Labourites' reflections admirable, he discerned that their ultimate goal was the establishment of a socialist system. Because of the church's unalterable opposition to socialism, he felt that he had to reject the plan, although he did derive two lessons from it: he learned the extent and depth of worldwide sentiment for social change in the wake of the war; and, as he said, "its favorable reception by the public seemed to me to indicate the need of a positive program from a Catholic source."[23] In short, with the bishops, Ryan was beginning to see how vitally important it was to compete for the affections of the working class.

Ryan found reconstruction programs more to his liking when he looked to sources other than the Labour party. He was particularly attracted by the plan offered by a group of twenty Quaker employers in Great Britain, which strongly championed labor's rights to organize and bargain collectively and advocated the erection of a semicooperative industrial system whereby labor would share in industrial management.[24] He also approved of the program prepared by the American Federation of Labor, which treated social reconstruction "under the three heads of trade union action, labor legislation, and general industrial and social legislation." Ryan was particularly heartened by the indication contained in that program that labor was ready and willing to assent to and cooperate in reform through governmental as well as union activity. These were precisely the two agencies for reform hallowed by Leo XIII's words, advocated by the postwar Progressives, and favored by Ryan himself. Ryan was, however, most impressed by the statement issued by the Interdenominational Conference of Social Service Unions of Great Britain, in which he discerned the proper mixture of principle and practical proposals for informing social action. He wrote that this program "declared that every human being is of inestimable worth; that legislation ought to recognize persons as

23. John A. Ryan, "Introductory: Some Other Reconstruction Programs," typed notes, p. 1, Ryan Papers, Correspondence 1939 (L–Z), Box B2-18, ACUA; Ryan, *Social Doctrine*, p. 144.

24. Ryan was so impressed by the Quaker program that he incorporated many of its ideas into his own and the bishops' program. See Abell, *American Catholicism and Social Action*, pp. 200–201.

more sacred than property, that the state ought to enforce a minimum living wage and enable the worker to obtain some control of industrial conditions, that the government ought to supplement private initiative in the provision of decent housing, prevent the occurrence of unemployment, remove the industrial and social conditions which hinder marriage and afford ample opportunities of education for all children." Ryan pronounced this statement's wise balance of ideal and detail "the most specific, comprehensive and sane declaration that has come from any group dealing with the problems of social reconstruction."[25]

Aided by his reading of these programs, Ryan began to formulate his own reconstruction ideas. In his admiration for and appropriation of the features in any of these programs, Ryan was guided both by his reverence for the ideal of social justice and his practical bent. Thus he could give his wholehearted approval to programs that, like the interdenominational and Quaker statements, envisioned the establishment of industrial democracy as the fullest and most ideal and idealistic realization of social justice and endorse the gradualist approach of reform by specific, cumulative measures advocated by the AFL because the latter ushered in changes that served justice on the practical level. For him, ideals were transcendent goals that inspired and directed action, but results were to be revered above all else because they were not transcendent but useful, and for him social utility was key.

In his appreciation for British programs, Ryan displayed the strange bifurcation of the mind that characterized the Progressives. The reformers were deeply convinced that America was a new creation and hence radically different from Europe. Especially at the end of the war, they reveled in America's enjoyment of special advantages and access to fresh opportunities because of being un-European. At the same time, the Progressives, and Ryan not least among them, insisted that all nations shared a congruence regarding industrial problems. Thus, for the reform-

25. Ryan, "Introductory," pp. 1–2. In a handwritten addition to the text of these notes, Ryan wrote, "prior to the appearance of the Bishop's [sic] Program." As with the Quaker program, Ryan would honor the interdenominational program by incorporating some of its proposals into his own program.

ers, foreign nations could guide America's attempts to deal with social problems in two contrasting ways: the fearful failures of other nations to check the rise of radicalism served as a spur to America to reject those reactionary policies that had led to an increase of radical sentiment overseas, and, at the same time, the successful adoption of ameliorative measures by foreign governments was seen as a vindicating laboratory for social experimentation. The expedient mind of the postwar Progressive was attracted to such measures in much the same way as it was attracted to America's wartime experiments, for they showed the feasibility of reform without subjecting the nation to uncontrolled or open-ended experimentation. The success of foreign social reforms redeemed the Progressives from charges of idle utopianism.

From his research, Ryan began to evolve plans for reconstruction which countenanced and advocated state intervention in industrial relations and the adoption of social legislation to establish full industrial democracy. These plans were new neither for Ryan, who had articulated a program of reform incorporating most of the features advocated by the postwar reconstructionists as early as 1909, nor for the Progressives, whose ideas were all but identical to Ryan's. What was surprising about Ryan's formulations in 1919 were that they seemed likely to be translated into action and that the church, which had always been leery of peacetime Progressivism, was about to identify herself fully with the reformers in rhetoric, in short-term reform proposals, and in the ultimate goals for the construction of a new social order.

Thus it would appear that in December of 1918, O'Grady and Ryan were in complementary positions. O'Grady was in search of a comprehensive plan of social reconstruction that would advertise the church's concern and wisdom to the nation, and Ryan was thinking along lines that could produce just such a program. The initial contact between the two men, however, was most unsatisfying. As O'Grady recounted the experience, he had turned to Kerby for advice. Kerby had told him, "You prepare a statement and have the Committee on War Activities approve it and then you can send it around to the four Bishops. You will not have any trouble with them." Upon leaving Kerby, O'Grady approached Ryan, who rebuffed him: "He was most apathetic. He did not think that I had a chance of getting out a statement and said he did not have any time to get to it." O'Grady was frantic and returned to see Ryan. Ryan had been working on a speech on reconstruction to be delivered before a Knights of Columbus convention in Louisville, but, as Francis L. Broderick notes, "dissatisfied with it, he had laid it aside in favor of a speech on the League of Nations." When O'Grady called on Ryan a second time, he noticed the piece in Ryan's typewriter and asked if he might see it. O'Grady read the speech and "told him [Ryan] that this was something that could be made a basis of a statement and I begged and pleaded with him to expand it." Ryan reluctantly agreed to undertake the task. In his autobiography he said the program was hammered out in whirlwind fashion: "Inasmuch as he seemed to be in a hurry to get the production, I refrained from rewriting it and merely dictated with a few verbal corrections the contents of the pencil draft to the operator of a typewriting machine and added a few carefully written paragraphs."[26]

Two days later, on 10 December 1918, O'Grady returned to review the revised version of Ryan's proposals. After some last-minute corrections and changes, he took the document to NCWC headquarters and gave it to his secretaries, who promptly typed it up. When the document was in a final and presentable form, O'Grady took it to the CSWA, which was then in session and eagerly awaiting the document it had demanded of Splaine and O'Grady two weeks before. O'Grady read "the entire document to the Committee almost without interruption." The CSWA was favorably impressed and moved "that the Committee on Special War Activities approve and endorse the article on Social Reconstruction submitted by Dr. O'Grady; that it be sent to the Administrative Committee of Bishops for approval with the request that the CSWA be permitted to pub-

26. John O'Grady, unpublished autobiography, pp. 30–31, National Conference of Catholic Charities Collection, ACUA; Broderick, *Right Reverend New Dealer,* p. 105; Ryan, *Social Doctrine,* p. 145. Broderick wryly notes that the program's final form testifies to its hasty composition: "The final production was a jungle of disorganization, betraying the hasty composition and inadequate editing." He goes on to say, however, "It was perhaps the most forward-looking document ever to have come from an official Catholic agency in the United States" (*Right Reverend New Dealer,* p. 105). Broderick's estimation of the stylistic merits of the document is wide of the mark, as I shall show below.

lish this paper, embodying the program of reconstruction, under the name of the National Catholic War Council." O'Grady's hard work was thus rewarded by the CSWA's endorsement. He did not fare so well at the hands of his own committee members, whom he had summoned to Washington to work out a program. When they arrived in Washington, some days after the program had already been forwarded to the Administrative Committee, the members of the reconstruction committee were angry with O'Grady and critical of the program.[27] There was, however, no turning back. The program was already in the hands of the bishops, and only the question of their approval stood in the way of its publication and circulation by Mead.

In recommending Ryan's program to the bishops for their approval, the members of the CSWA were endorsing and asking the church in America to espouse Progressive idealism and rhetoric in a significant way. Ryan's program was divided into two unequal parts, the first being a critical survey of the reconstruction programs offered by others and the second a prospectus of the solutions to reconstruction problems advocated by the bishops (really Ryan) themselves.

Ryan began his reflections on the social issues of the day and justified his indulging in the already widespread practice of offering reconstruction suggestions by quoting Francis Cardinal Bourne of Westminster: "It is admitted on all hands that a new order of things, new social conditions, new relations between the different sections in which society is divided will arise as a consequence of the destruction of the formerly existing conditions. . . . The very foundation of political and social life, of our economic system, of morals and religion are being sharply scrutinized and this not only by a few writers and speakers but by a very large number of people in every class of life, especially among the workers."[28] With Bourne, Ryan believed that the crises of the age demanded that the church put aside her former caution to address the problems all felt were threatening the very basis of society. In addition, following Leo XIII and Bourne,

27. O'Grady autobiography, p. 31; CSWA minutes, 10 December 1918, NCWC-CSWA (Minutes), ACUA.

28. John A. Ryan, "Social Reconstruction," draft, p. 1, NCWC (Rockford File), Box 6, folder 13, ACUA.

Ryan and the bishops believed that these were moral problems. Thus they felt that the church possessed that wisdom and clarity of vision which could save industrial society from destruction. Thus Burke offered the following formal introduction to the program when it was sent to the bishops: "The deep unrest so widely spread throughout the world is the most serious menace to the future peace of every nation and of the entire world. Great problems face us. They cannot be put aside. They must be met and solved with justice to all. In the hope of stating the lines that will best guide us in this situation, the following pronouncement is issued by the Administrative Committee, National Catholic War Council."[29] Burke's words and Ryan's program bore eloquent testimony to a new Catholic confidence in America and hinted at a reconciliation of the church with the American reform tradition.

Following his preliminary observations about the crisis of the age, Ryan presented a critical survey of the reconstruction schemes already current, divided into three areas, corresponding to three groups in society: labor, capital, and the church. Ryan gave unstinting praise to the proposals of the British Labour party concerning the "four pillars" of a just society, calling it "the most comprehensive and coherent program that has yet appeared on the industrial phase of reconstruction." He cautioned, however, that the Labourite program involved "a gradual approach toward socialism" and therefore had to be rejected as contrary to the teachings of the church. He then summarized three programs formulated by American labor groups, the California, Ohio, and Chicago Federations of Labor, all of which contained proposals for minimum wage legislation, social insurance, cooperative agricultural and industrial enterprises, and government ownership of natural monopolies. Ryan was sympathetic to these demands but concerned with the stress the California and Chicago programs placed on government ownership of monopolies. He called attention to the radical (that is, socialist) drift of these programs and failed to endorse them. Ryan could not approve of these plans because of his residual Catholic fear of radical socialism and its inroads among Ameri-

29. John J. Burke, Preface to Reconstruction Program, NCWC-CSWA (Burke), Box 15, folder 3, ACUA.

can workers. Ryan thus did not discover either the moderation nor the balance of principle and praxis that he desired among the labor plans.

He began his survey of plans from the world of business with the British Quaker industrialists, whom he praised. Their program called for a living wage (not a legal minimum wage—there was a difference between them in Ryan's mind), the recognition of the right of labor to organize and bargain collectively, measures to reduce unemployment and improve working conditions, and an orderly advance toward profit sharing and a cooperative industrial system. Ryan praised the altruistic spirit of the Quaker program, for he believed that if such a spirit permeated the social order, class division would be erased. Thus he singled out for praise one statement that summarized the Quaker plan and challenged American industrial mores: "We would ask all employers to consider very carefully whether their style of living and personal expenditure are restricted to what is needed in order to insure the efficient performance of their functions in society. More than this is waste, and is, moreover, a great cause of class division."[30]

Ryan had nothing but contempt for American businessmen. He characterized the plan for reconstruction advanced by the United States Chamber of Commerce as consisting of "proposals and demands in the interests of business," lambasted American capitalists for refusing "to concede the right of labor to be represented in determining its relations with capital"; and dismissed the program as "extremely disappointing."[31] Ryan's Progressive sympathies clearly were offended by the selfishness betrayed by America's leading capitalists. Together with radical labor, which showed a marked tendency to pursue its own ends without any thought for the position of management or the good of the public, arrogant and selfish capital posed a tremendous obstacle to social peace and order. Thus, on the surface, Ryan's critique of existing reconstruction programs seems to be merely a convenient method for voicing some time-honored Progressive reflections on the disruptive nature of class selfishness. His citing of the Quaker employers, however, revealed his

30. Ryan, "Social Reconstruction," pp. 1–3.
31. Ibid., pp. 3–4.

true intent. Ryan's choice of a specifically religious group of employers seems to argue that a religiously grounded sense of altruism was the only antidote to social unrest. His arguments were subtle and depended upon the cumulative evidence he was presenting to support his contention that the church alone, and specifically the American Catholic Church, could offer the nation the solution to its industrial problems.

When Ryan turned to the third source of reconstruction plans, the religious sphere, the inexorable logic of his argument became clear. He first considered the British Interdenominational Conference plan, which he praised. He cited with approval the ecumenical group's premise that "Christianity provides indispensable guiding principles and powerful motives of social reforms [in that] it lays down the basic proposition that every human person is of inestimable worth and that legislation should recognize persons as more sacred than property." The way it translated these basic natural law principles into concrete proposals for reform saved the interdenominational statement from being abstract, harmless, and platitudinous: "The statement of the Interdenominational Conference points out specific remedies for the evils it describes, specific measures, legislative or other, by which the principles may be realized in actual life." The interdenominational statement's blend of principle and detail and its insistence on translating principles into concrete and practical reform measures exactly mirrored Ryan's own methodology. Ryan did not, however, cite the interdenominational statement merely to praise it. He wished also to point out that a religious body had succeeded in crafting a program that, because it was based on sound and immutable principles, was devoid of any taint of self-interest and thus able to guide a true and lasting reform of social and industrial life. Ryan's point was unmistakable: the problems of the age were basically moral problems, and the church is the teacher of morality and the socially useful virtue of altruism. Thus America should look to the church for guidance in formulating specific principled proposals for dealing with social problems. When Ryan moved on to consider the American scene, he announced, "It is a pity that we Catholics of the United States have produced nothing to compare with this British document. We can however derive some consolation from the fact that every other religious body in America is in substantially the same predicament."[32] The conclusion to be drawn from Ryan's skillful argument was clear: since the British churches had produced the most promising program for reconstruction, the American church programs must likewise be the most beneficial. No such programs were extant, however, so the church must respond to the challenge and provide the nation with authoritative guidance. Ryan hoped to pattern the American Catholic program on the British interdenominational statement, carefully weaving principles and specifics together in a coherent, authoritative, and socially salvific plan for the future.

Ryan's survey of British and American reconstruction programs was much more than a simple overview of reform thought. It was a skillful and logical argument aimed both at justifying the bishops' (and his own) boldness in writing yet another reconstruction program and at persuading the nation at large of the urgent need of listening to the bishops if it ever hoped to achieve the Progressive ideal of a classless society based on justice.

After presenting this long justification for the program and his arguments for its salvific import for American society, Ryan sketched the program he and the bishops believed would lead to the erection of a just society. Informed by the method in the Interdenominational statement, he proposed to translate "our faith into works." He followed the Progressive path of establishing the feasibility of his reform proposals through an appeal to the nation's wartime industrial measures: "In the statements of immediate proposals we shall start wherever possible from those governmental agencies and legislative measures which have been to some extent in operation during the war. Those come before us with the prestige of experience and should therefore receive first consideration in any program that aims to be at once practical and persuasive." Thus armed with a sense of urgency and fortified by the reformers' war-born belief that reform was possible and workable, Ryan proposed to outline a program consisting of "those reforms that seem to be desirable and also attainable within a reasonable time and . . . those general principles which will serve as a guide to more distant de-

32. Ibid., pp. 4–5.

velopments."[33] He hoped to balance present possibility with future possibility, principle with praxis.

Following this methodological introduction, Ryan presented those practical measures whose adoption would hasten the development of a thoroughly just society. His proposals reflected postwar Progressive thinking in specifics as well as in method. He advocated land colonization for returning soldiers on the pragmatic grounds that such colonization "would afford employment to thousands upon thousands, would greatly increase the number of farm owners and independent farmers and would tend to lower the cost of living by increasing the amounts of agricultural products." (His pragmatic justifications did not entirely mask his and the Progressives' Jeffersonian belief that the yeoman farmer was the bulwark of American democracy.) He then pleaded for the retention of the United States Employment Agency because "the reinstatement of the soldiers and sailors in urban industries will no doubt be facilitated by [it]. . . . This agency has attained a fair degree of development and efficiency during the war." Ryan was arguing for present and future reform on the basis of wartime precedent. Ryan's third proposal called for the retirement of women workers from the industrial jobs they had held during the war. Because on the basis of natural law, women were "morally and physically" unsuited for industrial work, female representation in industry "ought to be kept within the smallest practical limits."[34] Here Ryan seemed willing to discard the lessons of the war, which had demonstrated the efficiency of women in the industrial sector. Clearly, in Ryan's mind, in a conflict between a Catholic understanding of natural law and a Progressive reverence for the industrial changes wrought by the war, Catholic morality took precedence.

In a move that pleased all parties in the postwar reform alliance, Ryan proposed the continuance of the War Labor Board for two reasons. First, he pointed out that "it prevented innumerable strikes, and raised wages to decent levels in many industries throughout the country." Thus, through its mediating power, the board had increased both the efficiency and the jus-

33. Ibid., p. 5.
34. Ibid., pp. 6–8.

tice of the American industrial system. These accomplishments alone would have been eloquent arguments for the adoption of Ryan's proposal. He went further, however, noting that the actions of the board were guided by principles that were close to his Leonine and Progressive heart: "a family living wage for all male adult laborers; recognition of the right of labor to organize, and to deal with employers through its chosen representatives; and no coercion of non-union laborers by members of the union." Further, through its judgments, the board had forced business to accept the practical (that is, monetary) consequences of a belief in these principles, thereby demonstrating the possibility of achieving principled reform and industrial cooperation. Ryan stated: "The principles, methods, machinery and results of this institution constitute a definite and far-reaching gain for social justice."[35] In short, the actions of the board accomplished that expedient and practical approximation of full justice which Ryan always favored.

In supporting the continuance of the War Labor Board, Ryan noted that its actions had effected a raise in wages in many national industries. Ryan's fifth proposal was that the high wage level attained during the war be sustained in the postwar period. This proposal amounted to a call for national acceptance of a living wage for all industrial workers. Although he justified this idea on practical and principled grounds, he felt more weight had to be given to the moral arguments. On the practical side, Ryan stated that wage levels should be maintained because "the average rate of pay has not increased faster than the cost of living." Therefore, merely to keep the wage earner from sinking into hopeless indebtedness, wage levels had to be continued at the war's high level. On the principled side, Ryan argued that the sharp increase of wages during the war had merely served to raise some workers' pay to a level that could be called a living wage. Confident that the war experience had set a precedent that would be difficult to reverse, Ryan pointed out that America's natural and industrial resources were "sufficient to provide more than a living wage for a very large proportion of the workers." Further, the rise in the amount of money in circulation as a result of higher wages would fuel industrial development.

35. Ibid., pp. 8–9.

Therefore, he concluded, "On grounds both of justice and sound economics, we should give our hearty support to all legitimate efforts made by labor to resist wage reductions." Thus Ryan's argument for the living wage was based on natural law principles, economic considerations, and practical wartime achievements. In his eighth proposal, he advocated the adoption of a legal minimum wage.[36] Because individuals and unions were not powerful enough to force industry to grant a living wage, which would allow a person to live a right and reasonable life, Ryan favored the use of legislation to accomplish that purpose.

The sixth plank of his reform program was a call for government housing for workers. Although he readily admitted that the federal government could not continue to provide housing for industrial workers in peacetime, the war had given a precedent, and he thought local governments should assume responsibility for providing public housing. Such a course of action was justified on the grounds that "industrial efficiency, civic health, good morals and religion" would be enhanced.[37]

Ryan next turned to ways of reducing the cost of living. Here he presented a two-tiered proposal that enshrined the age-old Progressive demands for the control of monopolies and the destruction of the middleman in the distribution process. Because monopolistic practices were responsible for exorbitant prices, it was only logical that the government should step in to check the monopolies, either by regulatory laws aimed at reducing or controlling monopolistic pricing policies or by direct government competition with monopolistic enterprises. As a second measure to control the skyrocketing cost of living, Ryan advocated the establishment of cooperative stores "under the ownership and management of the consumers," thereby eliminating unnecessary middlemen whose presence in the distribution chain added appreciably to the prices consumers paid for goods. Displaying the Progressive penchant for justifying and demonstrating the feasibility of their proposed domestic reforms on the basis of successful foreign experiments, Ryan cited the successful Rochdale system in England. His ultimate justification, however, reveals the depth of his Progressive sympathies: "the

36. Ibid., pp. 9–10, 12–13.
37. Ibid., pp. 10–11.

cooperative stores would train our working people and consumers generally in habits of saving, in careful expenditure, in business methods, and in the capacity for cooperation . . . they will be equipped to undertake a great variety of tasks and projects which benefit the community immediately, and all of its constituent members ultimately. They will then realize the folly of excessive selfishness and senseless individualism."[38] He meant that the people would see the wisdom of the Progressive vision of a classless (really middle-class) and altruistic society.

Ryan's ninth proposal was for the erection of a system of social insurance provided by the state and industry, which should "make comprehensive provision for insurance against illness, invalidity, unemployment and old age." Though calling for a comprehensive plan, however, Ryan made it clear that insurance funded by government and industry should be a temporary measure: "The ideal to be kept in mind is a condition in which all the workers would themselves have the income and the responsibility of providing for all the needs and contingencies of life, both present and future. Hence all forms of state insurance should be regarded as merely a lesser evil, and should be so organized and administered as to hasten the coming of the normal condition." Thus, even as he was framing proposals aimed at aiding the struggling lower classes, Ryan revealed his agreement with the Progressive dream of a classless society by making it clear that he did not favor a welfare system that "tends to separate the workers into a distinct and dependent class."[39] Instead, he viewed the establishment of a state-aided system of social insurance as a temporary and expedient measure aimed at hastening the arrival of the day when "normal" middle-class virtues had been instilled in the workers, the middle class extended, and the Progressive dream of a homogeneous society achieved. His Progressive tendencies were deep and well-developed.

In his tenth, eleventh, and twelfth proposals for postwar reconstruction, Ryan turned to three areas dear to the hearts of all the partners in the postwar reform alliance, especially laborers. In his tenth plank, Ryan called for labor participation in

38. Ibid., pp. 11–12.
39. Ibid., pp. 13–14.

industrial management as an antidote to social unrest. This idea involved the industrial democracy advocated by the reform alliance. Ryan reasoned that labor had a right to be represented at least in the "industrial" part of business management, the aspects of which he enumerated as "the control of processes and machinery; nature of product; engagement and dismissal of employees; hours of work; rates of pay bonuses, etc.; welfare work; shop discipline; relations with trade unions." Ryan believed that such a system would have many benefits: "There can be no doubt that a frank adoption of these means and ends by employers would not only promote the welfare of the workers, but vastly improve the relations between them and their employers, and increase the efficiency and productiveness of each establishment." In the next two proposals Ryan called for vocational training to prepare children for industrial work and for the adoption of child labor laws that would end the exploitation of children by industry.[40] These three proposals rounded out the roster of proposals Ryan deemed practical and able to be enacted within a reasonable period of time. These were not, however, Ryan's last words on the subject of reconstruction.

In what appears to be a note to the bishops, which surprisingly was not suppressed when the program was published, Ryan provided a rationale for the twelve reforms he had outlined. In words reminiscent of the Progressive urgings for the adoption of similar, if not identical, proposals, and responsive to the bishops' desire to garner a favorable hearing and positive publicity, Ryan argued that "substantially all of these methods, laws and recommendations have been recognized in principle by the United States during the war, or have been endorsed by important social and industrial groups and organizations. Therefore, they are objects that we can set before the people with good hope of obtaining a sympathetic and practical response. Were they all realized, a great step would have been taken in the direction of social justice." In other words, Ryan was arguing that the bishops needed such a program to solidify their position in America while advancing the cause of social justice. Sensitive to both the competitive denominational cli-

40. Ibid., pp. 14–15.

mate in which the church now found herself, and conscious of the need for long-range planning for ever greater approximations of the ideal of justice, however, Ryan pleaded with the bishops to incorporate a more philosophical section into the program: "Despite the practical and immediate character of the present statement, we cannot entirely neglect the question of ultimate aims and a systematic program; for other groups are busy issuing such systematic pronouncements, and we all need something of the kind as a philosophical foundation and as a satisfaction to our natural desire for comprehensive statements."[41]

Ryan was begging leave to expose the foundations of the Catholic reform (that is, Leonine) position and on this foundation to offer a principled critique of the American economic system. For Ryan, this was the chance of a lifetime to demonstrate the congruence between the Leonine Catholic and the Progressive positions. He had outlined his specific proposals in unabashedly Progressive terms, employing their rhetoric, espousing their plans, and using their war-based justifications for reform. In his more philosophical and long-term reflections and recommendations, he used Leonine thought to illuminate the righteousness of reform. Thus he presented Leonine Catholicism to a Progressive nation in thoroughly Progressive terms, at the same time that he presented American reformism to the church in thoroughly Leonine terms. It was his tour de force. Fortunately, the bishops acceded to his request.

In beginning his systematic reflections on the social problems of America, Ryan made it clear that he was following Leo's lead. He rejected socialism as a viable basis upon which to build a social order for "socialism would mean bureaucracy, political tyranny, the helplessness of the individual as a factor in the ordering of his own life, and in general social inefficiency and decadence." If he was harsh in his judgment of socialism, he was no less brutal in his assessment of capitalism's faults: "The present system stands in grievous need of considerable modifications and improvements. Its main defects are three: enormous inefficiency and waste in the production and distribution of commodities; insufficient incomes for the great majority of

41. Ibid., p. 16.

the wage earners; and unnecessarily large incomes for a small minority of privileged capitalists." Such a situation was unendurable to both Ryan and Leo. Though admitting that the proposals for reform outlined in the bishops' program would correct some of the abuses present in the industrial system, Ryan offered a more radical solution to industrial unrest that would ensure domestic tranquillity in the future. In reality, what Ryan proposed and what businessmen were to decry as rank socialism and Progressives would hail as the logical outcome of industrial democracy was Leo's by now old suggestion of a medievally inspired via media between socialism and capitalism. With words lifted almost verbatim from *Rerum Novarum,* Ryan stated, "The majority must somehow become owners, at least in part, of the instruments of production."[42]

This ideal, based on the medieval guildism which Leo revered, was to be achieved in the modern world, according to Ryan, by either one of two methods: by cooperative productive societies in which "the workers own and manage the industries themselves" or by copartnership arrangements in which "they [the workers] own a substantial part of the corporate stock and exercise a reasonable share in the management." Under either arrangement, workers would become masters of their own destinies and more fully conscious of their rights and their dignity. Ryan saw two major benefits from the adoption of either of these arrangements: production would be made more efficient and the danger of radical revolution would be eliminated from the American industrial scene. He acknowledged that adoption of either would involve "to a great extent the abolition of the wage system [but] . . . not the abolition of private ownership. The instruments of production would still be owned by individuals, not by the state." Thus Ryan envisioned a Leonine-inspired industrial democracy that would achieve the classless society dreamed of by the Progressives, not by destroying the right of private property but by extending it, thus creating a new and more inclusive middle class. Ryan thus presented the Leonine vision in terms the reformers understood. Ryan also subjected monopolies to a principled critique and found them of-

42. Ibid., pp. 16–17.

fensive to both morals and sound economics. He rounded out his reflections with a call for "a reform in the spirit of both labor and capital," a reform of labor's desire to "get a maximum return for a minimum of service," and a reform of the capitalist idea that labor is a mere commodity.[43]

Thus Ryan presented the bishops with a program that was thoroughly Leonine in its insistence on the need for radical and principled social change and thoroughly Progressive in its hopeful, possibilist spirit and its insistence that the shape of the future was to be discerned in the experiments of the wartime past. The CSWA approved the program at its 10 December 1918 meeting. Almost immediately Splaine forwarded a copy of it to Bishop Peter Muldoon, the chairman of the Administrative Committee, and the other members of the committee, stating that "the report represents the best personal thought of Reverend Doctor O'Grady," thereby attributing authorship of the program to O'Grady rather than to Ryan. Splaine also included a copy of the second report the reconstruction committee had prepared, which outlined the specific ways in which the church could cooperate with government agencies in postwar work and treated the delicate ways the CSWA should relate to the Knights of Columbus. In a sense, this second report translated the spirit of the bishops' program into practical action and answered part of the committee's mandate to provide a blueprint for coordinating all Catholic postwar work. It could be seen in another sense as the authoritative, internally directed complement to the program, which was addressed to the nation as a whole. This second report called for wholehearted support and cooperation on the part of the church with the work of the United States Employment Service, the Federal Board for Vocational Training, federal agencies charged with the rehabilitation of wounded servicemen, and federal bureaus overseeing the work of the Americanization of newly arrived immigrants.[44] The existence of these proposals for Catholic cooperation with federal

43. Ibid., pp. 17–19.

44. Splaine to Peter J. Muldoon, 11 December 1918, NCWC-CSWA (Ex. Sec.), Box 9, folder 10, ACUA; Reconstruction Committee Report, 11 December 1918, NCWC-CSWA (Ex. Sec.), pp. 1–9, Box 9, folder 10, ACUA.

agencies betokens the continuation of the war-born Catholic sense of acceptance in America, a new and surprising lack of fear of government intervention, and a willingness on the part of church leaders to advance the welfare of the church through public service.

Burke, the chairman of the CSWA, also wrote to Muldoon to plead for the bishops' endorsement of the program. Burke's letters reached Muldoon before Splaine's did, which accounted in part for Muldoon's initial response to the program. In his two letters, Burke told Muldoon that the program would serve a twofold educational purpose: it would guide Catholics in their postwar endeavors and provide valuable enlightenment to the nation: "We decided it was a leading pronouncement on what is uppermost in the public mind, will be a guide to our Catholic organizations and our Catholic people, and do invaluable work among all classes of present day leaders." In addition, Burke reminded Muldoon of the pressure under which the church was laboring because of its new exposure to the media: "We have been asked by several newspapers for an expression of our coming work. I'm eager to give them something; and I thought this program would be excellent." Thus, on the basis of a need to keep the church before the public eye and a desire to seize the opportunity to educate the Catholic population and the nation at large in the ways of Catholic reform, Burke urged Muldoon and his brother bishops to endorse and publish the program. As chairman of the Administrative Committee, Muldoon wired his approval of the program to Burke almost immediately. He did not, however, approve the text without some reservations: "As this is a most important and far-reaching document and will be very closely viewed by the hierarchy and by non-Catholics, and will be subject to the closest scrutiny, you must have every important statement carefully passed on by the very best authorities that we have in the Church."[45]

In advising caution, Muldoon told Burke that he would not

45. Burke to Muldoon, 10 December 1918, NCWC (Rockford File), Box 6, folder 13; Burke to Muldoon, 12 December 1918, NCWC-CSWA (Burke), Box 18, folder 15; Muldoon to Burke, 28 December 1918, NCWC (Rockford File), Box 10, folder 5; Muldoon to Burke, 14 December 1918, p. 1, NCWC (Rockford File), Box 6, folder 13, ACUA.

give final and formal approval for publication of the program until he had sounded out his brother bishops on the Administrative Committee. Muldoon's cautious attitude was wise. It also betrayed a keener awareness of the delicacy of the NCWC's position than was present at NCWC headquarters. Muldoon understood that, given its dubious canonical standing, the NCWC depended on the goodwill and visible unity of the bishops for its effectiveness. If at the appearance of a public statement purporting to represent the views of the bishops, any member of the hierarchy disavowed the pronouncement, the facade of unity would be broken, the church would look ridiculous, and her social mission would suffer an inestimable setback. Thus Muldoon's cautious insistence that the program be submitted to scrupulous prepublication scrutiny was reasonable.

Muldoon saw little problem with the text of the statement, although he did offer one trenchant criticism: "As a pronouncement I think it is very good indeed, but as a program it seems to me indefinite. Perhaps it is only intended as a pronouncement, but as soon as our people get this, they will necessarily ask the question—'What can we do and how are we to do it?' . . . In other words it is not made practical or applied." Muldoon wisely pointed out that without a program of specifics to direct the church's internal agencies on how to translate Ryan's ideas into action, the church's response to postwar problems would be diffuse, confused, and ineffective.[46] He was insistent that norms be provided to guide local parishes in the work of supporting and implementing the reforms called for in the pronouncement. He wanted specific ways of producing the unity of outlook and action the program seemed blithely to presume. As small-minded as Muldoon's objection to the program on the basis of its lack of applicability to the local parish level may sound at first, it was well-founded. After all, in forming the reconstruction committee, the bishops had charged the members with a twofold mandate: to formulate Catholic principles on postwar questions and to expose these principles to the Catho-

46. Muldoon to Burke, 14 December 1918, pp. 1–2. Muldoon wrote these reflections before he received Splaine's second report.

lic population and the nation in an educational enterprise; and to enunciate a strategy to coordinate the Catholic translation of these principles into action. In Muldoon's view, the program fulfilled the first part of the committee's mandate admirably. From his experience with the Social Service Commission of the American Federation of Catholic Societies, however, he had come to appreciate the sterility of pursuing a policy of issuing pronouncements that had no bearing on Catholic life. Muldoon reasoned in addition that even the educational value of such pronouncements was dubious if they were not made comprehensible to the Catholic people. Thus Muldoon was farsighted in realizing that the ultimate success of the Bishops' Program of Social Reconstruction did not depend on the immediate response it generated in the media, but rather on its ability to work a real transformation of Catholic thought on social issues. Hence he insisted on the need for providing the Catholic people with specific and concrete instructions that would link their local actions to the thought represented by the program. Only in this way did Muldoon believe that the social mission of the church could be advanced.

Muldoon did not so much object to the program as he insisted that the CSWA keep sight of the long-range goals which the hierarchical leadership had in mind in appointing the committee: the education of the Catholic population and the nation in Catholic social teaching.[47] By 16 December 1918, Muldoon had received Splaine's letter containing the second report of the committee. With this more practical document in hand, Muldoon withdrew his objections and gave his blessing to the program.[48] The other bishops concurred. Accordingly, Muldoon wrote to Burke, "I have just telegraphed you about program and to go ahead. I have heard from Bishop Schrembs and Bishop Russell—by telegrams. Bishop Hayes is lost somewhere in the

47. Significantly, Muldoon's thinking corresponded with O'Grady's desire to use the committee to produce a Catholic social literature of lasting value and Ryan's longing to bring about a passionate commitment to social justice in the Catholic community that would be grounded in principle and thus able to survive swings in public opinion and to avoid the expedient approach to reform that had marred the church's social ministry before 1919.

48. Muldoon to Burke, 16 December 1918, NCWC-CSWA (Burke), Box 18, folder 15, ACUA.

South. Go ahead then in God's name and may you meet with much success."[49] Burke was delighted, and the program was given to Mead for publication.

In less than a month, and under considerable pressure, the church had made substantial progress in her search for social justice. Before 26 November 1918, there had been no authoritative Catholic statement on postwar reconstruction, let alone on social problems in general, and no American strategy for dealing with those problems in a practical manner. By 16 December 1918, the American church was in possession of both. Armed with these documents, the church was determined to solidify her position in American life.

Although churchmen like O'Grady, Ryan, and Muldoon were concerned with the long-term effects the Bishops' Program of Social Reconstruction and the work of the reconstruction committee would have on the social consciousness of American Catholics, it is also undeniable that the NCWC-CSWA was at the same time aiming at the more immediate goal of sustaining the momentum of positive publicity the church had built up during the war years. In their drive to garner positive publicity, the bishops were especially eager to win a favorable hearing from two groups: the non-Catholic population of the country and the working classes, specifically the large number of Catholic workers. The bishops had different motivations for courting these two groups. In addressing the non-Catholic population, the church wished to reinforce their impression that the church was a loyal, responsible, and moral agent working to ensure the stability of American society. If this impression could be maintained during peacetime, the church would be able to solidify her position in American society. Among the working classes the bishops wanted to counter what they believed was a growing indifference to the church and her influence. Because of this diverse audience, the program's presentation had to be tailored in such a way that a broad and sympathetic hearing was gained, without sacrificing the integrity of the pronouncement. Therefore, the publicity for the program had to be handled delicately.

49. Hayes was on a tour of training camps in the South, in his capacity as the military vicar of the American Catholic soldiers. Muldoon to Burke, 16 December 1918, NCWC-CSWA (Burke), Box 18, folder 15, ACUA.

In addition, the bishops faced yet another problem in their attempts to ensure a wide circulation for the program. The extraordinarily large number of reconstruction programs already available made it highly improbable that the bishops would attract much attention with their words unless they were boldly aggressive in their public relations techniques. They had to grab the public's attention. Therefore, in presenting the program to the nation, the bishops had to balance boldness and tact. The task of maintaining this delicate balance was entrusted to Mead.

As soon as Burke handed over the program to him, Mead sprang into action. By 30 December 1918, he had prepared an ambitious and sophisticated plan for publicizing the program. He wrote to Burke and outlined an eight-part campaign in which he proposed to send the program in toto to all "class" newspapers and magazines; to provide a two-column story on the program, edited and ready for publication, to every urban daily in the country; to provide a similarly prepared three-column story to every weekly newspaper in the nation; to furnish stories to agricultural, labor, and Catholic organs; to arrange an interview with the *Saturday Evening Post* for O'Grady; and to make preparations for editorial interviews with all the principals involved in the production of the program. In addition, Mead sent Burke a comprehensive, annotated list of all the foreign newspapers which he believed should receive stories on, and if possible, copies of the program.[50] Clearly, such an ambitious program would gain the bishops the wide circulation they craved. Notice was one thing, however, and a sympathetic hearing was quite another.

As befitted a good press agent, Mead left nothing to chance. To ensure that the bishops would receive a sympathetic as well as a wide hearing for their words, he tailored the stories sent to the different organs outlined in his circulation scheme to the particular interests of their audiences. The bishops accepted Mead's plans. His sensitive and sensible treatment of them during the war had taught them how much he could accomplish

50. Larkin G. Mead to O'Grady, 30 December 1918, NCWC-CSWA (Reconstruction Committee), Box 6, folder 18; list of foreign newspapers, NCWC-CSWA (Burke), Box 22, folder 5, ACUA.

for the creation of a new and positive image for the church through the use of such methods. They trusted him, and they trusted that his methods would gain their words a sympathetic hearing as well as a wide exposure. Mead assumed his responsibilities with great energy and imagination. He wrote to O'Grady on 17 January 1919 asking that he let him know as soon as the program had received final confirmation. O'Grady responded that the program had received the authoritative approval of the bishops. He encouraged Mead to "make every possible effort to secure for us all the publicity you possibly can." When Mead presented his plans to the executive committee of the CSWA on 23 January 1919, the committee approved his program and gave its blessing to his work. On 8 February 1919 Mead wrote to Walter Hooke at the NCWC about his preparations: "The stage is all set now for our pronouncement publication—on which I've gone to the limit to get maximum results. I don't see how it can miss a huge spread all over the country. . . . Knocks and Boosts are going to fly thick on this pronouncement—but I've not talked with a single editor yet who wasn't impressed by it."[51] Mead was as good as his word. He did create a huge sensation throughout the country by his handling of the program. It attracted both praise and criticism. Above all, it kept the bishops in the public eye.

The bishops chose the date for the release of the program with great care. It was published on 12 February 1919, Lincoln's birthday. In choosing this date, the bishops connected their program with the spirit of the great liberator, linked the two reconstruction eras, and laid claim to a share in the wisdom and charity that had marked Lincoln's plans for Civil War Reconstruction. On that date heavy with symbolism, Mead's hard work began to show results.

There is no doubt that Mead's work was tremendously successful. As a result of his painstaking preparations, the Bishops'

51. Mead to O'Grady, 17 January 1919, NCWC-CSWA (Reconstruction Committee), Box 6, folder 8; O'Grady to Mead, 18 January 1919, and O'Grady to Mead, 22 January 1919, NCWC-CSWA (Reconstruction Committee), Box 6, folder 18 (see also Reconstruction Committee Report, 22 January 1919, NCWC-CSWA [Reconstruction Committee], Box 1, folder 1); CSWA minutes of 23 January 1919, NCWC-CSWA (Minutes); Mead to Hooke, 8 February 1919, NCWC-CSWA (Ex. Sec.), Box 10, folder 13, ACUA.

Program of Social Reconstruction did indeed create the spectacular impression he had promised. On the basis of the records he kept of the coverage afforded the program, he claimed that he had presented the program and other NCWC stories to "some sixty millions of readers" in "over six hundred communities throughout the United States." Arguing that a large percentage of his results were not reported to his office, he did not hesitate to boast that "I estimate that at least eighty millions of people in fully a thousand communities must have been reached." As a result of his labors, therefore, he told the bishops, "there is every indication throughout the secular press of this country that the editors of the nation have come to regard Catholic welfare activities as a vital and component part of the national news."[52] The variety and repetition of the coverage cited by Mead and the wide circulation he was able to substantiate for this coverage revealed him to be a man who served the bishops well and who understood the ways of publicity far better than they did. He presented the very event of the program's publication as newsworthy; he strove mightily to interest editors in its contents; and he created news out of the news he himself had created, accomplishing this last feat by calling the press' attention to the reaction of various segments of the press to the program. He created a sensation with his handling of the program and sought to sustain the momentum of publicity well past the date of the program's publication. At every turn, he painstakingly apprised the bishops of the progress of his campaign; he clipped newspaper stories as they appeared and forwarded them to NCWC headquarters with lists of the papers in which they appeared as well as the dates of publication. Throughout all of

52. Mead to Burke, 21 November 1919, NCWC (Rockford File), Appendix, p. 1, Box 9, folder 16, ACUA. Mead's figures are somewhat misleading. In citing these vast numbers, he failed to tell the bishops that they were composite figures, that is, whenever the same reader read two stories dealing with the same material on the NCWC, that reader was counted as two readers, and so on. Therefore, the figures must be viewed with extreme caution. Mead was, however, able to provide some concrete figures based on calculations of the circulations of the papers that carried his stories. Thus, for the coverage on the announcement of the publication of the program, he could cite a fairly reliable figure of 8,954,150; for a story on how labor responded to the plan, he could report a proven circulation of 2,030,525; and for editorials praising the NCWC reconstruction plan, he could cite a figure of 1,534,250.

this work, as he later told the bishops, he was conscious that he was creating a new and highly visible image of the American church in the eyes of the public; the image of a dignified, sober, serious church concerned with "the patriotic, civic and economic good of the whole nation."[53] Although there is a certain degree of flattery in Mead's statements about his service of the bishops (he wrote them when he was trying to get his NCWC contract renewed for another year), there is also an undeniable element of truth in what he told them. Everywhere they turned in 1919, they were confronted with evidence that their sophisticated media campaign had returned them large dividends of coverage and praise.

In the work of keeping the bishops' program before the public eye, Mead was enthusiastically joined by the officials of the National Catholic War Council. Indeed, the interest in the program among these men gave birth to a second public relations campaign that at first complemented and then replaced Mead's work when the NCWC's own actions resulted in the creation of a news service under NCWC auspices. At first the interest of the NCWC officials in the program found expression in a modest form. In mid-1919, the NCWC started the *NCWC Bulletin* (later *Catholic Action*), under the direction of Michael Williams. In his efforts to further the educational work of the War Council among the Catholic population, Williams endeavored to present to his readership the nation's positive reaction to the program. He wrote to editors throughout the country to solicit their responses to the program in an attempt to promote "a wide public interest in the work of the National Catholic War Council, particularly as that work is expressed in the wonderful platform of the bishops." With the passage of time, Williams grew bolder and began to do some of the work which Mead had been hired to do. When he realized that some of the major dail-

53. Ibid., Appendix, p. 3. Mead tried to counter the frivolous image of the church created by the Knights of Columbus. He denigrated the Knights' image as being "rather typical theatrical," presenting pictures of "priests . . . riding in tanks and aeroplanes; K of C secretaries were portrayed as scattering cigarettes broadcast in circus style." (Mead must have known, through his friendship with Walter Hooke at the NCWC headquarters, that the Knights of Columbus were a sensitive spot with the bishops. The hierarchy was tired of the Knights' sensational headlines and erroneous (at least to the episcopal mind) presentation of themselves as the complete and official Catholic agency in the public service.)

ies had neglected to cover the program, he undertook to rectify the situation. He wrote, for example, to Burton Kline, the editor of the *New York Tribune,* and begged him to cover the bishops' statement: "This program of social action I believe to be the one on which practical social reform may be safely based, so as to escape the danger of ultra-radicalism and state socialism on the one hand, and the almost equally grave danger of reactionary conservatism on the other. I will be very glad indeed to prepare an article for you dealing with this tremendous step taken by the Catholic Bishops."[54]

Williams also solicited articles by Catholic writers on the reconstruction statement and encouraged these writers to seek secular settings in which to present their views, so they might promote "the teaching mission of the Church so far as penmen may do." Finally, Williams arranged interviews with the media for those connected with the production of the program, and in June of 1919 he formulated plans for a "national advertising campaign in connection with the Reconstruction pamphlet."[55] Clearly, enthusiasm for the Catholic work of reconstruction was leading the NCWC leadership to usurp some of Mead's authority. This did not present a problem, however, because the program gained added exposure as a result of the combined efforts of Williams and Mead.

John J. Burke did not sit idly by either. Deeply conscious of the educational needs of the church and sharing Muldoon's view that the bishops' program's ultimate success depended on the reception it received in the pews, he wrote to all the priests of the nation asking that they use the program in their Labor Day sermons of 1919. In addition, he had the reconstruction committee prepare both a digest of the program for those who

54. O'Grady to Benedict Elder, 20 May 1919, NCWC-CSWA (Reconstruction Committee), Box 4, folder 11; Williams to Burton Kline, 22 May 1919, NCWC-CSWA (Reconstruction Committee), Box 9, folder 9, ACUA.

55. Williams to John Bunker, 29 May 1919, NCWC-CSWA (Reconstruction Committee), Box 9, folder 10; see also Williams to Michael Balco, 27 May 1919, NCWC-CSWA (Reconstruction Committee), Box 30, folder 22, ACUA. He arranged two such interviews for Muldoon in June of 1919 with the editors of the Sunday *New York World,* John O. Cosgrave and Arthur Bennington (O'Grady to Muldoon, 18 June 1919, NCWC-CSWA [Reconstruction Committee], Box 6, folder 22, ACUA). Williams to Frank Mulgrew, 19 June 1919, NCWC-CSWA (Reconstruction Committee), Box 7, folder 19, ACUA.

could not read all of it and a study guide, complete with questions and topics for discussion, to facilitate the dissemination of the ideas contained within the program among the Catholic population. Finally, he did everything he could to ensure that the program would receive serious consideration not only among the general public but also in academic circles. He sent copies of the document to all the colleges and seminaries (Catholic, Protestant, and secular) in America and asked that the program be discussed in classes.[56] Burke wished to ensure that the long-range goal of advancing the social education of American Catholics and Americans in general not be forgotten in the midst of the gratifying excitement stirred up by the publication of the program.

Although the bishops' program was but one part of the reconstruction work carried out by the NCWC, the reception it received soon overshadowed all other Catholic reconstruction work. It was a rare and exciting moment for the NCWC and the bishops, and they savored it. As a result of Mead's good work, the reaction to the bishops' statement was voluminous and quick in coming. Although the reports of the reconstruction committee were, for the most part, laconic about the reception accorded the program, mentioning the pamphlet as one small part of the larger work, occasionally the committee allowed itself to exult. Thus, in one of its reports, the members of the reconstruction committee boasted of the electrifying effects of the program's publication: "The general educational program of the War Council was of a more far-reaching character than any educational work which has been undertaken during the past twenty-five years. In January 1919, the world was in confusion. Everybody felt that we needed a statement of principles of justice and right to suit the newer conditions. Never in her history did the Church have a better opportunity to take the lead and very quickly did she realize her opportunity. Her clear and bold statement of principles . . . surpassed anything that had been published in half a century."[57]

56. Burke to All Clergy, 10 August 1919, NCWC-CSWA (Burke), Box 25, folder 10; Burke to Schools, February 1919, NCWC-CSWA (Ex. Sec.), Box 9, folder 7, ACUA.

57. See Reconstruction Committee Report, n.d., p. 4, NCWC-CSWA (Reconstruction Committee), Box 33, folder 5, ACUA.

The reconstruction committee hailed the publication of the program as an epochal event in American Catholic history, for it marked the emergence of the Catholic Church as the definitive, and in their eyes at least, the universally recognized voice of moral authority on the American scene. Its sponsors believed that the program was a landmark document for the church in her relations with the outside world. For the church and her understanding of her social mission in the modern world, the committee believed it was equally epochal, because it demonstrated the feasibility of applying "Christian [that is, natural law] principles to present day problems."[58] In short, the program had given the American church a method for engaging in constructive and up-to-date criticism of the pressing social problems of the age, on the basis of which she could confidently approach her mission. Of course, this was Leo's method. Ryan had taken the opportunity afforded by the writing of the program to demonstrate its utility to the American church. The committee rejoiced in the discovery of this useful tool and used it in its subsequent pamphlets. Thus the publication of the program was a step forward in the American church's search for its Leonine heritage.

Later NCWC reflections on the meaning of the program for the church bear witness to the belief that it had worked a significant transformation in both the internal educational mission of the church and her external leadership of the nation. The NCWC leaders, however, were not dreamers. They wisely realized that although the bishops' program endowed the church with a method of social criticism and laid claim to national moral leadership for the church, it was only the first step. To solidify the church's claim to effective moral leadership, the NCWC leaders understood that the church's membership would have to be coaxed into a passionate commitment to the contents and spirit of the document and educated in the effective use of its methods. In short, the program was as much a challenge as a triumph. The NCWC strove mightily to convince the church's membership to rise and meet the challenge. While engaged in this work of persuasion, the program's sponsors revealed the complex of motivations behind the document's for-

58. Ibid., p. 5.

mulation and publication and the link between the varying motives. In an appeal addressed to the laity, the NCWC leaders stated, "It is expected that the pronouncement of the Catholic bishops will result in a keener and more wide-spread interest among both individual Catholics and Catholic organizations in the great social problems which we are facing. If the program does not attain this end, it will have failed in its purpose."[59]

Herein was enshrined the statement of the long-range goal desired by Ryan, O'Grady, and Muldoon: the bold advance of Catholic social consciousness in ways that liberated the American church from its old timidity: "It points out rather definitely how far he may go without being at variance with the best Catholic thought and tradition." Hence the NCWC strove to educate the Catholic population in Catholic social thought. This education was sought for a thoroughly practical reason. The NCWC leaders saw education as the first step in a process of shaping American society and its future along lines that were informed by Catholic principles: "In the future, the layman must take his part in bringing the influence of the Church to bear both in the legislative and practical problems of the hour." The NCWC stressed that if Catholic laymen did not cooperate in this work, it would "be taken up by others who are not of our Faith: Protestant organizations have been interesting themselves a long time in the education and enlightenment of our people."[60] Such statements are startling for a number of reasons. On the positive side, they are eloquent testimony that the church now felt at home in the competitive denominational atmosphere of American religious life. (Indeed, Walter Hooke fairly crowed when, reflecting on the prestige the program had brought the church, he said, "When the [reconstruction] Committee began its work it found that the practical mouthpiece of the opinion on religious questions of the country was the Federal Council of Churches. It is no longer."[61]) On the negative side, these NCWC statements and the ambitious desires they bespeak could have given rise to Nativist fears of Catholic aggression

59. Ibid., p. 4.
60. Ibid., pp. 1, 4, 5.
61. Walter G. Hooke, Report of the Executive Secretary, February 1919, NCWC-CSWA (Ex. Sec.), Box 1, folder 1, p. 5, ACUA.

such as had caused the church problems throughout her American sojourn. In 1919, the church escaped these old fears because the goals and measures outlined in the bishops' program corresponded with the Progressive aspirations of the age.

The public reception accorded the bishops' program left the staff and Administrative Committee of the NCWC fairly euphoric and seemed to lend substance to their hopes that the church could claim a large and effective position of moral leadership in the country, which it could translate into political power capable of shaping a future informed by Catholic social principles.

In a certain sense, however, the program was not an official document of the magisterium. Although it was issued over the signatures of four bishops, the program had the same tenuous canonical standing as did its sponsoring agency, the NCWC. Therefore, whereas the document seemed to bear the stamp of approval of the entire American church and to enunciate a new and unified Catholic stand on social issues, it was actually merely educational and directive, not binding. Although its framers and supporters called attention to its moral authority, they could never claim that the document had any legal authority. Therefore, its effectiveness in the public eye depended on the maintenance of a united public front of support among the bishops. If any bishop publicly questioned or disavowed the document, its status among the Catholic population would be compromised, and Mead's work would be undercut.

Given the delicacy of the situation, the members of the NCWC Administrative Committee and their staff were gratified to hear the positive feedback of the metropolitans on the program. Edward J. Hanna, the archbishop of San Francisco and later president of the Welfare Council, wrote to praise the program and to offer his help in spreading its teachings: "I know not how to say enough about 'Social Reconstruction,' and I consider it the most timely statement which has come from any group in the Church since the beginning of the War—How can I help you to give it greater vogue?" The archbishop of New Orleans, J. W. Shaw, also wrote to commend the document and to lament the sorry condition in the church with regard to social questions: "After a cursory perusal I find the pamphlet very instructive and directive. I need not tell you that I feel very keenly my inability to carry out the reforms which are imperatively needed by the changed conditions of society through the fortunes of war. With limited means and few persons who are disposed to take up the great work . . . I am at a loss to know what to do."[62] James Cardinal Gibbons, the archbishop of Baltimore, was cordial in his support of the program and did his utmost to rally episcopal support for the document. Patrick Hayes, the auxiliary bishop of New York, who succeeded John Cardinal Farley as archbishop of New York in 1919, continued his support for the program when he left the NCWC Administrative Committee to assume his new responsibilities. The leadership of the Chicago Archdiocese, ever sensitive to the needs of the large number of industrial workers under its care, gave vocal and consistent support to the program in the *New World,* the archdiocesan newspaper. Thus, many of the more visible and vocal members of the hierarchy praised the program. Indeed, when Ryan asked Muldoon about the episcopal reaction, Muldoon told him that he knew of no hierarchical criticism of the document.[63]

This remarkable unity was startling, especially since before the war, the bishops had resolutely followed a social strategy of "masterful inactivity." To understand this new openness to social action, it is helpful to remember, first, that Peter Muldoon of Rockford had, during his tenure on the Social Service Commission of the American Federation of Catholic Societies, long advocated a positive Catholic response to social questions; that Joseph Schrembs of Toledo had been educated in the German-American community, which had developed a lively if not wholly realistic tradition of social concern; and that Patrick Hayes was a pioneer in his own diocese in the drive to bring Catholic charities in line with Progressive advances in social work. Therefore, a majority of the members of the NCWC Administrative Committee were sensitive to social issues and believed the church should align herself with the most advanced social thinking of the nation. Second, as Edward Roddy notes,

62. Edward J. Hanna to Peter J. Muldoon, n.d., NCWC-CSWA (Burke), Box 15, folder 3; J. W. Shaw to Burke, 22 March 1919, NCWC-CSWA (Burke), Box 15, folder 5, ACUA.

63. Ryan, *Social Doctrine,* p. 149.

death had removed many of the more conservative prelates from the American scene: "It must be recalled that no few influential, conservative prelates died between 1912 and 1919, and their places had been taken by younger men with new ideas." These younger men showed a willingness to follow the liberal directions outlined by the NCWC's leaders. Third, with the decline of immigration, "these new leaders were free to devote more thought and attention to the problems touching the lives of their flock." Finally, as Roddy points out, the church benefited from the acceptance she had won as a result of her work during the war: "It is quite possible also, that Catholic patriotism and loyalty to the United States, which so clearly proved itself during the war, lessened anti-Catholic prejudices and thus made it easier for Church authorities to address the nation."[64] The hierarchy wished to take advantage of the providential moment to solidify the church's position. Therefore there were no voices raised to protest an action that could advance the cause of the church.

There were, however, fissures that broke the facade of unity initially presented by the hierarchy. Muldoon may never have heard of any episcopal rumblings against the program, but clearly there were some misgivings among the hierarchy. Shortly after the pronouncement's publication, Archbishop John Bonzano, the apostolic delegate, told Bishop William Russell that he had some serious reservations about the program. As Russell reported to the NCWC, he said, "It seems that some Bishop or Archbishop has complained." Russell advised the Administrative Committee to send a representative to the delegate to smooth matters over and to halt the NCWC's publicity campaign until his misgivings were answered.[65] Mead's campaign was halted temporarily, and Burke visited Bonzano to plead the NCWC's case.[66] Burke answered Bonzano's questions satisfactorily, and the publicity campaign was resumed. Bonzano, how-

64. Roddy, "Catholic Newspaper Press," pp. 293, 232.

65. William T. Russell to Burke, 6 June 1919, NCWC-CSWA (Burke), Box 21, folder 22, ACUA. There is a tantalizing lacuna in the evidence because the apostolic delegate's files are closed for at least the next twenty-five years.

66. Burke to Muldoon, 7 June 1919, NCWC (Rockford File), Box 9, folder 5, ACUA.

ever, was not the only prelate who questioned the program. Vincent Wehrle, O.S.B., the bishop of Bismarck, North Dakota, wrote to Cardinal Gibbons to demand that the NCWC disavow the document because radicals in his socially progressive state were claiming that the bishops "were in favor of their own program, namely, a socialistic state."[67]

Other bishops were incensed by specifics contained in the program. Bishop William Turner of Buffalo was particularly annoyed by the document's espousal of social insurance, and when the NCWC sent a lecturer to his diocese to plead with Catholic voters to support the Davenport health insurance bill before the New York legislature in 1920, Turner thundered his disapproval: "The lecturer sent out by the Catholic War Council gave the impression in a recent speech that the authority of the Catholic bishops was behind the advocacy of the bill. . . . I oppose this pernicious measure. . . . It is a plank in the socialist platform."[68] William Cardinal O'Connell, archbishop of Boston, objected to the program's call for a child labor amendment or child labor laws because he believed that such measures were socialist in inspiration. Thus, when Ryan lectured in Boston on behalf of a child labor amendment in the 1920s, O'Connell wrote to Archbishop Michael Curley of Baltimore to protest Ryan's stand and his apparent use of the church's authority to further his own plans: "Yesterday this city was flooded with the nefarious and false views on the amendment supposed falsely to be in the interests of the Child, sent out from Washington by sly methods in which he seems to be an expert, by Rev. J. A. Ryan. . . . From this vicious propaganda it is made to appear that we Catholics who oppose this soviet legislation are incapable of reading plain English."[69] O'Connell believed Ryan's words compromised his own teaching authority. He advised Curley to silence Ryan and to expel him from the faculty of the Catholic University. O'Connell closed his diocese to Ryan and nursed his grudge against Ryan and the Social Action Department of the

67. Ellis, *Life of Gibbons,* 1:541–42.

68. Quoted in Roddy, "Catholic Newspaper Press," p. 217.

69. William O'Connell to Michael Curley, 2 November 1924, Ryan Papers, Ref. N–Po, Box B2-41, ACUA.

Welfare Council with such unrelenting bitterness that he later spearheaded an episcopal drive to quash the NCWC and thereby to silence its troublesome social voice.

The objections to the program offered by these various bishops show how vulnerable the NCWC was. During the war, episcopal unity had served to advance the church's prestige and to check the budding hubris of the Knights of Columbus. Hence the bishops were willing to lend their support, however lukewarm, to the NCWC, for they received benefits with no real loss of authority. In short, the church had everything to gain and the bishops lost nothing as a result of their wartime unity. The program, however, seemed to jeopardize their authority in their own sees. Therefore the bishops did not hesitate to voice their objections. O'Connell's vicious and largely clandestine campaign to abolish the NCWC showed the lengths to which episcopal jealousy could go. Conversely, O'Connell's, Turner's, and Wehrle's anger at the advancement of Progressive views in the bishops' names demonstrated, albeit rather obliquely, that the bishops understood that unity brought them power. The social liberals knew when they agreed to the publication of the program that its effectiveness on the national scene would depend on the public's construing it as the unified and authoritative Catholic response to social questions. Indeed, they hoped that this impression would gain them a wider hearing.

Conservative prelates resented this fact because it not only limited their own freedom in teaching but seemed to commit them to positions diametrically opposed to their own. The conservatives did not so much object to the power unity brought as to their inability to shape the social stands that would benefit from the use of that power. The objections to the program voiced by the three dissenting bishops show that a fear of socialism remained deeply ingrained in the minds of some members of the American hierarchy. If the conservative prelates succeeded in quashing the program because it seemed to countenance socialism, the American church would be condemned to a sterile and altogether unsatisfactory social program once again.

That there were still bishops who could serenely contemplate such a turn of events made Muldoon's initial observations on the program and its ultimate goals seem all the wiser. Muldoon had insisted that the program not be seen as a one-shot bid for glory, but rather as the beginning of an ongoing education in Catholic social principles and the contemporary application of those principles to American life. He rightly perceived that the only way out of the prison of the church's past social sterility was through a grounding in principles so solid and so unquestionably Catholic that fear would give way to passionate conviction as the foundation of American Catholic social action. The enunciation of these objections by some members of the hierarchy therefore reveals the state of the church, the vulnerability and potential strength of the NCWC, and the continuing presence of episcopal jealousies. It was indeed fortunate that in the first months following the program's publication the fractious bishops did not publicly broadcast their objections or the passions that gave birth to them. To be sure, a storm was gathering, but in February 1919, the liberals seemed to have captured the American Catholic Church and charted a new course for her.

In summary, then, the Bishops' Program of Social Reconstruction marked a decisive turning point in the Catholic involvement in the mainstream of American life and in the American Catholic search for social justice. The mere fact and mode of its publication and advertisement throughout the nation argue for its importance in American Catholic life. Its publication amounted to a bold proclamation that the church was abandoning its timid social strategy of masterful inactivity, and the language it employed and the proposals it espoused proclaimed that the church was embracing a decidedly Progressive position, which was shocking in light of the church's prior coldness toward the reformers. To be sure, this transit from distrust to alliance was facilitated by the church's wholehearted participation in the Progressive crusade of the Great War, but the circuitous route the church followed in her shift does not detract either from the importance or the consequences of this realignment. Through her war work, the church learned to speak the righteous rhetoric of the reformers, and in the course of the war she appropriated both the vocabulary and the spirit behind this rhetoric. Thus she emerged from the war sharing the same idealism as did the Progressives and believing as they did in both the desirability and the feasibility of reform along lines suggested by wartime experiments in industrial life. On the basis of this shared ideology, the bishops issued the remarkably Progressive bishops' program, thereby giving "authoritative sanction to reforms for which Ryan had long struggled" and entering the mainstream of American reform.[70]

In addition to marking a new Catholic alliance with the American reform tradition, the program also marked a first institutional step toward the American church's appropriation of Leo XIII's vision of the church's mission in modern industrial society. Its author, John A. Ryan, hoped through the program to demonstrate both the effectiveness and the elasticity of Leo's method and the applicability of Leonine principles to the American scene. He accomplished this task admirably. (Raymond McGowan was later to defend the program by citing Leo as its inspiration: "The Bishops' Program had developed somewhat and made certain specific application of Leo's encyclical to American life."[71]) Seen in this light, it is clear that in addition to being a pivotal document in American Catholic history, it was also a bridge document. It sought to represent the best Catholic social thought to the nation in terms that were partially Progressive and partially Leonine. It was able to use these two sets of terms because its roots and the roots of its author were in both traditions. Indeed, it was precisely because of its divided pedigree that the document was able to serve as a bridge between the two traditions. For that same reason, however, the program was also problematic. As time went on and attacks were launched against it, it had to be defended on two fronts: to Catholic critics, it had to be shown to be fully and convincingly Catholic; to American critics it had to be justified as fully American. In the supercharged postwar era, when battles raged as to the true meaning of Americanism, this second task was to

70. Broderick, *Right Reverend New Dealer*, p. 107. "The Bishops' Program, along with a bewildering number of similar manifestoes issued about the same time, reflected the wartime feeling that only a reconstituted society based on social justice could redeem the four years of carnage. Tactically, the times seemed right. The increase in governmental activity incident to the war gave reformers their chance: the problem was not to force government into unwanted areas, but to hold existing ground against abrupt withdrawal, to catch public favor at a time of decision and to bed down favored reforms in the moment of victory" (ibid.).

71. Raymond A. McGowan, "Catholic Work in the United States for Social Justice," *Catholic Action* 18, no. 5 (1936):5.

prove no less wearying than the first, and the NCWC had to face the formidable opposition of William Cardinal O'Connell. Exhaustion was the reward of the righteous.

The mode of the program's advertisement throughout the country was also important. The bishops' sophisticated use of modern public relations techniques to broadcast their message to America and their expressed desire to compete with Protestant groups to shape the religious outlook of the nation show that through the war work and the publication of the program, the church had come to appreciate the practical meaning of religious pluralism. The American Catholic Church of 1919 was willing and even eager to compete and to compete aggressively in the religious marketplace of America.

Thus it was that the bishops' program, written by Ryan, issued by the bishops, launched by Mead, and hoped for by many within the church came to be. Through it, the church hoped to solidify her position in American life. In many ways, her new image and her future role in society rode on its public reception.

Chapter v

The Reception and Defense of the Program

Before the publication of the Bishops' Program of Social Reconstruction, Mead had stated that because of his extensive and meticulous plan for its publicity, it could not fail to create a sensation. When Williams later reflected upon the reception the document received, he bore witness to the effectiveness of Mead's work: "Probably no other document ever put out from a Catholic source in this country attracted nearly so much attention. . . . It may be useful to remark in passing that the success of the Catholic War Council in getting notices from the daily papers for this program was due mainly to good press-agent work—a circumstance that holds a lesson for Catholics in many other departments of activity." Williams was not willing, however, to give Mead all the credit for the program's success. Citing the "vital character" of the document, Williams believed that the public had taken to the program precisely because "the publication of this pamphlet was a social event of primary importance, for it put a platform of practicality beneath the manifold efforts being made on all sides to reconstruct our shaken social order."[1] In other words, Williams believed that the program had attracted a positive public response because, though it was fully at one with the Progressive spirit of the age, its practical bent set it off from other more philosophical statements and thus redeemed it from rank utopianism.

The wide and positive national response to the bishops' document, however, can be only partially explained by its unity with the spirit of Progressivism, its salutary practicality, its so-

1. Williams, *American Catholics in the War,* p. 315, 307. John A. Ryan agreed that the success of the program was due largely to the publicity work of Larkin Mead (*Social Reconstruction* [New York: Macmillan, 1920], p. 5).

phisticated media presentation, or even a combination of these factors. The program received wide currency also because it took the nation by surprise.[2] History had taught the American public to expect the church's leadership to issue lackluster social statements that buttressed the status quo and gave comfort to America's business class. The spectacularly public abandonment of such a stance proclaimed by the publication of the bishops' program therefore surprised the nation, altering the received image of the church and, thanks to Mead's work, in a sensationally public way. Not only were the American bishops no longer fragmented, defensive, timid on social issues; they were unified, self-confident, and aggressively interested in social problems. And they were loud. In short, in the view of the public, the program signaled a complete and disconcertingly public break with the American church's past. People scrambled to account for and respond to this startling transformation.

Progressives and other social liberals, long used to Catholic intransigence on social issues, tried to come to terms with the church's shift and ultimately welcomed her to the emerging postwar reform alliance, although some reformers remained skeptical about the passion and depth of the church's conversion. Organized labor, too, was heartened by the program and hailed the bishops as economic sages but also wondered about the depth of commitment to reform the document heralded. The business community was stung by the defection of a trusted ally and wondered aloud if the bishops had gone mad or red. The Catholic population was stunned because its leaders seemed both to be animated by a new missionary spirit and to espouse a new role for the church in industrial society. In short, surprise was general. This element of surprise, which gave rise to shock and even outrage in some cases, contributed substantially to the sensation the program created.

The church in turn realized that she faced a twofold long-term educational challenge. To secular doubters, she had to prove by her actions that the program was not merely a onetime event. She would have to testify to a deeply felt conversion to passionate social concern by committing herself to concrete

2. Abell, *American Catholicism and Social Action,* p. 199. See also Ellis, *Life of Gibbons,* 1:541.

programs for social change. Among her own flock, the church faced a similar challenge. She would have to justify her actions in terms of her tradition, and she would have to educate and prepare the flock to commit themselves to the reform activity her new missionary image dictated. Through internal social catechesis and conspicuous external social involvement, the church would have to redeem the startling public promise of change contained within the program. Much of the NCWC's activity in the months and years that followed the publication of the bishops' program was directed to meeting this double challenge.

As both Williams and Ryan noted, the secular response to the program, expressed both in private correspondence and in the media, was extensive and gratifying. The letters addressed to the leaders of the War Council reveal that the program struck a responsive note among non-Catholic Americans. W. B. Ashley, an official of the Boy Scouts of America and the editor of the religious news section of the *Scouts' Magazine,* wrote Williams that he found the document to be of "exceptional value" and he would alter the usual format of his column so as to bring the program to the attention of his readers and religious leaders throughout the nation. The editors of the *New York World,* a liberal newspaper sympathetic to reform wrote to O'Grady requesting an interview with Bishop Muldoon. O'Grady advised Muldoon to jump at the opportunity to keep the program before the public eye: "The article will be given front page of the editorial section of the *Sunday World.* and would do our movement a world of good—if you will pardon the pun." If O'Grady and Muldoon were flattered and gratified by the *World*'s request, they were startled by the kind words that came from William Knowles Cooper, the general secretary of the Washington, D.C., office of the YMCA: "I read the article [in the *Nation*] with very deep interest. It is the word which I have long desired to hear uttered by responsible religious authority. I am sorry our organized Protestantism has not delivered a similar statement." Then, in a move that was sure to please the NCWC, Cooper told Muldoon that he had praised the program to William Jennings Bryan and that "if you would like to have me do so," he would be happy to give copies of the document to Bryan as well as to half a dozen leaders of American Protestantism. Muldoon directed that Cooper receive twice the number of copies he asked for.[3] Praise continued to pour in, together with requests for more copies that could spread the bishops' gospel of reform. The NCWC was gratified by these expressions of approval and frequently turned admirers into collaborators and evangelists.

As they read their correspondence, the bishops grew daily more confident that the program's proposals were the sure cure for social unrest. Indeed, they began to believe that the applicability of their message knew no bounds—no geographical bounds, that is. They forwarded copies to Charles Murphy, a member of the Canadian Parliament, for publication and distribution in Canada; and Splaine wrote to John O'Grady that "I understand that our pamphlet on Reconstruction has been sent to Lenine [sic] in Russia for his guidance and salvation."[4] Clearly the bishops believed that they had uttered the words of eternal life.

Although all of these developments and responses were heartening, the most gratifying response came from Raymond Fosdick: "I am weighing my words when I say that I am thrilled with its message. . . . The fine spirit of liberalism that lies behind the whole document, the fearlessness with which the suggestions are treated, as well as the clarity of the presentation make the pamphlet a real landmark in industrial thinking." Fosdick, however, did more than merely praise the document. By placing the pronouncement in its historical context, he expressed the grateful surprise that made the program so important and accounts for the sensation it caused: "I am amazed that such a statement should come from the Church. . . . With thousands of others I have become in recent years increasingly discouraged at the attitude of our spiritual leaders in matters of industrial reconstruction. . . . The Church has seemed to be too

3. W. B. Ashley to Michael Williams, 28 May 1919, NCWC-CSWA (Reconstruction Committee), Box 9, folder 10; John O'Grady to Peter J. Muldoon, 11 June 1919, NCWC-CSWA (Reconstruction Committee), Box 6, folder 22; William K. Cooper to Muldoon, 3 April 1919, NCWC-CSWA (Burke), Box 18, folder 17, ACUA.

4. Charles Murphy to Walter G. Hooke, 15 May 1919, NCWC-CSWA (Ex. Sec.), Box 2, folder 11 (promising that he would make sure the copies "are distributed where they will do the most good"); Michael J. Splaine to John O'Grady, 31 March 1919, NCWC-CSWA (Reconstruction Committee), Box 7, folder 5, ACUA.

much an agency that protected and bolstered up the established order regardless of its justice." Fosdick ended his note with a veiled challenge for the church to bring to completion the good work it had begun. In his response to Fosdick's flattering letter, Muldoon accepted both the praise and the challenge. Voicing his own old belief that the program's effectiveness over the long term could be judged only by its success or failure in raising the Catholic social consciousness and fostering practical action, Muldoon assured Fosdick: "We hope, in the National Catholic War Council Bulletin, to follow up this program and to explain it more fully. To be of value it must be insisted on and made even clearer still for the ordinary working man. . . . I can assure you, my dear Mr. Fosdick, that your kind words of approbation are most encouraging and will prompt us to uphold the principles outlined in the program."[5]

The letters the leaders of the NCWC received in response to the publication of the program indicated first, that the nation believed that a radical change had occurred in the American church. Second, in response to this perceived change, Progressives such as Fosdick and Cooper welcomed the church to the reformist fold, thereby opening up the possibility of a warmer rapprochement between the church and the reform camp. Third, it seemed to many that the Roman Catholic Church had assumed an unprecedented and hence unexpected role of leadership in social action in the country.[6] Finally, it was clear that the grandly public way in which the church had laid claim to this social leadership had, in addition to destroying the old image of the church, created new expectations for its social role, which in turn created new challenges for the church. Publicity was not an unmixed blessing.

As gratifying as the bishops' private correspondence was, the real impact and importance of the Bishops' Program of Social Reconstruction can more adequately be gauged by its reception at the hands of the press. The program received extensive cov-

5. Raymond B. Fosdick to Muldoon, 9 June 1919, NCWC-CSWA (Ex. Sec.), Box 1, folder 19; Muldoon to Fosdick, 14 June 1919, NCWC (Rockford File), Box 9, folder 29, ACUA.

6. This was, of course, the perception Ryan and the bishops wished to foster. They had hoped to present the church as a sage and sober presence in American society that could be trusted with the awesome task of shaping the nation's future.

erage.[7] It must not be supposed, however, that the readers Mead counted had read the same story. Mead had devised an ambitious and sophisticated distribution scheme, tailoring the stories that he provided to different publications to the special interests of their respective audiences. Therefore, the coverage of and editorial reactions to the program reflected the various emphases Mead gave to his reports.

Mead supplied the general daily press with a news release that contained an innocuous two-paragraph introduction and excerpts from the program.[8] The Associated Press and United Press International were provided with the same article and instructed to release it on 12 and 13 February 1919. Several writers in the secular press offered comments on the program and thus expanded on the initial coverage requested by Mead. William Marion Reedy of the *Saint Louis Mirror* commended the document and suggested that its composition was motivated by the Church's particularly close relationship with the working classes. He also believed that it marked a turning point in Catholic social action: "Why is it put forth at this time? Because the Catholic Church is very close to the people and knows what the people are thinking and feeling. . . . It is no longer going to leave to its 'separated brethren' the task and glory of doing something for the salvation of man in the here and now." William Hard, who was to become one of the program's most vocal supporters, was even more extravagant in his praise of the church and the bishops' pronouncement. Writing for Hearst's *Metropolitan Magazine* in January 1920, Hard said, "We do not see simply an economic program by wise persons. We see the oldest and largest of Churches brought by its human social situation to a new refreshment of its ancient gift of prophecy for the poor."[9]

Whereas Reedy and Hard interpreted both the motivation and the message of the program in religious terms, other segments of the secular media called attention to its more secular implications. Under a headline proclaiming a "Real Revolution in the

7. Less than two months after its publication, Burke told Muldoon that it had been read by 20 million people (Burke to Muldoon, 2 April 1919, NCWC-CSWA (Burke), Box 18, folder 17). This figure seems exaggerated and conflicts with Mead's "proven" figure of 7.8 million.

8. "Catholic Call to Reconstruction," NCWC news release, 13 February 1919, NCWC (Historical Materials), chap. 14, ACUA.

9. Quoted in Ryan, *Social Reconstruction*, pp. 16, 18.

Catholic Church," *Current Opinion* noted that "it endorses the movement of labor to obtain a voice in the management of companies, and leans toward what is coming to be known as Guild Socialism." *Current Opinion* was not alone in calling attention to the radical cast of the program's proposals and its analysis of the shortcomings of the capitalist system, nor were such observations the gratuitous products of either fearful conservative or fervently radical minds. As part of his campaign to win the program a wide and sympathetic hearing Mead had carefully supplied newspapers in Wisconsin (the home of Robert LaFollette), North Dakota (the site of many postwar experiments in social welfare), as well as the industrial areas of Ohio, Pennsylvania, California, Illinois, and New York with a story that highlighted the more radical appearing elements of the program, such as its resemblance to the program advanced by the British Labour party and its insistence on long-range reforms in the American economic system which would eventually usher in complete industrial democracy. The newspapers in these areas printed Mead's article without alteration and with evident approval. Under the headline "Catholic Church Turns Socialistic," the *El Cajon* (California) *News* indicated its approval by reproducing the article that was supplied by Mead's news service. The paper stated, "In many respects, the program resembles that of the British Labour Party. It endorses many social and economic doctrines heretofore pronounced socialistic by conservative thinkers." In addition, using Mead's words, the paper was happy to note, "It is generally understood that every line of the pronouncement issued today has been carefully studied and passed upon by practically every notable prelate in the United States before being made public. The program therefore, may be said to be an official statement of the attitude of the American Catholics toward social and economic problems now engaging the attention of all thinkers."[10] The unmistakable message of the article was that the church had thrown her en-

10. "A Real Revolution in the Catholic Church," *Current Opinion,* May 1919, p. 312; "Catholic Church Turns Socialistic," *El Cajon* (California) *News,* 8 March 1919, p. 8. Mead forwarded a list of twenty-seven newspapers in which this same article appeared. Among them were the *Baltimore Sun,* the *Chicago Evening Post,* the *San Francisco Daily News,* the *Los Angeles Record,* the *Brooklyn Citizen,* the *Rochester Times,* and the *Cleveland Press.*

tire weight behind the cause of social reform. The image of the church was well on its way to being altered among the working classes. Of course, there were some dangers in tailoring the news to the audience. Some bishops were appalled at the "radical" program.[11] Despite occasional trouble caused by Mead's shrewd actions, however, his activities brought the bishops the attention they craved.

As a result of Mead's work, the program attracted attention in the socialist press as well. Upton Sinclair called the document a "Catholic miracle." The *New York Call* was thunderstruck and said, "Did you read it a couple of days ago? The real revolution in the Catholic Church? Did you see what that august organization is standing for? Notice it well, for it is a real portent, a real sign of the times." Recovering a bit from its surprise, the *Call* stated: "This official pronouncement of the Catholic Church can be held up to strengthen men who are starting on a new road to an understanding of the new world that is to be." Although the *Call* took encouragement from the program, it reserved the right to remain skeptical about the document's long-term effects on the social mission of the church. In view of the hostile relationship between the church and socialism, the socialists' skepticism was understandable,[12] and it is surprising that the *Call* was willing to praise the bishops' program even grudgingly. Publicity, however, had a price: while Mead's leftward-slanting articles won a wide audience, they also raised a red specter that came back to haunt the bishops before many months had passed.

Although Mead undoubtedly flirted with trouble and shaded

11. As was noted in Chapter IV, when the Most Reverend Vincent Wehrle, O.S.B., the bishop of Bismarck, North Dakota, was confronted with the spectacle of socialists blithely claiming Catholic support for their program, a notion they derived from Mead's article, he was dismayed and angered. On the other hand, the Most Reverend John F. R. Canevin, the bishop of Pittsburgh, when confronted with a similar situation in his industrial diocese, wrote to the NCWC asking it to make it clear that the program was theirs and did not come from socialist sources because some socialists in the Pittsburgh area were claiming credit for it.

12. Sinclair quoted in Ryan, *Social Reconstruction,* p. 13; "Catholic Church Speaks Out," *New York Call,* 4 March 1919, p. 8. The *Call* was skeptical of religious groups, their actions, and their motives. It praised only the Quakers, the Saint Andrew Brotherhood, and Harry F. Ward. Usually the paper identified Christianity with oppression.

the truth somewhat when he sought to win a sympathetic hearing for the bishops' proposals among the disaffected, the articles he supplied to more moderate newspapers presented the program in a more moderate and ultimately more truthful light. For these papers, Mead composed a basic article that stressed the bishops' calls for standard Progressive reforms such as minimum wage laws, the maintenance of the War Labor Board on a permanent peacetime footing, and social insurance. In short, he emphasized the sober, gradualist approach to reform which the document advocated in the foreseeable future and played down the more radical long-term changes advocated in its final section.[13]

When scores of moderate newspapers presented the contents of the bishops' platform to the public on 13 February 1919, the program appeared in a strikingly different light than it did in the more left-leaning papers. Mead's moderate article created the impression that the bishops were sober sages who would be able to lead the nation into an era of unparalleled domestic tranquillity. Indeed, one moderate newspaper, the *Chicago Daily News*, printed an editorial commenting on the startling difference between the radical and the Catholic approaches to reform. Under the headline "Social Justice vs. Socialism," the *Daily News* praised the sober approach outlined by the bishops: "Not state socialism, with its tyranny and inefficiency, not Bolshevism, but gradual and orderly transfer of ownership by means of peopleizing corporate securities, of inducing workmen to acquire a stake in the industry that pays wages and dividends should be the ideal of enlightened and fair-minded advocates or righteousness in economic relations."[14]

Although almost all segments of the secular media were re-

13. Mead supplied the bishops with a list of 130 newspapers that used the moderate article he had supplied. Among them were the *New York Globe*, the *New York World*, the *New York Evening Telegram*, the *New York Times*, the *Oakland Labor Review*, the *Brooklyn Standard Union*, the *Toledo Bee*, the *Boston Transcript*, the *Fall River Globe*, the *Albany Times-Union*, the *Buffalo Times*, the *Buffalo Courier*, the *New Orleans Star*, the *Milwaukee Leader*, the *Minneapolis Journal*, the *Boston Globe*, the *Providence Bulletin*, and virtually all the Catholic diocesan newspapers of the nation.

14. Quoted in the *Good of the Order: A Fortnightly* 14, no. 167 (1919): 8. This review collected many of the reactions of the national press and published them in a special number on 1 September 1919.

sponsive to the bishops' program, the group that was most favorable was, not surprisingly, the Progressive press. LaFollette's magazine praised it, and the editors of the *New Republic* hailed it as a sign of the times, which for them meant that it was a sign that reform fervor had reached such heights that full reform of the American economic system would be achieved: "One of the most important signs of the times is the new interest exhibited by the churches in the industrial problem. The latest evidence of this tendency toward broader views is afforded by the report of the Administrative Committee of the National Catholic War Council. . . . It is opposed to anything savoring of a collectivist organization, but demands substantial modification of the existing system. . . . If this sort of thing goes on unchecked, we shall soon arrive at a pass where the real standpatter will be quite unable to find a spiritual fold." The journal *Reconstruction* reiterated the *New Republic*'s observations and suggested that a powerful reform alliance was coalescing: "Nothing more clearly indicates than the changed attitude of clergymen and churches the extent to which the claims of the people for economic justice are reaching the conscience of mankind." *Reconstruction* acknowledged not only that the church was at one with reform sentiment but that it had assumed a position of leadership in the reform movement. The journal asserted that the program "is in advance even of anything that the progressive wing either of the Republican or Democratic party has ever advocated." Such sentiments were not uncommon. Writing for the *Nation,* Raymond Swing went so far as to say that it was better than anything produced by the AFL. The reformist editors of the *Survey* seemed to speak for reformers in general when they welcomed the bishops to the liberal fold: "Once again the Catholic hierarchy in America has expressed its profound sympathy with the forces in the national life that make for orderly social progress. . . . Its attitude toward the immediate political and social problems was discussed, and in the famous reconstruction program of the four bishops of the administrative committee of the National Catholic War Council endorsed."[15]

15. Robert LaFollette, "Social Reconstruction," *LaFollette's Magazine,* April 1919, p. 58; editorial comment, *New Republic,* 22 February 1919, p. 99; editorial

The reformers found the entire program worthy of praise, but they were particularly drawn to it because they perceived a link between their own desire for the establishment of full industrial democracy and the bishops' call for copartnership in industry. William Hard noticed this congruence, and using words that betrayed a common Progressive belief that laissez-faire capitalism was based on a selfishness that all reformers found reprehensible, he praised the program for stressing a collectivism that would enshrine human rights and promote altruism: "The bishops seem to think that the collective spirit will not be satisfied, and should not be, with 'representation.' The collective spirit demands ownership. The Spirit of Man demands ownership in the earth, in the earth's machines, for assured self-preservation. If it cannot get that ownership except collectively, it will get it collectively. The Bishops prefer a certain collectivism to a certain senseless individualism."[16] In the light of Hard's words, it is no wonder that the Progressives fairly rushed to embrace the bishops. Clearly, the two groups shared a common critical attitude on social issues, an almost identical rhetoric, and a fierce devotion to the evolutionary transformation of society that would result in the final victory of democracy.

The general Progressive praise for the program was tempered by misgivings about some of the specific proposals advocated by the bishops and questions regarding the motives behind their decision to publish it. For instance, *Reconstruction* was upset about the proposals for cooperative stores. The editors of the journal preferred to put their faith in government control: "We believe a better remedy would be arbitrarily to create a margin between wages and the cost of living by the enactment of minimum wage laws." Apparently, the old Progressive distrust of self-help and the corresponding belief in noblesse oblige died hard in some quarters. On the question of motives, Raymond Swing, in a generally favorable article in the *Nation* (which was matched by an equally positive piece in *America* at the same time), which brought a swift rebuttal from Muldoon, suggested

comment, *Reconstruction,* April 1919, p. 128; Raymond Swing, "The Catholic View of Reconstruction," *Nation,* 29 March 1919, p. 467; "Catholic After War Work," *Survey* 4 (October 1919): 21.

16. William Hard, "The Catholic Church Accepts the Challenge," *Metropolitan Magazine,* January 1920, p. 27.

that the bishops were opportunistic and somewhat calculating: he charged that they were motivated by a desire to make headlines and to cement the church's ties with labor.[17]

In spite of these critical comments, however, the initial response to the program in the secular and especially in the Progressive press was on balance one of incredulous delight. This reception shows that the bishops' program represented a significant turning point in the history of social Catholicism in America. The oft-repeated expressions of surprise, however, also pointed out with striking clarity that such a radical break with the past required that the bishops follow the statement with subsequent statements and strenuous actions that would solidify the gains represented by the program. Hence, R. H. Tierney, S.J., advised Muldoon: "The Bishops' Program is causing intense, if quiet discussion, and even those who are delighted with its contents are wondering if it is sincere, if the Church really intends to actualize it. . . . The Bishops 'scored a beat,' as newspapers put it, and Socialists and Methodists are none too well pleased. The latter are making heroic efforts to put their own program into effect. . . . Another pronouncement from one of our bishops would help to convince them that Catholics are really in earnest."[18] The church had achieved much through the publication of the program but had also set a challenge for herself to redeem the promise inherent in her words.

Thanks to Mead's careful planning, the second party in the postwar reform alliance also noticed the program. In the article Mead prepared for the labor journals, he stressed issues that were close to the laborers' hearts, such as the rights of labor to organize, to bargain collectively, and to a living wage as a minimum of justice and the bishops' plea that the War Labor Board be maintained in peacetime.[19] Labor's response to the program

17. Editorial comment, *Reconstruction,* May 1919, p. 155; Swing, "Catholic View of Reconstruction," p. 467. The bishops were delighted by Swing's generally positive reaction to the program, but they did not wish to appear calculating in the eyes of the general public. As a result, they followed a divided course in dealing with him: they asked his publisher for more copies of his articles so that they could circulate them, and they wrote letters protesting his charges of opportunism.

18. R. H. Tierney to Peter J. Muldoon, 9 April 1919, NCWC (Rockford File), Box 6, folder 13, ACUA.

19. See list of newspapers in note 13 above. In addition consult "Church Op-

and to Mead's article was diverse, ranging from wildly enthusiastic endorsement to a more wait-and-see skepticism, with most appraisals falling between these two extremes. On the one hand, in a widely reproduced article that appeared in October of 1919 under the headline "Church Program Pleases Labor," John Fitzpatrick, the president of the Chicago Federation of Labor, assessed labor's response to the bishops' words: "Nothing has appeared in a long time that will be of more substantial benefit to the cause of organized labor and of economic justice than the social reconstruction program of the National Catholic War Council. The four bishops who have signed this program and issued it to the world are entitled to the heartiest thanks of every wage earner who has the interests of his fellows at heart, and both they and the Church will receive his thanks and appreciation in full measure."[20]

Fitzpatrick's words amounted to a joyous acknowledgment that the labor movement had found a new and strong advocate of the rights of the workingman. J. W. McConaughty, an industrial relations expert, went one step further and fairly canonized the bishops for their perspicacity: "In providing for an immediate and gradually increasing participation by labor in the management of industry, the reconstruction program of the Catholic bishops points to the only visible means of saving our industrial civilization." The *Seattle Union Record*, however, remained skeptical of the ultimate effects of the much-heralded plan: "We are glad that the Catholic Church is seeing the coming of a new day. Of course, we do not disguise from ourselves the fact that the bishops chosen to formulate a reconstruction platform were naturally somewhat in advance of others in these matters. We

---

poses Reducing Wages," *Labor Record* (Youngstown), 22 February 1919, p. 5; "For New Era for Labor," *New York Times*, 14 February 1919, p. 11; "Church Program Warns against Wage-Cutting," *Railway Conductor*, August 1919, pp. 428–30; "Reconstruction Suggestions," *Federal Employee*, 13 December 1919, pp. 725–26. All of these stories stressed the bread-and-butter issues addressed by the program.

20. John Fitzpatrick, "Church Program Pleases Labor," *Skaneateles Democrat*, 3 October 1919, p. 1. Mead forwarded a list of more than sixty newspapers in which the article appeared. Among them were the *White Plains Argus*, the *Mankato Review*, the *Faribault Daily News*, the *Lansing Farmer*, the *Bloomington World*, the *Richmond* (Cal.) *Independent*, the *Valley City* (N.D.) *Times Record*, the *Thief River* (Minn.) *Falls Times*, the *Hartford* (Wisc.) *Press*, the *Appleton Crescent*, the *Bucyrus Independent*, and the *Mechanicsburg* (Pa.) *Journal*.

do not expect all the bishops to side forthwith with the working classes in their struggles."[21]

Overall, however, labor journalists seemed to want the rank and file of their respective unions to read and appreciate the document. The *Machinists' Monthly Journal* recommended the program to its audience:

> The work of this committee is extremely commendable and should receive the serious consideration of not alone our national and State legislative bodies, but of organizations of both capital and labor. We are sure that organized labor is ready to cooperate in any movement that has for its purpose the establishment of industrial democracy—which is virtually what the reconstruction programs of the American Federation of Labor and the Administrative Committee of the National Catholic War Council advocate, and both programs should receive the hearty support of all good citizens who have the welfare of the nation at heart.

The *Shoeworkers' Journal* echoed the machinists' call and praised the bishops' right thinking on wage issues close to labor's heart.[22]

Although the labor leaders were willing to acknowledge the wisdom of the program's proposals and recommend the document to their colleagues, they could not help but notice, as had the liberal commentators, that the program signaled a radical break with the Catholic past. Thus, even as he praised the program, Fitzpatrick reminded the church of the hostility toward religion which her past actions had fostered among the ranks of labor: "It would seem useless and foolish to blink the fact that many workers have been more or less estranged from the Church during recent years by reason of their preoccupation with the struggle for economic justice and industrial freedom . . . there have not been wanting plausible propagandists who have striven to show that the Church is on the side of special privilege in the battle between privilege and democracy." Nevertheless, Fitzpatrick said, "Today we are rewarded by a pronouncement that is undoubtedly the greatest ever put forth by any religious body on this subject." In other words, as Frank

21. Quoted in Ryan, *Social Reconstruction*, pp. 14, 13.

22. "Reconstruction Program," editorial comment, *Machinists' Monthly Magazine*, March 1919, p. 267; "Reconstruction Program," editorial comment, *Shoeworkers' Journal*, March 1919, p. 15.

Walsh put it, the program could only serve to renew relations between the two bodies and thus help the church "in retaining and strengthening its hold on the people."[23] If the program brought labor closer to the church, it would fulfill one of the bishops' fondest hopes: it would have secured the church a place in the affections of the working classes and assured her a place in the brave new world being built in the postwar era.

Given the history of the hostility or indifference between labor and the church in the prewar period, labor's embrace of the church seems a bit precipitous. There were, however, ideological and strategic reasons for labor's new cordiality toward the church. The ideological reasons were founded upon two mutually supportive perceptions of the church which the program produced among laborers. First, the short-term proposals gave labor the impression that the church was in favor of granting those very bread-and-butter concessions for which the labor movement had long struggled. Thus, in recommending the bishops' program to its readers, the *Shoeworkers' Journal* praised the bishops' advocacy of a living wage for all employees; both the *Seamen's Journal* and the *Miner's Magazine* were attracted by the plan's insistence that the high wage levels achieved during the war be maintained; and the national union newspaper *Labor* found all the practical proposals worthy of praise.[24]

Second, when they read the long-term reforms advocated in the final section of the plan, labor leaders believed that the

23. John Fitzpatrick, "The Bishops' Labor Programme," *National Catholic War Council Bulletin*, July 1919, p. 9; Frank P. Walsh, "The Significance of the Bishops' Labor Program," *National Catholic War Council Bulletin*, August 1919, p. 18. The national union newspaper, *Labor*, agreed: "One of the most hopeful signs of the times is that such men as Bp. McConnell of the Methodist Church, Bp. Williams of the Episcopal Church, and Dr. John A. Ryan of the Catholic Church are denouncing in the press and from the pulpit the wickedness of low wages, or unreasonably long hours and of unhealthful working conditions . . . most important of all—through their conduct they have done more to re-establish the workers' faith in the Church and its doctrines than any other body of men in our time" (*Labor*, 26 February 1920, p. 4).

24. "Social Reconstruction," editorial comment, *Shoeworkers' Journal*, March 1919, pp. 15–16; Lawrence Todd, "Our Washington Letter," *Seamen's Journal*, 5 March 1919, p. 8; "Church Opposes Reducing Wages," *Miners' Magazine*, March 1919, p. 1; "Father Ryan's New Book on 'Social Reconstruction,'" *Labor*, 1 January 1921, p. 3.

church was committing herself to helping establish industrial democracy in America, which seemed to indicate a congruence between the church's goals and those of the unions. Thus the *Shoeworkers' Journal* heaped praise on the bishops: "The wisdom of their conclusions is shown particularly in their statement that labor ought gradually to receive greater representation in the industrial part of business management. . . . These are all matters that the trade union movement attempts to deal with." The *Seamen's Journal* echoed the shoeworkers' sentiments and exulted that "virtually all the religious bodies of the United States are thus brought to the point where they not only concede but preach that the laborer is worthy of his hire and competent to say whether its terms are just and wholesome."[25] The labor journalists rejoiced that the war experience had created a groundswell of support for their goals.

Thus the laborers saw the bishops as their ideological kinsmen, and because they recognized a common rhetoric they also saw the churchmen as potential and strategically well-placed allies in the struggle against the entrenched power of the industrialists. In this battle, labor was at a decided disadvantage. Therefore, it showed a willingness to enter into power-strengthening alliances in the hope that association with other groups would enhance its image, advance its cause, and fulfill its dreams. Labor leaders thus sought to cement a strategic alliance with the Catholic Church. On the basis of his reading of the bishops' program, Frank Walsh, the former joint chairman of the War Labor Board, announced that a complete identity existed between the causes of labor and the church: "It is a triumph for true religion just as it is a triumph for the cause of economic democracy. For the interests of the two can never be far apart. The heart of organized labor believes that it is working in that same cause of human brotherhood to which the Church is pledged, and it is impossible to exaggerate the heartening and inspiring effect of this proof that the leaders of organized Christianity recognize and acclaim this identity of interests."[26] This

25. "Social Reconstruction," editorial comment, *Shoeworkers' Journal,* March 1919, p. 26; Lawrence Todd, "Our Washington Letter," *Seamen's Journal,* 30 July 1919, p. 8.

26. Walsh, "Significance of the Bishops' Labor Program," p. 18.

proclamation of an identity of interest was especially beneficial to the cause of labor for its identification with the traditionally conservative and moral influence of the church could provide a shield against the barbs of businessmen.[27] It is no wonder that labor journalists rushed to embrace the bishops' pronouncement. In the months following the program's appearance, the relationship between labor and Catholicism grew stronger. In the years that followed, however, this new friendship would be severely tested.

The Social Gospellers joined the Progressives and the laborers in responding to the bishops' program, echoing the sentiments expressed by their coreformers. The *World Tomorrow,* a radical Fellowship of Reconciliation newspaper, reviewed it favorably, as did Tyler Dennett, the publicity agent of the Interchurch World Movement, who saw it as an indication of Catholicism's ability to adapt to changing conditions and acknowledged that the bishops had established themselves as Christianity's moral leaders in industrial America by presenting a platform "which is far more explicit and more in line with the democratic movement of the age in industry than many a Protestant denomination can claim," an accolade seconded by F. Ernest Johnson, one of the leading social figures of the Federal Council of Churches.[28] Thus at the highest levels of the Social Gospel hi-

27. John Fitzpatrick also stressed the conservative nature of the program: "It is not a visionary programme; it is not the picture of a Utopia to be realized in the far distant future. It is what labor demands now, and those who wish to avoid the excesses and dangers of a violent and bitter upheaval can do nothing better than to acknowledge its true conservatism and aid organized labor in putting it into effect" ("Bishops' Labor Programme," p. 9). Labor was not the only party to benefit from the new alliance. The church regained the affections of the working classes, as Philip E. Ziegler reported: "Their ringing declarations in favor of Labor's aims, the establishment of human brotherhood and the elimination of economic injustice, has, I believe, done much to restore the workers' interest and renew their contact with the Church" ("Labor's Criticism of the Church," *Literary Digest,* 1 September 1923, p. 35). In addition, the church gained a loyal and vocal friend. When the NCWC came under sharp attack from the National Civic Federation for the supposedly radical nature of the bishops' program, the *Seamen's Journal* sprang to its defense: "Ralph M. Easley . . . has decided that the NCWC is too radical in its reconstruction program dealing with labor issues. . . . Just who has authorized Ralph Easley to speak for the American labor movement is a mystery. . . . Perhaps his authority to speak for the Catholic Church membership is similarly self-bestowed" (Lawrence Todd, "Our Washington Letter," *Seamen's Journal,* 14 May 1919, p. 8).

28. "Are the Churches Awakening?" *World Tomorrow,* March 1919, p. 81;

erarchy there was praise for the program and an evident willingness to acknowledge the bishops as colleagues—indeed even as leaders—in the fight for the ultimate triumph of virtue.

Although the liberal Protestants were heartened by the program, like their reforming colleagues among the Progressives and the laborers, they were frankly surprised by the spectacle of the supposedly conservative American hierarchy enunciating plans that were so clearly at odds with the church's earlier, conservative social statements. Surprise gave birth to wonder, which in turn gave rise to questioning and a search for the motives behind the bishops' actions. Alva Taylor, the secretary of the Disciples of Christ's Board of Temperance and Social Welfare, writing in the *Christian Century,* suggested that the program was rooted in practical necessity. Taylor argued that since the Catholic Church in America was a working-class church, the bishops were bound to champion the cause of labor: "It seemed surprising to many that Catholic ecclesiastics should make so Progressive and forward-looking a pronouncement. It is really not to be wondered at, for what an institution will do in such matters depends largely upon the nature of its clientele, and the great mass of Catholics in this country belong to the laboring class."[29] Taylor thought the program contained many laudable proposals, but it seemed somehow opportunistic, the product of the same astute calculation to which Raymond Swing had referred in the *Nation.* The editors of *World Tomorrow,* however, refused to countenance any suggestion that the program was motivated by self-interest. On the contrary, that

---

Tyler Dennett, *A Better World* (New York: George H. Doran, 1920), p. 75. Johnson said: "Probably it must be admitted too, that the Protestant communions have been much slower in coming to conscious recognition of industrial problems as calling for a specific treatment by the Church. Spiritual responsibility for a very large section of the working world has given rise to a body of Catholic doctrine bearing upon industrial conditions and relations that is quite without parallel in Protestantism. . . . Thus it happens that the Catholic Church, which has maintained the doctrinal tradition of Christianity substantially unmodified and which therefore appears to be theologically conservative as compared with Protestantism, is at the same time more liberal in its explicit teaching with references to matters economic and industrial" ("The Teaching of the Protestant Church," *Annals of the American Academy of Political and Social Science* 103 [1922]: 81–82).

29. Alva Taylor, "The Church and Industrial Democracy: Quakers and Catholics," *Christian Century,* 17 April 1919, p. 14.

journal believed that the church's solidarity with the poor created a sympathetic bond with the laboring classes, and it insisted that the program grew out of the humanitarianism that such sympathy nurtured: "For ourselves we reject the implication that the Catholic Church is animated solely by this unworthy fear [of losing workers to radicals]. Without doubt there is a section of the clergy and laity within the Roman Church who have both the wisdom and intimate contact with plain people to make them sincerely desirous to have the Church stand squarely in the new era with labor rather than with the great vested interests." The Protestant William Hard also defended the program against those who wished to see self-serving motives behind its publication by saying with reverent awe: "The Roman Catholic Church in America, for reasons which flow from the foot of the cross to this instant hour of the sins of the world proposes to abolish the wage system."[30]

Although the liberal Protestants' response was one of pleasant surprise, they too reserved the right to remain skeptical. Even the editors of *World Tomorrow* said, "It remains to be seen, however, whether an organization as essentially autocratic as the Roman Catholic Church can come to terms of lasting harmony with the free spirit of modern democracy." The *Christian Century* adopted the same wait-and-see attitude.[31]

On the whole, however, the Social Gospellers responded favorably to the bishops' program and welcomed their Catholic brethren to an ecumenical fellowship that was united both by a common desire to advance the cause of social justice and by the righteous rhetoric that cemented the reform alliance of the postwar era. Their expressions of surprise that the bishops should issue such a forward-looking statement, their scrambling for explanations of the bishops' motives, and their polite skepticism do not detract from their enthusiasm. If anything, the questions raised by the liberal Protestants testify to the extraordinary transformation of the church's image wrought by the program's publication. Before 1919, the Social Gospellers

30. *World Tomorrow* quoted in "The Bishops' Pastoral as Others See It," *America*, 22 March 1919, p. 624; Hard, "Catholic Church Accepts the Challenge," p. 16.

31. "Are the Churches Awakening?" p. 81; "A Medieval Shrine or a Program for Labor," *Christian Century*, 9 October 1919, p. 4.

had seen only evidence that the church was socially reactionary. The program called many old prejudices into question. Thus their questions were understandable and their skepticism reasonable. Apparently Mead, Ryan, and Muldoon had succeeded in creating a completely new image for the American church. The liberal Protestants blinked with gratified wonder and a touch of disbelief to hear their rhetoric coming from such an unaccustomed source.

As recently as the turn of the century, Mark Hanna had praised and courted the Catholic Church as a stay against radical confusion. Hanna had good reason for this view. The church leadership, partly in response to business overtures, partly because of a sincere belief in the virtues of the capitalist system, and partly because of a deep and abiding fear of radical socialism, had consistently acted to steer its working-class flocks away from radical causes. As a result, the business community looked upon the church as a loyal and useful friend, and none appreciated the bishops' program's radical nature so fully as did big business. Indeed, capital saw the program as a bitter betrayal of trust and a shocking departure from the past. As a result, business' response to the program was quick and venomous, although more often than not, it was couched in ingratiating—even patronizing—terms that seemed to suggest that businessmen thought they could shock the church to her senses and lure her back to the old and comfortable relationship of the past.

Shortly after the appearance of the program, Stephen C. Mason, the president of the National Association of Manufacturers, wrote to Cardinal Gibbons demanding that he have the church withdraw the statement. He reminded Gibbons that in the past the church had always publicly denounced the evils of socialism and therefore the bishops' plan could only be construed as a reversal of policy. He denounced the statement as a "covert effort to disseminate what he termed 'partisan, prolabor union, socialistic propaganda under the official insignia of the Roman Catholic Church.'" Gibbons dismissed the criticism and advised Mason to reread the statement.[32] Mason's private expression of anger did not exhaust big business' bitterness.

32. Quoted in Ellis, *Life of Gibbons,* 1:541.

Business took its case to the public. Feigning reluctance and using honeyed words, *Industry* launched a vicious attack on the church: "It is with the greatest reluctance and sadness of spirit that the editor of *Industry* calls attention to this deplorable situation. There is not the slightest desire to detract from the nobility and greatness of those religious denominations which have endured through the changing ages, nor from the wonderful work in behalf of human betterment of the philanthropic organizations, but American business principles are questioned and American businessmen maligned to a point where 'forebearance ceases to be a virtue.'" *Industry* then entered the fray in earnest. Its arguments followed a time-honored pattern. The editor first pointed out the absurdity of the church's taking any stand on economic matters: "It is hard to understand how the Church feels confident and competent enough in its knowledge of industrial conditions to endorse these measures [such as collective bargaining] in its pastoral letters and in its creeds particularly since not many instances are on record of the Church's asking advice of the employers of either great or small numbers of workmen in the representative industries."[33]

The editors wished the church to return to the pulpit and confine her sermons to the spiritual realm. As time went on, business became even more critical of the church's stand on social issues, and when the Interchurch World Movement published its report on the notorious steel strike of 1919, which was critical of Judge Elbert Gary and business in general, Marshall Olds attributed the radical contagion sweeping all of the churches to the influence of the hated bishops' program: "In July [actually February] 1919, a certain organization within the Catholic Church made a general public announcement of policy which undoubtedly materially influenced the formation by the (Protestant) Interchurch World Movement of its Industrial Relations Department. . . . After the appearance of this announcement by a faction of the other religious body of the country, the Interchurch faction that had long urged that policy now insisted

33. "Announcing a Series of Articles on 'The Industrial Fallacies of Certain Religious and Secular Organizations,'" *Industry,* 15 May 1920, p. 3; "Industrial Fallacies of Certain Religious and Secular Organizations," *Industry,* 15 June 1920, p. 2.

that the Interchurch World Movement should extend its influence and activities into the industrial field."[34] Thus through sweet reason and blunt criticism the business community responded to the new image of the church by trying to get the church to return to the fold. These efforts were to no avail. Business was forced to admit that the church had emerged as a new and formidable adversary that was passionately opposed to capital's dreams of normalcy. As a result, during the years that followed, business bent all its energies to the task of blunting the NCWC's criticism of its practices.

Although the reaction of big business to the program was venomous and persistent, it was not surprising. Both more surprising and potentially more damaging was the criticism directed against the plan by the National Civic Federation and its leader, Ralph M. Easley.[35] In the years immediately before the war, the federation had become increasingly concerned with what it perceived to be the Bolshevist tendencies of America's reformers. As Marguerite Green notes, the reform ideal of industrial democracy began to strike fear into the hearts of Easley and his followers.[36]

As a result of this fear and the radicalism from which it seemed to spring, the federation became more favorably disposed toward the business community and more wary of radical elements among both the laborers and the intellectuals of the country. Easley decided that since the American Federation of Labor, under the safely conservative leadership of Samuel Gom-

34. Marshall Olds, *Analysis of the Interchurch World Movement Report on the Steel Strike* (New York: G. P. Putnam's Sons, 1922), pp. 394–95.

35. The National Civic Federation was an organization composed of representatives of business, labor, and the public who came together to examine social issues with a view to fostering social harmony among classes for the public good. Its close ties to Samuel Gompers and its labor sympathies led to strained relations with the National Association of Manufacturers. The manufacturers' opposition notwithstanding, the federation was a powerful group in America, and through its *Review,* its policies gained wide publication. There are particular ironies connected with the federation's opposition to the program. Gibbons's name appeared on the organization's letterhead, as did that of Nicholas Frederick Brady, the brother-in-law of Francis P. Garvan, who paid for the public relations campaign that won the program such a wide hearing in America.

36. Marguerite Green, *The National Civic Federation and the American Labor Movement, 1900–1925* (Washington: Catholic University of America Press, 1956), pp. 362–63.

pers, could see to the extirpation of radicalism from the labor movement, "the NCF should undertake to clean them [radicals] out from the Churches, the colleges, the universities and the various places which the labor movement could not reach."[37] To accomplish this winnowing, Easley proposed to form a committee that would investigate the radical elements in the country. The National Civic Federation leadership approved the formation of the committee and entrusted its leadership to Easley, Conde Pallen, and Everett Wheeler. On 12 February 1919, they spied yet another center of radical thought (the NCWC) and another radical manifesto, the Bishops' Program of Social Reconstruction.

Within a month of the program's publication, Easley launched an attack on it.[38] He and his committee issued a report condemning the plan in terms that were similar to those used by the business community:

> It is, however, a matter of concern to the Committee that there is a small, but active and well-organized group in the Churches which appears to be impatient with the slow and orderly process of political and economic evolution and has espoused Marxian doctrines as supplying the only solution for existing problems . . . there are other clergymen . . . who while not frankly accepting the principles of socialism or communism, foster and aid the groups represented by such philosophy. . . . This latter group is by far the most dangerous and difficult to deal with. . . . They are men who are unfitted by training and ability to deal with the complex and difficult problems presented in the realm of governmental reform and political economy.

The Catholic member of the committee, Conde Pallen, made the reference to Catholicism explicit when he said, "While the Catholic Church . . . is steadfast in its support of law and order, there are to be found certain priests whose viewpoints on social and economic questions meet with the hearty support and applause of the radical and revolutionary elements in our country."[39]

The War Council realized that the Easley report and the comments of Pallen, a widely respected Catholic journalist and the

37. Ibid., pp. 371, 389.

38. Abell, *American Catholicism and Social Action*, pp. 204–5.

39. Conde Pallen, "A Belated Complaint," *Catholic Charities Review* 5 (1921): 271.

editor of the *Catholic Encyclopedia* project, were as potentially damaging as they were embarrassing. When he first learned of the appearance of the Easley report, Burke put on a brave front and wrote to Muldoon, discounting its significance by saying, "from the history of the man this was to be expected."[40] Nevertheless, the NCWC leadership realized that Easley's report was a real threat because his many connections made it probable that his views would find their way into many business journals.[41] In his report as well as in articles in the *National Civic Federation Review,* Easley charged that the plan advanced by the bishops was unofficial (and hence not binding for Catholics), novel (and hence out of keeping with the church's tradition), and dangerously radical. Clearly, measures would have to be taken to answer his charges and blunt his attack.

Accordingly, O'Grady fired off a letter to Easley demanding the right to rebut his charges in print. Easley acceded to the request. O'Grady's published letter met Easley's criticisms head-on. Easley, however, printed O'Grady's letter with a repetition of his own charges, which he assured his readers were supported by the testimony of a group of Catholics whom he declined to name. Exasperated, O'Grady took up his pen once again and wrote both to protest Easley's treatment and to answer the charges anew.[42]

O'Grady's line of reasoning leads one to believe that the NCWC was especially stung by the revelation that Catholics were aiding Easley in undermining the authority of the program. These Catholics were, O'Grady's comments to the contrary notwithstanding, well-versed in canon law. They understood full well that the NCWC was of dubious canonical standing and that consequently its pronouncements had only a tenuous claim to authority. O'Grady knew that if such assertions were left unchallenged, the program's standing among American Catholics would be seriously compromised. Accordingly, he sought to establish and defend the moral authority of the doc-

40. John J. Burke to Peter J. Muldoon, 4 April 1919, NCWC (Rockford File), Box 8, folder 6, ACUA.

41. Murray, *Red Scare,* p. 87.

42. John O'Grady to Ralph M. Easley, 3 April 1919, Easley to O'Grady, 4 April 1919, O'Grady to Easley, 9 April 1919, NCWC-CSWA (Reconstruction Committee), Box 4, folder 10, ACUA.

ument. His argument was divided into two parts. To the assertion that the bishops' plan was unofficial because it represented the opinions of only four members of the hierarchy, he contended that "all the bishops were consulted concerning the organization of the archbishops in the War Council. . . . Therefore, the Four Bishops who issued the Reconstruction Program represent the entire hierarchy." O'Grady deftly skirted the tricky question of the canonical status of the NCWC, which was the question on which the controversy turned, by saying that since the anonymous critics refused to reveal their identities and thus to present their credentials to enter into a debate on the finer points of canon law, "we cannot accept them as qualified authorities on the jurisdiction of episcopal committees." O'Grady dismissed the critics' assertions that the bishops did not intend to endorse the particulars of the program: "The anonymous writer would have his readers believe that the Four Bishops said in effect: 'While we are in favor of wider social justice, we do not pass judgment upon the particular measures advocated in this Program.' That would be no doubt highly satisfactory to those persons who hold the social views of the anonymous writer, but to attribute it to the Four Bishops is not to credit them with a high order of seriousness or of intelligence."[43]

O'Grady bravely tried to turn back Easley's attacks, but he was clearly nervous about the long-range damage the charges would inflict on the program's credibility. In addition, he was uneasy about having to joust with anonymous opponents. In his letters to Easley, he tried to coax or shame the critics into the open but to no avail. In desperation, he enlisted the aid of Colonel Patrick Callahan, who wrote to Easley to ascertain the names of the offending parties. Easley responded with a tantalizing, "Confidentially, I will say to you that it was some important Catholic people who brought the Reconstruction pamphlet to me and they stated that it was not authorized by the hierarchy and therefore did not represent the Catholic Church."[44] He did not, however, reveal any names. Callahan forwarded the correspondence to the NCWC headquarters in Washington. The

43. O'Grady to Easley, 9 April 1919.

44. Easley to Patrick H. Callahan, 11 April 1919, NCWC-CSWA (Reconstruction Committee), Box 4, folder 10, ACUA.

mystery remained, and the NCWC continued at a disadvantage in the exchange.

Easley did not let up in his attacks. In September of 1920, the *National Civic Federation Review* published an article by P. Tecumseh Sherman that continued the onslaught.[45] The fallout from Easley's attacks was not confined to the pages of the *Review.* New York State's Joint Legislative Committee Investigating Seditious Activities (the Lusk Committee) took up Easley's charges and made them even more pointed by fingering Ryan as the guilty party who had dragged American Catholicism into the socialist camp.[46] Clearly, Easley and the questions he raised about the novel, radical, and unofficial character of the program would have to be met squarely. Private correspondence and rational argument had failed to silence Easley and his colleagues. The NCWC finally resorted to a lively public defense that was entrusted to Ryan's care.

In assembling the reconstruction committee and defining its tasks, O'Grady, Muldoon, and Splaine had made it clear that they wished to use the committee to produce a Catholic social literature of lasting value that would raise the social consciousness of American Catholics. The bishops' program was the first pamphlet the committee produced in its attempt to fulfill its mission. Therefore, although the non-Catholic reception of the program is important for understanding how the document remade the image of the church in America, in many ways the Catholic reaction was even more important.

The Catholic reaction to the program was mixed. In general, however, it generated a surprisingly positive response. Intellectuals were laudatory in the extreme. Williams called the program "an achievement of the most momentous consequence, one which was so bold at first seeming, and so startling in its results upon public opinion as to alarm many ultra-conservatives both outside and within the Church. And yet the action referred to was perhaps the most thoroughly Catholic thing done by the Council." Williams believed that the publi-

45. P. Tecumseh Sherman, "Catholic Reconstruction Program Analyzed," *National Civic Federation Review,* 25 September 1920, p. 24.

46. Clayton Lusk et al., *Revolutionary Radicalism: Its History, Purpose and Tactics: Being the Report of the Joint Legislative Committee Investigating Seditious Activities,* 2 vols. (Albany: J. B. Lyon, 1920), 1:1139.

cation of the program indicated the church's acceptance of her authoritative teaching role in the modern world. Shane Leslie wrote from England to inform the bishops that he fully believed that "a hundred years hence the only surviving statement by any of the modern Episcopacy will be that to which you and your colleagues gave your names." The wise and intellectually alert labor priest Peter Dietz commended the plan: "If it is not a vindication of all that I suffer for and have been oftentimes blamed for, what is it? Your episcopal War Council document of recent date gave me much joy and on that program I surely have a mission."[47]

The reactions of the intellectuals and the social activists were encouraging to the bishops, but because they were most often expressed in private letters, they were of dubious value in advancing the educational mission that Muldoon favored. American Catholicism's published responses to the program, however, were crucial to this mission. Catholic editors rose to meet the challenge and through their vigorous support of the bishops' platform strove mightily to raise the American Catholic social consciousness in ways that Muldoon had envisioned.

The national Catholic press was dominated by three journals sponsored by religious orders and directed toward three different audiences: the Paulist Fathers' *Catholic World,* a journal of thought and opinion aimed at a literate audience; the Jesuits' *America,* a newsweekly aimed at a general although fairly educated clientele; and the Holy Cross Fathers' *Ave Maria,* a popular devotional monthly that was addressed to a wide popular audience. All three supported the program. The *Catholic World* published George Schuster's reflections on the bishops' words, which corresponded with the Paulist vision of the church's mission and place in American life. Schuster saw the publication of the platform as a move by the church to assume her rightful position at the center of American life. He rejoiced at this new development and invited his readers to see the program as an event and a document of immense importance for the church

47. Williams, *American Catholics in the War,* pp. 304–5; Shane Leslie to Muldoon, n.d., NCWC (Rockford File), Box 6, folder 13, ACUA; Dietz quoted in Fox, *Peter Dietz,* p. 140. Dietz was not without some misgivings, as shall be seen later.

and the world: "We proclaimed the Reconstruction Program and proved to the world that we had not forgotten our free descent from Christian men. I think that the future historian of American Catholicism, looking back over decades of splendid effort, will mark this as a critical place in our story; for here we broke the fast of silence. . . . There is shown clearly the importance of considering the Church as a world force."[48] He was extravagant in his praise and urgent in his insistence that the entire American church realize that the earth had shifted and that a new creation had been brought forth.

The Jesuit *America* rendered the bishops invaluable assistance in informing Catholics on the meaning of the plan. The editors turned one issue of the magazine into a forum for exposing the platform to its readers. They gathered articles by Raymond Swing, a leading liberal, J. W. McConaughty, a labor sympathizer and former assistant secretary of the War Labor Board, and William Maloney, a laborer, added their own editorial observations on the meaning of the program, and continued to keep their readers informed on the progress and meaning of the plan for the church. Through their extensive coverage of the program, *America*'s editors strove to present the bishops' words as moderate, wise, and fully in accord with Catholic tradition. *America* was happy to publish both William Maloney's remarks: "There is in all this, as can be readily seen, not the slightest tinge of a Socialistic tendency, since the entire purpose is to promote the extension and not the abolition of private property," and Joseph Husslein's article "Popes' and Bishops' Labor Program." It would appear that *America*'s enthusiasm for the program knew no bounds. In addition to defending the plan against Swing's criticism in the *Nation*, R. H. Tierney, S.J., the editor of *America*, wrote to Muldoon that he was moving might and main to interest secular editors in New York in covering the program.[49]

48. George N. Schuster, "Catholic Literature as a World Force," *Catholic World*, July 1920, p. 462, 454–55.

49. See *America*, 29 March 1919; also ibid., 14 June 1919; William J. M. A. Maloney, "The Contents of the Bishops' Labor Program," ibid., 22 March 1919, p. 602; Joseph Husslein, "Popes' and Bishops' Labor Program," ibid., 14 June 1919, pp. 248–50; R. H. Tierney to Peter J. Muldoon, 9 April 1919, NCWC (Rockford File), Box 6, folder 13, ACUA.

Ave Maria was no less enthusiastic in its support of the program. D. E. Hudson, C.S.C., told his readers that the bishops were continuing the moral crusade of the war in their reconstruction proposals: "The quartet of Catholic prelates . . . evidently do not look upon the signing of the Armistice as an indication that their usefulness has ceased or that their occupation is gone. In common with other judicious citizens, they are convinced that after-the-war problems are likely to prove as difficult of solution as was the eventual winning of the great world conflict." Hudson rebuffed the charges that the plan was novel: "Imperfect knowledge of the Church's position as to Socialism is the explanation of such statements. The Catholic press is never tired of reiterating that, while the Church opposes Socialism, she is by no means antagonistic to many and many a social reform." The national Catholic treatment of the program was rounded out by the contribution of the *NCWC Bulletin,* which, because it was a house organ and was edited by the liberal Michael Williams, praised the plan and justified it as the natural outgrowth of Catholic social teaching. Williams wrote: "Deriving from the immutable standards of spiritual and moral values committed by God to his Church, the traditional social principles and programmes of the Church have in all ages been the norm of practical and worthy social systems . . . today as in all other epochs . . . the world has need of the social principles laid down by the Church." Williams seemed to rejoice in critics' reactions to the program, which he thought only served to prove "it [the Bishops' Program] is so alive. . . . It does not utter soporific generalities. It suggests practical and workable social remedies." The national Catholic press thus did yeoman service in trying to bring the program to the attention of Catholic audiences and in presenting a fully Catholic justification for the proposals it contained.[50]

As laudatory as the national Catholic journals were in their treatment of the bishops' program, their contribution to the

50. D. E. Hudson, "Notes and Remarks," *Ave Maria,* 1 March 1919, p. 277; D. E. Hudson, "Notes and Remarks," ibid., 12 July 1919, pp. 53–54; Michael Williams, "The Catholic Programme of Reconstruction," *National Catholic War Council Bulletin,* June 1919, p. 8. One other national Catholic organ championed the program: the *Catholic Charities Review.* The *Review* was edited by John A. Ryan and thus became a major defender of the bishops' words.

educational enterprise outlined by Muldoon was negligible for the simple reason that their readership was small. As a result, the task of educating the Catholic public fell mostly on the shoulders of the editors of the diocesan newspapers, which, although individually small in circulation, were collectively able to reach a far wider audience than the national journals could. These newspapers met the challenge and sought through their coverage of the program to inform and thus transform the Catholic social consciousness. The coverage they devoted to the program was diverse but overwhelmingly positive. Some commented on the novel and radical nature of the bishops' actions; others staunchly maintained that the program was traditional in nature and conservative (that is, antiradical) in both its intent and the possible consequences it envisioned for the American industrial system. Behind the elation of those papers that stressed the novel and radical cast of the program there lurked a sense of relief that the church had finally broken her long and inopportune silence on social issues by presenting the bishops' plan. Father Peter Gannon, writing for Omaha's *True Voice,* expressed this relief at the same time that he scolded the bishops for their tardiness in becoming involved in social issues: "There is much work to be done and we are glad the Bishops are to take the lead in it. Lack of their direction and leadership was the one thing that defeated so much well meant Catholic endeavor in the past fifteen years." Anne O'Hara McCormick, writing in the Columbus *Catholic Universe,* voiced the same relief: "Those of us who have wished that the Church in America might take some authoritative and official part in the solution of almost overwhelming social problems . . . will derive great satisfaction from the [bishops' program]. . . . It is time the Catholics of the country stood behind some such constructive program."[51]

In their praise of the action of the bishops, Gannon and McCormick were acknowledging a great transformation of the church's social mission. They were also agreeing with some of the church's critics who insisted that the program represented a radical departure from the American church's traditional and conservative behavior. In a burst of enthusiasm, the *New World* of the Archdiocese of Chicago, which was outspokenly prolabor

51. Quoted in Roddy, "Catholic Newspaper Press," pp. 237–38.

in its editorial stance, went beyond Gannon and McCormick when it said: "It is as radical as could possibly be expected and it is as timely as the most modern conditions could warrant. It stamps as absurd and mischievous the damning compliment that attempts so often to malign the Church, that it is a sort of sublimating policeman to guard all wealth, good and bad, and to be the barrier against rational discontent. . . . The conclusion is made plain that the era of capitalism is over. Like feudalism, it has had its day and must be discarded. The new world is to be for the worker. . . . Backed by the Church, the workman may take heart that his day will be hastened."[52] These were brave words well calculated to endear the church and her plans to the working classes. In the frightened and frightening days following the war, however, when radicalism seemed to many to threaten America and its stability, they were also words redolent with revolution. The sentiments expressed by the *New World* would return to haunt the program's defenders and make their apologetic task all the more difficult.

Overall, however, the line expressed by Gannon, McCormick, and the *New World* was not taken up by most of the program's apologists, most of whom adamantly refused to concede that the plan was novel. Instead, sensitive to charges of radicalism and novelty, they insisted that since the program was rooted in the nation's and the church's traditions (which they frequently pointed out were complementary), it was essentially a sober and conservative document.[53] Thus the *Brooklyn Tablet* (which believed that the program's publication was the most momentous event in American Catholic history since Baltimore III[54]) boldly defended the program as the embodiment of the ideals of the republic: "Feeling that America is not yet free of danger and that the Catholic Church still has a most important part to bear in protecting and preserving the country of Lincoln and Washington our Hierarchy has seen fit to keep intact our organization. What their future work will amount to can be recognized by reading their priceless document on 'Social Reconstruction.'

52. Editorial comment, *New World,* 21 February 1919, p. 4.

53. The church would have to argue that the action was both old and new: old in that it was rooted in tradition and new—good for the American church.

54. Editorial comment, *Brooklyn Tablet,* 15 February 1919, p. 1.

. . . Its conservative, impartial, just, Catholic and American tone will win the support of Government, of capital and labor, of citizens of every walk of life."[55] The *Tablet* believed that the program's conservative and thoroughly American emphasis on democracy made it the ultimate antidote to the radical sentiment that was sweeping and threatening the nation.

The *Tablet* defended the program's conservatism on the basis of its conformity to American values and ideals; other newspapers located its conservative inspiration in its connections with the Catholic tradition. The *Saint Louis Western Watchman* said, "It does try one's patience to read the comments of ignorant critics who affect surprise at what they deem a radical departure from the past on the part of the Church. There is nothing novel in this evidence of interest in the problems of living men and the authors had but to adapt traditional principles to the actual situation to formulate the Program." The *Boston Pilot* echoed these sentiments when it staunchly insisted that the program was merely a contemporary practical application of Catholic principles which were the only effective cure for radicalism: "No one can accuse the Catholic Church of the error of being impractical in her treatment of the social question. She is ever ready to adapt her tried and true principles to the changing conditions of the times. She opposes socialism and its variants, but she proposes social reform. . . . As a practical alternative to Bolshevism, we commend this remarkable document to the earnest consideration of all serious minded students of the social question." The *Buffalo Echo*, reflecting its largely German Catholic readership, justified the traditional Catholic nature of the document by telling its readers that the program was influenced by the work of Bishop Wilhelm von Ketteler and the Austrian Catholic reformers, but most Catholic writers found the program's warrant in Pope Leo XIII's writings. Thus the *Hartford Catholic Transcript* assured its readers that "the report bears all the earmarks of a thorough study of Pope Leo's Encyclical on 'The Condition of Labor' [*Rerum Novarum*] and the application of principles admitted by Catholic sociologists and Catholic students of economic conditions."[56]

55. Quoted in *Good of the Order*, p. 2.

56. *Western Watchman* quoted in Ryan, *Social Reconstruction*, p. 11; edito-

Whether individual papers chose to rejoice that the program signaled a new and salutary departure from the church's past social somnolence or to call attention to its traditional Catholic and American roots, all were agreed that though the program continued the church's opposition to socialism, it also enunciated a positive, constructive social program that represented a real opening to the cause of labor. Thus the program altered the church's image among the working classes. In this, all the editors rejoiced. Therefore, the *Hartford Catholic Transcript*, echoing the *Chicago New World*, said, "Labor agitators who have been given to representing the Catholic Church as inimical to well-directed labor movements will find scant comfort in perusing this report. . . . As the first authoritative pronouncement in the United States of the Catholic attitude toward economic affairs, the report will be welcomed by Churchmen and the labor world as an illuminating, directive document." The *Salesianum* of Milwaukee's Saint Francis de Sales Seminary went so far as to say that the document would cement the relationship between church and labor: "It is a pamphlet well worth the study of every priest in our country. Who more than he should be interested in the welfare of the laboring classes? They are in the greatest majority in every parish throughout the land—faithful, true-hearted members of every congregation—the very backbone of our Church in the United States. Their cause should be our cause—their interest ours."[57]

Clearly, the Catholic press believed that with the publication of the program, the American church had arrived at the threshold of a new age, bright with promise. Answering Muldoon's call for an education in the social principles that would guide the church in this brave new world, the editors did all they could to recommend the bishops' statement to their readers.[58]

---

rial comment, *Boston Pilot*, 3 May 1919, p. 4; *Buffalo Echo*, quoted in *Good of the Order*, p. 11; editorial comment, *Catholic Transcript*, 27 February 1919, p. 4. See also the *Tablet*, cited in *Good of the Order*, p. 4.

57. Editorial comment, *Catholic Transcript*, 27 February 1919, p. 4; editorial comment, *Salesianum* 14 (1919): 44–45.

58. It might be argued that the diocesan editors had to praise this new American Leonine document and that therefore their coverage of it is of dubious value for assessing the impact and import of the bishops' plan for the American church. Before 1919, however, the social record of American Catholic newspapers was undistinguished. With the exception of John Boyle O'Reilly's *Boston*

The editor of the *Brooklyn Tablet* spoke for all the editors when, drawing upon the war experience and its rhetoric, he said, "The same unity we showed in the war must be awakened anew. Here is a definite, constructive social program to counteract everything of a radical or reactionary nature. Let us one and all fall in line behind our peerless generals and strive again to win new victories for God and Country."[59]

Although the program met with widespread approval among American Catholics, it would be wrong to assume that the entire Catholic population was delighted with what the bishops had said and done. There were some loud negative reactions to the document. Perhaps the most surprising criticism came from Peter Dietz, a labor priest with close ties to the AFL. Although Dietz was generally favorable toward the program, he had some misgivings about some of its proposals. As Mary H. Fox notes, Dietz was especially scornful of the idea of labor cooperation in management. He thought such proposals were irredeemably naive or unspeakably foolish.[60] Dietz felt it was far wiser to concentrate on practical measures that guaranteed labor concessions on bread-and-butter issues for which the unions had struggled for so long. Dietz's complaints about the program reflected the disdain which some of his friends in the AFL still entertained for the ideology of the reformers.

Tablet and George Dering Wolff's *Philadelphia Union and Times,* the newspapers had given only lip service to a few Leonine ideas. The Catholic editors were so afraid of aiding the growth of socialism that they had very little of a constructive nature to say on social issues. Indeed, more often than not, they had defended the economic status quo, a strange situation given the working-class nature of the church's American flock. As Edward Roddy notes, with the publication of the bishops' program, all that changed. A seismic shift took place in the world of American Catholic journalism: "The Catholic press, responding to this startling manifestation of Church leadership, transformed itself into a willing handmaiden of the social justice movement. Shedding—in large measure—former prejudices and fears, it courageously defended trade unionism, criticized capital and 'exposed' the sinister influences behind the 'red hysteria'" (Roddy, "Catholic Newspaper Press," pp. 227–28).

Roddy finds a note of irony in this radical shift: "Because of the admittedly radical nature of some of the provisions of the Bishops' Program, it is all the more surprising to note the lack of raised eyebrows among the more conservative Catholic newspapers. Overnight, as it were, these right-wing journals found the Catholic Church publicly endorsing measures which they had fought as 'socialistic' in previous years" (ibid., p. 242).

59. Editorial comment, *Brooklyn Tablet,* 15 February 1919, p. 4.

60. Fox, *Peter Dietz,* p. 140.

A far more serious source of discontent was the German-American Catholic community. The normally voluble Arthur Preuss, the editor of the *American Catholic Fortnightly Review*, maintained a tantalizing silence on the program, which reflected Preuss's pique that the Irish social theorists at the Catholic University had managed to foist their views on the entire American Catholic community with the blessing of the bishops. Together with his fellow Germans, Preuss believed that the Irish cadre headed by Ryan and Kerby was naive and wrongheaded because of its failure to understand and endorse German Catholic social thought. The German Catholic Central Verein was of two minds about the document. As Philip Gleason points out, its initial reaction was favorable, although somewhat reserved: "The *Central Blatt*'s [the organ of the Verein] formal treatment of the Bishops' Program was by Father Charles Bruehl, a regular contributor on reform matters. His discussion was generally favorable, although he noted that the Program failed entirely to consider the Mittelstand problem and that parts of it would undermine the energy and initiative of the middle class." The Reverend Albert Muntsch also covered the program for the *Central Blatt*, and he followed Bruehl's lead. He too offered cautious praise for the document, saying, "The Program of 1919, though it is rather a Program of Labor Reform than a complete social reconstruction platform, has been met with the widest acceptance, being called by one authority, 'the most courageous step ever taken by the Church in America.'"[61]

Grudging praise, however, soon gave way to animosity. William J. Engelen warned the *Central Blatt*'s readers: "Even at present, although we are said to have entered upon an era of reconstruction, the average Catholic as well as non-Catholic will read the following expression by Dr. John Ryan with a sense of doubt: 'The spirit and traditions of the Church are much less favorable to the current claims and pretensions of capitalism than the uninformed reader would be likely to infer from a study of Catholic writers. The latter are so pre-occupied refuting Socialism and defending the present order, that they go to

61. Gleason, *Conservative Reformers*, p. 195; Albert Muntsch, "Another Reconstruction Program," *Central Blatt and Social Justice*, February 1920, pp. 348–49.

the opposite extreme, understating the amount of truth in the claims of Socialism.'"[62] Ryan's statement in general and the bishops' program in particular made Engelen see red—figuratively and literally. He believed that Ryan's great reliance on state intervention would lead to rank socialism, a prospect the Germans could not abide. Finding the bishops' words of questionable wisdom and dubious practical value, Engelen lumped the program together with other reconstruction schemes current at the time and dismissed them all: "In a certain sense, the above programs deny the necessity of reconstruction, and demand a remodelling, or as a speaker lately expressed it, demand 'reconstruction for Europe and a readjustment for our country.' The study of this question and the development of a uniform program from admitted principles may be difficult, but it must also be possible." He was equally unkind in his treatment of Ryan.[63] Engelen's reaction was understandable. He believed that German Catholic social thought boasted a longer pedigree and possessed greater wisdom than did Ryan and his Catholic University colleagues. Piqued by the bishops' oversight, the Germans refused to lend their wholehearted approval to the program. Instead, in the pages of the *Central Blatt*, the Germans presented their own comprehensive program for social reconstruction, which stood in marked contrast to that of the bishops.

The Germans were not the only Catholics dismayed with what the NCWC had wrought. Conservatives came in many stripes and gave the bishops a great deal of trouble.[64] The most

62. W. J. Engelen, "Social Reflections: Reconstruction by Force," *Central Blatt and Social Justice*, December 1919, p. 279.

63. Gleason, *Conservative Reformers*, p. 194; W. J. Engelen, "Social Reflections: Reconstruction Programs," *Central Blatt and Social Justice*, October 1919, p. 204. Referring to people who cited Ryan as an expert on social questions and Ryan's proposals as the only sure way to a just social order, he said icily, "I know that a goodly number of people are not so certain about the saving force of these practical applications" (W. J. Engelen, "Social Reflections: The Corner Stone of Reconstruction," *Central Blatt and Social Justice*, March 1920, p. 381).

64. "A notable example of this [Catholic opposition to the NCWC] was the strong criticism directed at the Bishops' Program by conservatives. They considered it dangerously radical and the administrative committee tainted with socialism. John A. Ryan, the actual author, was suspected of being a Marxist sympathizer and a National Civic Federation committee studying socialism spoke of priests who are in important positions in Catholic organizations and who

famous and notable antagonist of the bishops' program and its author was Conde Pallen, who wrote the Civic Federation report which attacked the program with great viciousness and with damaging results. Pallen's reaction to the program and to Ryan's work was not, however, exhausted by his work on the committee. He carried on a lively and vitriolic correspondence with Ryan and wrote to Archbishop Edward J. Hanna of San Francisco and the NCWC to demand that the bishops order Ryan to stop using the bishops' authority to publicize his own dangerously radical social ideas.[65] The program was clearly not a source of joy to all the Catholic people.

The bishops had hoped that their program of social reconstruction would have a wide circulation among the American people, and the coverage accorded its publication redeemed their hopes and cheered their hearts. Among both friends and foes, however, the same notes kept cropping up in the reviews given the program: all were struck by the novelty of the church's breaking with her cautious past performance on social issues. To the socially active Catholics, the Progressives, laborers, and Social Gospellers, this break was welcome and encouraging. To conservative Catholics and businessmen, the shift was a bitter disappointment and an occasion for concern.

To discredit the program its opponents consistently attacked its novelty, its radical tendencies, and its dubious magisterial standing in the church.[66] These three criticisms set the terms

---

'sympathize with, foster and aid' Marxist-oriented philosophy. In view of a situation that developed in 1922, it seems probable that a few bishops were among the critics of the War Council, but John A. Ryan did say that no bishop publicly attacked the Bishops' Program" (Sheerin, *Never Look Back,* pp. 53–54).

65. McKeown, "War and Welfare," p. 248.

66. As McKeown notes, the charges of radicalism were lodged against the long-range goals enunciated by the program: "The average middle class American suspected that the least interference with the wage system was a step toward socialism; he did not understand that producers' cooperatives and partnership arrangements were designed to re-establish private enterprise through the cooperation of like-minded individuals working independently of government" ("War and Welfare," p. xxix). The problem of the program's legality was potentially dangerous—indeed, the most dangerous of all. In a hierarchical church, a statement of dubious canonical standing and hence of questionable magisterial weight could easily be dismissed, and the laity would be left with perfect freedom to follow their own lights. This could wreck the educational enterprise on which the bishops had embarked.

upon which both opponents and defenders of the program argued its merits and flaws. The defenders had to argue their case with reference to these three points and on two simultaneous fronts. To the Catholic faithful who were concerned about its dubious magisterial standing and its roots in Catholic tradition, the program's champions had to establish the moral (as opposed to the legal) authority of the plan by demonstrating its essential continuity with the church's corpus of social teaching and especially with the Leonine tradition. This endeavor gave rise to fights between liberals and conservatives concerning the legitimate interpretation of Leo XIII's thought. Second, the program's supporters had to demonstrate its essentially conservative nature in the American context in which it appeared. In 1919, this meant that they had to prove that instead of participating in radicalism, the program was an effective antidote to radical agitation and was at one with American values and ideals. Of the two fronts on which the battle to defend the program had to be fought, clearly the bishops and their partisans believed that the fight to establish its traditional Catholic pedigree was the more important. On first blush, this may seem strange, but on closer inspection, it makes sense for two strategic reasons: first, as Muldoon had noted even before its publication, the program could be counted a success only if it produced a social metanoia among Catholics. If doubts persisted concerning its Catholicity, hesitant Catholics could easily dismiss it and thus lessen its impact on the church. Second, since the conservatism of the church was legendary, if the bishops and their colleagues at the NCWC could demonstrate the program's continuity with Catholic teaching, charges of radicalism would appear more than a bit ridiculous. On the question of why the bishops did little to defend its American roots, it would seem that the war had created such a feeling of self-confidence among American Catholics that they did not feel the need to prove their patriotism. Perhaps Ryan had succeeded in convincing the bishops that Leonine social Catholicism was synonymous with good Progressivism and both were synonymous with good Americanism.

To complicate matters, the program's spectacular media coverage dictated that the church's leaders pursue a line of defense and explanation that was equally public. Confronted with this situation, the NCWC intensified its publicity campaign and committed itself ever more fully to a systematic educational program.

In this undertaking, Bishop Muldoon took the lead in defending the program to the American public as a conservative Catholic document with salutary public implications. Using the appeal to Catholic tradition, Muldoon said that since the bishops' program was grounded in those immutable Christian principles which alone can serve as the basis of a just and stable society, it was doubly conservative: it was conservative in its inspiration and conserving in its effects.[67] Ryan followed Muldoon's lead in discounting the charge of radicalism when he said: "Were those who express surprise at the contents of the Bishops' Program . . . acquainted with the traditional social principles of the Church, they would realize that this programme is merely an adaptation of those principles to conditions and needs of the time in which we live."[68] Elsewhere, he maintained that "our position was easily shown to be in accord with the authoritative Catholic teaching, as found in Papal Encyclicals." Ryan and Muldoon were joined by *America*, which further specified the

67. In writing to the *Nation*, Muldoon said, "However much men may differ about certain minor details contained in the Programme, it is based upon immutable principles of justice and charity which the Church holds, has held and will ever hold. . . . To us it appeared that the world, and in particular the United States, was willing to listen to representatives of the Church, which throughout the ages has strived not only to protect the workman but to further his progress in all ways consistent with Christian morality. In this you have the reason why the Bishops have brought forth once again the old, old principles of justice" (Peter J. Muldoon, "Correspondence," *Nation*, 19 April 1919, p. 608).

68. Quoted in Williams, "Catholic Programme of Reconstruction," p. 10. In a more sanguine moment, Ryan freely admitted the "radical" nature of the program: "It contains some proposals of social and industrial reform which are more nearly 'radical' than anything of the sort that had ever before proceeded from episcopal sources in the United States" (John A. Ryan, "The Bishops' Program of Social Reconstruction," address delivered at Sydney Mines, N.S., 29 July 1921, Ryan Papers, Writings Miscellaneous, Box B2-24, ACUA). In an unguarded moment, he admitted to his sister, Sister Mary John Ryan, "The Bishops' names are on the Reconstruction Program because they made it their own and we all want the authority that it derives from that fact. My name attached to it would defeat this purpose entirely. Most people who are acquainted with these matters know that I am sufficiently radical. What they did not realize is that such doctrines pass muster with the bishops. I think that this action . . . is a vindication of all the theories that my name has been associated with and indirectly of all that I have done in this field." (Broderick, *Right Reverend New Dealer*, p. 108).

program's link to traditional Catholic teaching: "A closer knowledge of the labor encyclicals of Pope Leo and a more intimate acquaintance with the history of the Church's activities in the Middle Ages . . . will show the consistency of the present program with the past history of the Church."[69] Ryan, Muldoon, and *America* believed that this argument established the program's pedigree and rescued it from charges of novelty and radicalism. Thus they dismissed their opponents' attacks as absurd.

In one quarter, however, the charges of radicalism and novelty did not abate. The National Civic Federation continued to attack the program. Moreover, the sophistication of its charges led to a fight over the authoritative interpretation of the Catholic tradition, and especially the works of Leo XIII, the very ground on which the church had chosen to rebut the accusations of radicalism.[70] In the battle to claim this treasure, John A. Ryan clashed with his most worthy and erudite opponent, Pallen.[71]

Stung by what he considered to be Pallen's "defection" from the church and furious that Pallen's arguments had proved so troublesome and damaging, Ryan initiated a correspondence with Pallen which is filled with a viciousness and pedantry that does credit to neither man. After introductory sparring in which the contestants exchanged mutual charges of bad faith, the heart of the disagreement was finally broached. Answering Ryan's contention that the program represented the best thought of the church, Pallen said acidly, "Pardon me if I fail to see in you and Dr. McGowan in Washington the sole depositories of the wisdom of the Holy Ghost in matters economic. I am content to accept Leo XIII's principles and teachings on

69. Ryan, *Social Doctrine,* p. 158; John A. Ryan, "The Bishops' Pastoral as Others See It," *America,* 22 March 1919, p. 624.

70. The fight with Easley and Pallen was first taken up in the pages of the *Catholic Charities Review,* a journal Ryan edited. In the *Review,* Ryan stated that Easley should be disregarded and his charges dismissed because he was a reactionary who did not know what he was talking about. See John A. Ryan, "Anonymous Critics of the Bishops' Reconstruction Programme," *Catholic Charities Review* 3 (1919): 163–65. Ryan was joined in rebutting Easley's charges in the *Review* by John Hearley, whose sophomoric attacks on the National Civic Federation were ad hominen and ineffective. See John Hearley, "Plutocracy Ascends the Pulpit," *Catholic Charities Review* 5 (1921): 116.

71. The conflict between Ryan and Pallen was carried initially through private correspondence, which was published in the *Winona Courier,* the organ of the Diocese of Winona. Thus the conflict entered the public arena.

these matters as set forth in his Encyclical 'Rerum Novarum.' Indeed I am quite confident that Rome has a much stronger and juster claim to be the seat of infallibility than Washington." Ryan responded that he too accepted Leo, but he accused Pallen of accepting Easley as the ultimate arbiter of the meaning of the church's social doctrines. In a flourish that wounded Ryan deeply because he believed himself largely responsible for the American rediscovery of Leonine social and economic thought, Pallen refused to accept Ryan as the authoritative interpreter of Leo: "You seem to think that the only economic orthodoxy is your 'doxy, and that anyone who presumes to criticize any phase of your 'doxy is a knave, a prevaricator and a conspirator against the peace of injured innocence."[72] The correspondence flowed back and forth between the two contestants. Of course, the mutual vituperations did nothing to convert either one to the other's position. The correspondence did have two beneficial results, however. It revealed the core of controversy hiding behind the charges of radicalism and novelty that were leveled against the program: both accusations were rooted in the question of the program's consistency with the Leonine social tradition. In addition, and consequently, the correspondence revealed the urgent need for the church to begin the educational work of exposing and explaining the Catholic social tradition to her flock.

In his remonstrations with Ryan, Pallen inadvertently pinpointed the problems that would be encountered in such an educational venture. Pallen had made it clear that he accepted Leo's social teachings without reservation. For Pallen, however, this meant merely accepting what Leo had said. Thus he revered the Leonine letter. He violently opposed Ryan's and the bishops' contentions that the specifics of their plan represented a proper application of Leonine principles to the American social situation. Thus the real controversy concerned the spirit of Leo's teaching rather than the letter of his written words. In other words, the contest was in the area of methodology.

Ryan's understanding of Leo's teaching led him to believe, as a good neo-Thomist, that there were two poles to Leonine

72. John A. Ryan and Conde Pallen, "Correspondence," *Winona Courier* 12, no. 3 (1921): 26–28.

thought: the immutable principles of natural law and the ingenious and elastic translation of these principles into a modern and localized industrial idiom, which would allow the church to speak out on contemporary problems. Ryan saw the principle of expediency mediating and informing the transit from principle to praxis. For him, expediency did not taint or compromise the validity of the principled base of his social discourse. Rather, for Ryan, the principle of expediency rescued Catholic thought from both moral torpor and utopianism. Roman Catholic social thought did not ambition the full realization of the Kingdom of God on earth. Instead, ardently believing that grace cooperated with nature, Ryan believed that social amelioration was achieved through the advocacy of specific and practical measures that established an incremental approximation of full justice. Thus, as Ryan understood it, Leonine social thought possessed an elasticity that worked two ways: it enshrined the ideals of full justice as the transcendent goal that judged and directed human social behavior; and it was patient of imperfection on the practical level at which measures were advocated to bring about approximations of justice. For Ryan and others, Leo had enunciated a social morality that was at once lofty and possibilist. Hence, in seeking to educate the Catholic population, the bishops wished to demonstrate how Leo's spirit and method had inspired the specific proposals in the program. This was an ambitious undertaking answering a tremendous challenge, but if it could be successfully accomplished, it would yield both short-term and long-term benefits. In the short run, the temporally conditioned practical and expedient Progressive measures contained in the program would be vindicated as truly traditional and thus neither radical nor novel. In the long run, if the noncompromising nature of the operation of the principle of expediency could be demonstrated, Catholics could be taught the necessity of committing themselves to future practical measures of reform that aimed at establishing social justice with the assurance that in doing so they were not mistaking the temporary for the eternal but merely giving their temporary allegiance to measures that seemed to serve the ideal.

Stung by Pallen's attacks, Ryan shouldered the task of educating the American Catholic population in Leonine thought and the ways in which it was enshrined in the program. Through lectures, interviews, and articles, he strove to defend the program and to advance the social education of American Catholics. In November of 1919, Ryan was invited to give the Mulry Lectures at Fordham University in New York. He seized the opportunity afforded by this forum to address the program's critics.[73] (These lectures were rushed into print by Macmillan and Company and thus reached a much wider audience than the group of social work students to whom they were first delivered.) Because the lectures were originally intended for a specifically Catholic audience, they were couched in particularly Catholic terms. Because of Ryan's own passionate belief in the essential congruence between the Leonine and American reform traditions, however, Progressive ideas and argumentation are evident throughout the lectures.[74] Specifically, Ryan employed such Progressive arguments as appealing to the success of the government's wartime experiments in the regulation of industrial relations to justify the continuation of such measures in peacetime;[75] calling for legislation as the most effective and acceptable way of achieving social reform; and appealing to the success of foreign experiments in alleviating social evils to jus-

73. Throughout his remarks, Ryan employed a tantalizing third-person mode of speech. He insisted on referring to the bishops as the authors of the document, even though it was already well known that he was the true author. He doubtless insisted on the bishops' authorship because he believed that such an attribution would buttress the moral authority of the program in the eyes of the Catholic population, for, in the course of the lectures, Ryan said, "It is true that these facts do not show that the Program has the stamp of official authority . . . on the other hand, it represents something more than the individual opinions of the bishops who issued it . . . it would not have official authority in the strict sense because no group of bishops has legislative authority except when they meet in provincial council or in a national council. However, the Program has a great deal of moral authority inasmuch as it comes from four bishops who must have realized that they were representing in a general way all the archbishops and bishops of the country" (Ryan, *Social Reconstruction*, pp. 8–9).

74. Ryan seemed to acknowledge that the church's entrance into the Progressive war crusade both made the program possible and generally gave the document its shape and direction: "Possibly they [the bishops] would not have issued it if they, like the rest of us, had not been at the time breathing the psychological atmosphere of the war" (ibid., pp. 20–21).

75. "The Program, therefore, starts with these problems created by the war, and also with certain agencies which were set up by the government during the war, on the theory that these agencies may be of value in time of peace" (ibid., p. 26).

tify the adoption of similar measures in the United States.[76] At the heart of Ryan's defense of the bishops' program to his Catholic audience, however, were his adamant belief that the document represented a valid extension and application of Leo XIII's thought and method to the American scene and his strenuous attempt to demonstrate the truth of this belief. In a sense, then, Ryan was engaged in his usual twofold task: he was attempting above all to prove the Leonine inspiration of the bishops' statement. Coincidentally, and equally important, he was trying to show the congruence between American Progressivism and the Catholic tradition of social reform.

Early in the lecture series, Ryan addressed the question of the continuity of the program with the tradition of the church. Keenly aware that Americans in general and American Catholics in particular were ignorant of the traditional social teachings of the church, he began by citing Bishop Muldoon's statement that the document "is based upon the immutable principles of justice and charity which the Church holds, has held and will ever hold." Ryan then set out to justify his statement by connecting the program to the thought of Leo XIII. In his arguments to vindicate the Leonine nature of the program and its specific proposals, Ryan relied heavily on a few key concepts found in traditional Catholic natural law morality, which underlaid the program: the first was the belief that the dignity of the individual, buttressed by inviolable natural rights, was to be honored and preserved at all costs. The second was that the natural law theory of the state required that the state take an active and positive role in the promotion and preservation of natural rights.[77] In addition, Ryan tied as many specific proposals as he could to Leo's doctrine of the living wage, which was also safely Catholic in origin and expression. Finally, and in answer to questions as to the propriety of the church involving herself in social issues, Ryan insisted that, as the authoritative interpreter of the natural law, the church had a responsibility to involve

76. In the Mulry Lectures, Ryan continued and expanded on the Progressive logic that he had enunciated in his initial outline of the proposals of the program. This argumentation is discussed in Chapter V.

77. Ryan, *Social Reconstruction*, pp. 19–20, 10, 75.

herself in social criticism. This was not an option for ministry—it was a duty. Natural law thus undergirded Ryan's entire exposition of the program and Catholic social teaching in general.

On the question of particulars within the program, some proposals were justified as Leonine with dispatch. In *Rerum Novarum,* for example, Leo had clearly defended the laborer's right to a living wage. Therefore, Ryan had merely to cite *Rerum Novarum* to prove the traditional basis for the program's advocacy of minimum wage legislation: "Pope Leo says the worker has a right to a living wage; that it is not merely desirable that he should have this reasonable minimum . . . but that he has a moral right to this much, a right having the same moral force as the right we assert to our money if somebody attempts to take it away from us." To those who believed that the use of legislation to assure laborers of receiving a living wage bordered on socialism, Ryan retorted that right reason and the Leonine natural law theory of the state sanctioned the use of legislation:

> We cannot look to economic forces to provide the laborer with a living wage. We cannot rely upon the benevolence of employers either because the majority of employers in competitive industries cannot pay much more than they are paying. . . . The labor unions will not be able to provide a guarantee of living wages to all the workers, because those groups of the laboring class that need living wages most are the ones that are least able to organize. . . . The only method of bringing about living wages universally is that of legislation. . . . The Catholic theory of the state is not the laissez-faire theory. . . . The Catholic doctrine is that . . . it must protect all natural rights . . . and the right to a living wage is one of the natural rights.[78]

Thus there could no question that the minimum wage plank of the program was thoroughly consistent with Leonine natural law morality.

Not all the short-term proposals contained in the program could be justified on Leonine grounds with such ease. Indeed, considerable mental sleight of hand was required to square some specifics in the program with Leonine thought. Ryan was equal to the task. In addressing the question of a national employment service, for example, he defended the Leonine pedi-

78. Ibid., pp. 66, 74–75.

gree of the proposal by saying, "A national employment service may be regarded as implicitly contained in the living wage doctrine. Laborers have a claim to a living wage because it is necessary for their welfare; they must get a living. . . . But the living wage is not of much use unless the workers have an opportunity to earn it by labor." Common sense and expediency therefore required that means be devised whereby men and women could be guaranteed that full measure of natural rights to which they were entitled. The employment service thus appeared as a Leonine-warranted measure to ensure the workers the full and untrammeled possession of their rights. Ryan dismissed objections that the bishops' advocacy of state-sponsored social insurance was dangerously paternalistic by returning to his favorite Leonine principle: "It seems to me then, that social insurance of the workers against sickness, accidents, old age, invalidity and unemployment is a necessary means of protecting those who do not have wages sufficient to enable them to obtain such protection for themselves; and that it is entirely in accord with the principle laid down by Pope Leo XIII: 'Whenever the community or any particular class suffers or is threatened with injury which can in no other way be met, it is the duty of the State to step in and prevent it.'" Through such reasoning Ryan was able to demonstrate the Leonine inspiration and warrant for all of the proposals for short-term reform contained within the program. Indeed, in a burst of bravura, he claimed: "In a word, we can see that nearly all of these proposals for immediate reform which are contained in the Bishops' Program are immediately or remotely deductible from the one general idea or general principle of a decent livelihood which is contained in the living wage doctrine of Pope Leo XIII."[79] Ryan was perhaps overstating his case in attributing the inspiration for all the proposals to the living wage doctrine. It would have been more correct to say that the entire program was permeated by natural law morality with its absolute insistence that the dignity of the human person be preserved, promoted, and honored in social relations and through social reform.

Certainly in defending the traditional nature of the most controversial of all the program's proposals—the advocacy of the

79. Ibid., pp. 204, 99, 205.

erection of an industrial system based on copartnership—Ryan did not follow the same slavish line he pursued in justifying the short-term reform proposals. Instead, he defended the plank on the basis of natural law, social utility, and Leonine sympathy with the idea. Thus, he argued, "The first reason [for advocating copartnership] is one that is fundamental to human nature . . . they [the workers] share in some degree the desire which is native in every adult human being to have some voice in determining the material conditions in which he lives and works."[80] Therefore, the duty to honor and promote human dignity enshrined in natural law morality seemed to necessitate the erection of industrial democracy, with its emphasis on partnership. Ryan buttressed the claim of natural law by pointing out that copartnership would reduce the militant hostility that marred industrial relations under the capitalistic system, thus improving social conditions for the general public.[81] As his final argument, demonstrating the traditional nature of the proposal, Ryan not surprisingly turned to Pope Leo: "The remedy recommended for the situation is again a principle contained in Pope Leo's Encyclical on 'The Condition of Labor,' or rather a general proposal; namely, a wider distribution of private property."[82] (Ryan believed that copartnership would extend rather than destroy the ownership of private property. He continued to wed Progressive sympathies with Leonine ideas.) The result of Ryan's defense of the short-term and long-term reform proposals in the program in Leonine terms was that he presented a Catholic argument for strenuous Catholic support for American Progressive reform ideas. He had bridged the gap that had previously existed between the two traditions.

By answering the challenge raised by the program's critics, Ryan initiated the educational enterprise entrusted to the social

80. Ibid., pp. 141–42.

81. "The second reason why labor should have some share in industrial management is one that concerns the public, concerns all of us. The labor union is essentially a militant organization, essentially a fighting organization. . . . Now that is the main purpose of the union, to fight for the welfare of its members, and the methods that it uses may be contrary to the welfare of the people as a whole, and may be directed toward a small instead of a large product" (ibid., p. 145).

82. Ibid., pp. 206–7.

teachers of the American church by Bishop Peter J. Muldoon. Ryan used the opportunity to introduce the church to the intricate, socially useful, and critical thought of Pope Leo XIII and to demonstrate the congruence or complementarity between Leonine principles and specific Progressive reform proposals. Above all else, Ryan strove mightily to expose the American church to the spirit and method of Leo (the spirit revered ideals, the method sought application in the practical order) in the belief that an understanding of Leonine method and spirit would open up American Catholics to the ongoing task of social reform. Thus although Ryan's task in the Mulry Lectures was to defend the specific measures of a specific program, he did not merely seek to canonize those particular measures as the guarantees of full justice. His own devotion to those proposals was passionate but temporary and expedient. His real passion was for justice, but he was not a utopian. Therefore, he embraced and he urged the American church to embrace any concrete practical measure that could bring about a greater approximation of full justice. In the years between 1906 and 1919, he believed that the platform of the American Progressives contained those expedient and temporally conditioned measures that were most conducive to the advancement of American society toward the transcendent goal of full social justice, a goal that animated his every action. Because of his natural law grounding and his use of the principle of expediency, however, he was able to disengage himself from specific platforms or proposals when those plans showed no possibility of enactment and thus offered no pragmatic hope of advancing the cause of justice. During the 1920s, when the nation turned more and more toward what Warren G. Harding called normalcy, he tried to convince the Catholic population to support those agents and measures that offered the greatest hope of social reform. In this work of educating Catholics in the need to cooperate in possibilist schemes for social reform, Ryan offered his Social Action Department and himself as models for the faithful to follow. He exhorted, urged, and cajoled the Catholic population to greater social awareness, to more passionate love for the ideal of full justice, and to more openness to cooperation with American reformers who sought, through incremental reforms, to approximate the ideal. It was a difficult task and one just begun in the Mulry Lectures. Ryan would wear himself out answering the challenges of Bishop Muldoon and Pope Leo XIII.

The Bishops' Program of Social Reconstruction was published with great fanfare, received with wonder, and defended with ingenuity. Gratified by the wide reception their words had received, but somewhat embarrassed by everyone's surprise at the novelty of such a statement proceeding from such a supposedly conservative group, the bishops were forced to admit privately that their previous policy of masterly inactivity on social issues had been a sterile approach. Chastened by the shock that the program had caused among all segments of the population, the bishops committed themselves to the work of appropriating the Leonine heritage that they had overlooked in the past. In addition, because of their spectacular and public breaking of their social silence with the program, the bishops had, of necessity, to redeem the promise of social involvement contained in the program in equally public ways, both among the faithful and before the eyes of the nation. During the 1920s, the bishops showed an amazing—even a quixotic—devotion to the tasks of solidifying and substantiating the new image of the church created by the program and of laying definitive claim to the position of moral leadership they had claimed on the basis of the program's public reception. At long last, the American Catholic Church had emerged from social somnolence.

Chapter VI

The Legacy of the Program and Its Place in Two Traditions

The Bishops' Program of Social Reconstruction of 1919 was a spectacular public announcement of the American Catholic resolve to effect a rapprochement with American Progressivism and Leonine Social Catholicism. The glare of the spotlight and the publicity the church had sought made it almost impossible to renege on the program's promise of social involvement. The nation was watching. No longer could timidity inform or direct the church's social ministry. In the future, a passionate and principled commitment to the cause of reform would have to direct her every social action. The events of 1919 tested the church's resolve to redeem the promise of the program and revealed the depth of her commitment to the cause of reform, thereby bearing witness to the impact the program had on the American church.

The year 1919 matched bloody 1877 as a time of labor unrest and industrial violence. Despite the national hope that the signing of the armistice would usher in a new age of brotherhood, prosperity, and progressive social advances, it actually opened an era of anxiety, bitterness, and unrestrained industrial warfare. All of America seemed to erupt in the course of the year as labor and capital sought to consolidate or repudiate the industrial changes wrought by the war. The Seattle general strike, the Boston police strike, the great steel strike of 1919, and numerous other strikes plunged the country into social and industrial chaos, mocking the hopes of the reformers and creating a reactionary mood.

The greatest social trial of the year occurred when, on 22 September 1919, America's steelworkers struck to protest both working conditions and the paternalism of the steel companies that denied them the rights to organize on their own terms and to bargain collectively through their chosen representatives.[1] The steel strike involved far more than questions of wages, benefits, or procedures in any one industry. In many ways, it was the battleground on which labor and capital fought to determine which side was the true heir to and representative of American values. Both parties in the conflict used the rhetoric of patriotism spawned by the war in their efforts to advance their respective causes. In addition, both sides courted public opinion and continued to seek alliances with the centers of power and influence in American life.[2] Both labor and capital courted the churches, thereby severely testing the churches' commitment to the causes of labor and industrial reform.

In taking its case before the court of public opinion, big business had several advantages. By and large, the daily press was either controlled by or sympathetic to big business. As Elizabeth Stevenson points out, the papers "condemned the strikers, presenting a picture of them as dangerous aliens and radicals." Such journalistic reports played upon and seemed to lend credence to widespread fears that Bolshevism would soon overrun America. As William Leuchtenberg notes, "the growing militancy of organized labor in 1919 appeared to align labor unions with worldwide radicalism."[3] Labor, however, was not the only force in America whose cause was jeopardized by the public's fear of a Bolshevist onslaught. Many other groups saw a sinister and radical aspect in the reformers' calls for alterations in the American economic system. Thus the hysteria of the Red Scare provided the captains of industry with a great advantage over their reform and labor opponents. In a nation touched with mad fears, businessmen convincingly presented themselves as bulwarks of stability and preservers of American values.

1. Miller, *American Protestantism and Social Issues*, p. 210.

2. In this regard, Robert K. Murray says, "That anti-unionites were well aware of this fact [that public opinion was the most powerful force for the suppression of radical ideas] is undisputed. Shortly after the steel and coal strikes, organized labor demonstrated its increasing awareness of the indispensable asset of a favorable public opinion by establishing the Federated Press, the first national news service owned and operated by labor unions" (Murray, *Red Scare*,. p. 163).

3. Elizabeth Stevenson, *Babbitts and Bohemians: The American 1920's* (New York: Macmillan, 1967), p. 54; Irving Werstein, *Shattered Decade, 1919–1929* (New York: Charles Scribner's Sons, 1970), p. 17; Leuchtenberg, *Perils of Prosperity*, p. 70.

During the steel strike, however, capital did not limit its campaign to a sophisticated use of the daily press. True to its overall postwar strategy, business sought in addition to ally itself with that age-old foe of radicalism, the Catholic Church, believing as always that such an alliance would enhance its image as a moral influence on American life. Hence, in the course of the strike, capital assiduously tried to convince the public that a community of interest—a shared hatred of radicalism—existed between the church and the business community. Accordingly, accounts of Catholic clergymen condemning the strikers in general and William Zebulon Foster, the strike organizer, in particular, received wide publicity. The *Manufacturers' Record* was happy to inform its readers:

> That the Catholic Church is bitterly opposed to socialism is well known, but not as widely known as it should be. In this respect the Catholic Church sets a wise example for all the Churches of this and all other lands. Many Catholic priests are taking a very vigorous part against the men who are now on strike. The failure of the strike leaders to call out five thousand men from the Bethlehem plant of Baltimore is credited largely to the work in opposition thereto of a priest who warned his constituents against the activities of the strike leaders. The denunciation of these strike leaders by the Rev. Mr. Molyneux, pastor of the Catholic Church in Braddock Pennsylvania, is one of the most scathing criticisms ever made against radical labor leaders.[4]

Molyneux became something of a folk hero among the business class, and his words and example were cited extensively to buttress the business community's claims to moral authority. Capital had good reason to claim Molyneux as one of its own, for he thundered against the strikers with words that linked Americanism, Catholicism, and business in a holy alliance against radicalism, foreigners, and atheism:

> The strike is not being brought about by intelligent English-speaking workmen, but by men who have no interest in the community, are not an element of our community, and who do not have the welfare of our men at heart. . . . William Z. Foster, the transplanted strike leader and fomentor of trouble among the steel workers, is a rank blood thirsty socialist. His philosophy is that of a madhouse. . . . I consider him both a fool positive and an ass superlative . . . no man could be more solic-

4. "The Fight against Socialistic Strikes by the Catholic Church," *Manufacturers' Record,* 2 October 1919, p. 106.

itous for those under him than the leaders of these mills are. They have left nothing undone to provide for the welfare of their men that could be done. I think they have reached perfection in this way.[5]

The *Manufacturers' Record* was even more pleased with the testimony of the Reverend Thomas Devlin of Pittsburgh, who warned his congregation that if they dared to join the strikers, they would be "apostates of the Catholic faith, traitors to their country, and enemies to authority." Holding up Devlin and Molyneux as examples for all the clergy of the nation to follow, the *Record* issued a strong challenge to all to fall in line behind God, country, and the United States Steel Corporation: "The minister who at this time fails to recognize his responsibility to proclaim the truth so strongly presented by these priests . . . is faithless to his solemn duty to his country, and to his God."[6]

Labor was equally interested in associating its cause with that of the church, and for the same reason—to gain divine or at least ecclesiastical approval for its battle against capital. The church responded with more enthusiasm to labor's need than to that of capital, and the prolabor activities of her steel region clergy were recognized and praised by a variety of commentators. Foster was heartened by the brave support offered by prolabor priests,[7] and the Progressive journalist William Hard chronicled the strike's events and claimed that the clergy's behavior in the steel strike proved that the church had thrown in her lot with the cause of labor. In searching for the reason for such a stance, Hard attributed the church's sympathy with labor to the influence of the bishops' program:

Those principles, as declared by the Bishops of the National Catholic War Council, began to be much on the lips of Catholics even in this strike. There was an occasion, for instance, when a sermon by a priest against the strike was brought to the desk of another priest for answer.

5. Rev. P. Molyneux, "A Sermon on the Steel Strike," *Open Shop Review*, January 1920, pp. 26–29.

6. "Fight against Socialistic Strikes," p. 106.

7. William Z. Foster, *The Great Steel Strike and Its Lessons* (New York: B. W. Huebsch, 1920), p. 117. Foster makes the point that the few clergymen who rallied to the strikers received their full support. They were, however, the exception, as was the Interchurch World Commission of Inquiry. Foster's treatment of the conduct of the churches in the strike was generally critical. See ibid., pp. 117–18.

> The fact of the sermon was notorious, but the answering priest was bland. "Ah, my friends," said he, "this is terrible. Let me read you out of the Bishops' 'Social Reconstruction Program.' You see that these bishops are for collective bargaining; and then, beyond good collective bargaining, they are for greater representation of Labor in the industrial part of management."[8]

Hard and Foster were not alone in their praise for the behavior of the steel region's Catholic clergy during the strike. The *World Tomorrow,* which had earlier expressed doubts about the church's ability to sustain the social stance enunciated in the bishops' program, reported: "For actual worth the finest recent contribution of the Church to the cause of labor and of freedom was made by the Catholic priests in the Pittsburgh district who identified themselves with their people against the whole might of the Steel Trust."[9] The acts of these individual priests seemed to indicate that the church was well on the way to solidifying its new image in the eyes of the public.

There are many indications that the transformation of the church in the steel regions was representative of a larger, indeed, a national change. More than the public perception of the church seemed to have changed in the wake of the publication of the bishops' program. Not surprisingly, the steel strike elicited a response from the church's social activists. Although he criticized what he called radical labor for its violations of just contracts and its violent strike methods, Ryan saw the steel controversy as an example of the new Bourbon attitudes of the industrial autocracy. Ryan ridiculed Judge Elbert Gary's assertion that his employees did not need a union because his brand of welfare capitalism provided for their every need. He called such patent paternalism an insidious form of "industrial feudalism," which denied laborers their basic human right to self-determination.[10] Analyzing the issues disputed in the strike, Ryan concluded that the steel magnates were the irresponsible parties, for their denial of human rights and their intransigence

8. William Hard, "After the Strike," *New Republic,* 28 January 1920, p. 260.
9. "The Church and the Cause of Freedom," *World Tomorrow,* March 1920, p. 91.
10. John A. Ryan, "Radical Labor and Autocratic Capital," pp. 1, 4–5, address for a Knights of Columbus convention, n.d., Ryan Papers, Writings Miscellaneous, Box B2-24, ACUA.

had caused the strike. Ryan's view was shared by a large segment of the Catholic population, and the Catholic press broadcast similar sentiments throughout the nation.[11]

The papers flayed Gary and "decried the tendency to label any complaint against injustice as Bolshevism." In light of the timid and often confused social thinking of many Catholic editors before 1919, this wholesale defection from the business camp was heartening to labor and a bitter disappointment to business. It was also startling. In searching for an explanation for such an unexpected unified Catholic journalistic response to the steel strike, Roddy arrives at the same conclusion as had Hard: the Bishops' Program of Social Reconstruction had transformed Catholic social consciousness.[12] The editors had undergone a conversion, and they strove to pass on the insights of their enlightenment to their readers.

As a result of the rash of strikes of 1919 and the bitterness they left behind, labor and its allies suffered from significant and continuing problems. Labor especially faced hard times. Labor's wartime advances had attracted large numbers of workers to the unions, but the repeated failures to win concessions from big business through strikes had caused their numerical strength to dwindle when many workers began to believe that welfare capitalism offered them a surer path to security than did strikes and confrontation. In addition, external forces conspired to undermine labor's wartime gains. First, as Burl Noggle points out, the disbanding of the wartime regulatory agencies that had provided official approval of labor's demands and dreams seemed to indicate that the unions had fallen out of favor in Washington. Second, the fiercely antiunion animus of the business community, which had been somewhat muted during the war, resurfaced with renewed vigor, venom, and a determination

11. Edward Roddy asserts that the Catholic press was distinguished from the daily press in its staunch defense of the strikers ("Catholic Newspaper Press," p. 184).

12. Ibid., pp. 165–66. The Catholic papers did not maintain a totally united front on the strike issue, as Roddy notes: "With an editorial silence which must have been deafening, Father McMahon's *Catholic Universe* of Cleveland ran full-page anti-strike, anti-union, anti-Bolshevist advertisements paid for by the American Steel and Wire Company" (ibid., p. 174).

to discredit labor's program.[13] Finally, as a result of capital's masterful public relations work, the public adulation the unions had enjoyed as a result of their wholehearted support for the war evaporated in the midst of the strike turmoil. As Ellis W. Hawley writes, "They were being blamed for the rising cost of living and lagging productivity; and in a public mind inflamed with anti-Bolshevik hysteria the distinction between good American unions and those bent on social revolution had become increasingly dim."[14] The public believed that labor's demands were exorbitant, its grievances groundless, and its intentions revolutionary.[15] Try as they might, unionists could not convince the American public of the justice or desirability of their demands. Capital succeeded in using propaganda to convince people of its stabilizing and stable influence. The public began increasingly to pin its hopes for a more prosperous future on the expertise of industry and its leaders. Capital had begun to solidify its claim to the right to shape America's future, and a grateful public seemed ready to anoint businessmen, and not the reforming alliance, as the true prophets of the American scene.

As the organizers and the potential beneficiaries of the strikes, it was almost inevitable that the unions would suffer as a result of the agitation of 1919. To an extent, however, the churches shared the same fate. In the strikes, they were caught between two radically different sets of expectations. Labor de-

13. Mark Perlman, "Labor in Eclipse," in *Change and Continuity in Twentieth Century America: The 1920's*, ed. John Braeman, Robert H. Bremner, and David Brody (Columbus: Ohio State University Press, 1968), pp. 105, 133, 113; Noggle, *Into the Twenties*, p. 67.

14. Hawley, *Great War*, pp. 48–49. See also Roddy, "Catholic Newspaper Press," p. 229.

15. Irving Bernstein notes: "Income inequality and the relatively low standard of living of American workers, however, did not arouse social protest. There were two principal reasons for this silence. The first, doubtless the more important, was that the material well-being of the employed sector of the labor force was improving. . . . The other reason for the failure of social protest to emerge was that the standard of living among American workmen, regardless of its deficiencies, was among the highest in the world, a consideration of no mean importance to urban masses who were largely immigrants themselves or the children of immigrants" (*A History of the American Worker, 1920–1933: The Lean Years* [Boston: Houghton Mifflin, 1960], p. 65).

manded an ecclesiastical show of solidarity with its cause. Radical labor, and radicals in general, were especially urgent in their challenges to the churches.[16] Capital was no less urgent in pressing its demands. As the year wore on, business grew increasingly bitter and impatient with the churches' wayward behavior. Businessmen nursed their bitterness and vented their anger by attacking the churches with largely unfounded assertions of radicalism.[17] In response, the two great branches of organized Christianity in America, Protestantism and Catholicism, took decisive steps to translate their social concern into action. At tremendous cost to themselves, both groups continued to identify with labor and to push for industrial reform. The depth of the churches' commitment to social justice may be gauged on the basis of that cost.

American Protestantism was convulsed as a result of the churches' advocacy of labor. The Interchurch World Movement saw its hopes of converting the world in a generation evaporate when contributions from its wealthy supporters declined following the publication of its critical report on the behavior of industry in the steel strike, and the Federal Council of Churches was vilified for its prolabor stance. Moreover during the 1920s, social Christianity went into decline as conservative Protestants reacted against the "modernism" of the Social Gospellers.

Although the Catholic responses to the bloody events of 1919 were not as costly or as spectacular as that of the Interchurch World Movement, they were important. On the basis of its past expedient and timid social performance, the church might have been expected to beat a hasty, prudent, and strategic retreat from her exposed and vulnerable social position, especially considering the hierarchy's sensitivity to questions raised by the mainstream culture about Catholic patriotism. By the end of 1919, employers had made it seem that conformity to their industrial policy and social vision was a patriotic duty. To be against big business was un-American. In this ticklish situation, the hierarchy acted with a hitherto unparalleled decisiveness. During

16. See, for instance, "Sins of Omission," *World Tomorrow*,. February 1920, p. 41.

17. Murray, *Red Scare*, p. 175.

the war, the bishops had led the church into an American mainstream that defined true Americanism as conformity to Progressive idealism. Even as the dreams of the reformers were being mocked by business' victory over idealism, the bishops decided, in a move that was as quixotic as it was decisive, to reaffirm their loyalty to the American ideals they had embraced during the war by committing themselves and the church to the causes of reform and labor rights at a moment when neither was in vogue. The prelates expressed their commitment in word and deed. In both cases, they testified to the importance and influence of the program.

The expression of shock, dismay, and surprise that greeted the Bishops' Program of Social Reconstruction had frankly surprised the bishops. Therefore, when he convoked a plenary session of the American hierarchy in mid-1919, Cardinal Gibbons told the bishops that they had to disabuse the nation of the impression that the hierarchy had acted out of character in issuing the program:

> Three things, in my opinion, are needed. First, the presentation, definite, clear and forceful, of Catholic social principles. Second, more knowledge as to the best methods of Catholic social and charitable work. Third, a more general impulse to put our social principles and methods into operation. Society never had greater need of guidance. . . . Too often we must admit, our principles, the principles of the Gospel, have lain so hidden in our theologies, so much so that the recent pamphlet on Social Reconstruction appeared to many a complete novelty. The Church has a great work of social education and social welfare lying before it.[18]

Gibbons was challenging his fellow bishops to go on record as favoring the program in a plenary session. Such an action would buttress the document's claim to moral authority within the church and solidify the church's new social image in the eyes of both the faithful and the nation. The hierarchy responded to Gibbons's request by embracing the educational mission he enjoined and by issuing a wide-ranging pastoral letter.

The Pastoral Letter of 1919 addressed the social question with great vigor. In their introductory remarks, the bishops ac-

18. James Gibbons, "Letter to the Hierarchy," 5 May 1919, *Ecclesiastical Review* 61 (1919): 12.

knowledged the gravity of the social situation in the nation: "At present, however, we are confronted with problems at home that give us the gravest concern. Intent as we are on restoring the order of Europe, we did not sufficiently heed the symptoms of unrest in our own country, nor did we reckon with movements which, in their final result, would undo both our recent achievement and all that America has so far accomplished." Echoing the Progressive idealism they had embraced during the war, the bishops lamented that party spirit was threatening the common good of the republic: "In the prosecution of their respective claims, the parties have apparently disregarded the fact that the people as a whole have a prior claim. The great number of unnecessary strikes which have occurred within the last few months is evidence that justice has been widely violated as regards the rights and needs of the public. To assume that the only rights involved in an industrial dispute are those of capital and labor is a radical error." After that nod to classic Progressive idealism, however, the bishops proclaimed their unflagging support for the cause of labor: "The right of labor to organize, and the great benefit to be derived from workingmen's associations, were plainly set forth by Pope Leo XIII. . . . The right of labor to a living wage, authoritatively and eloquently reasserted more than a quarter of a century ago by Pope Leo XIII, is happily no longer denied by any considerable number of persons. What is principally needed now is that its content should be adequately defined and that it should be made universal in practice, through whatever means will be at once legitimate and effective." The Pastoral Letter went on, at least implicitly, to accept and defend the militancy of labor unions as a necessary fact of industrial life and ended its consideration of the social question with a reaffirmation of Ryan's idea of copartnership, which was really the Progressive idea of industrial democracy.[19]

The Pastoral Letter was significant because it was animated by the same spirit and contained the same mixture of Progressive and Leonine rhetoric that had marked the bishops' program, even though it lacked the specificity of the earlier docu-

19. Pastoral Letter of 1919, in *Pastoral Letters of the American Hierarchy, 1792–1970*, ed. Hugh J. Nolan (Huntington, Ind.: Our Sunday Visitor, 1971), pp. 233, 246–48.

ment. In addition, because the Pastoral Letter was an official document issued by the entire American episcopate, its appearance made it clear that the bishops wished to commit themselves in an incontrovertible way to the spirit and mission outlined in the earlier episcopal document. Hence critics who wished to discount the program's authority in the Catholic community by pointing to its unofficial character were confounded by the spectacle of the entire hierarchy making a public commitment to the program outlined and announced in February of 1919. Clearly the church was moving to reaffirm her new image and mission in industrial society.

The Catholic response to the industrial unrest of the postwar era was not exhausted by the publication of the Pastoral Letter of 1919. At the time of the program's publication, both Muldoon and Gibbons had sensed the urgent need for the church to embark upon an extensive program to advance the knowledge of social thought among Catholics in the hope that such knowledge would enable them to influence the formation of a new social order. Although the Pastoral Letter undoubtedly contributed to this educational enterprise, it did not outline any long-range strategy for continuing the pedagogical work which Gibbons and Muldoon thought was essential for the church's future in America. What was needed was a permanent agency that could systematically and continuously reflect on current social problems from a Catholic point of view and provide the Catholic community with guidelines on how to respond to these problems. As early as June of 1919, the Committee on Special War Activities had recognized the need for just such an agency. At the June 1919 meeting of the CSWA, the members of the executive committee asked that the NCWC look for ways "to utilize to the fullest possible extent in Catholic welfare work in the future the experience it has gained from the war." In their petition, the members of the executive committee, using words that echoed those of Pope Leo XIII, reminded the NCWC that religion was the "supreme factor underlying all individual and social realtions" and that the church should face her social responsibilities squarely. Her future work should be directed toward bringing about institutional (that is, systemic) economic change and a recognition of the rights of labor. The CSWA was asking the hierarchy to establish an agency that would coordinate Catholic efforts to bring about the immediate and long-range systemic reforms outlined in the program.[20]

Convinced of the wisdom and timeliness of this request, the hierarchy acceded to the wishes of the CSWA. When the American episcopate established the National Catholic Welfare Council in November of 1919, the Social Action Department (SAD) was formed as one of its constituent departments. As Karl Cerny notes, with the formation of the SAD, "advocates of a constructive Catholic social program now had, for the first time, a national platform from which to propagate their message."[21] Indeed, the formation of the SAD gave hierarchical sanction and direction to Catholic social action in America. The benefits from such a national social action agency soon became evident to the bishops: in a bureaucratic society, a national voice enabled the church effectively to deal with the national centers of power, providing a platform from which to influence lawmakers to frame legislation in conformity with Catholic principles. In addition, the SAD's hierarchical support and a national headquarters enabled it to resist local pressure groups that opposed social change and the social activism of the Christian churches.[22] Hence the SAD was not as vulnerable to monetary blackmail as was the Interchurch Movement and was able to function effectively as a voice for reform even in the conservative climate of the 1920s.

To fulfill its mandate from the bishops, the SAD joined with Catholic and non-Catholic organizations to advance the cause of reform. Its main thrust, however, was educational, and as Cerny notes, the pedagogical mission was twofold and marvelously Ryanesque: "On the one hand, it was constantly engaged in furthering an awareness and comprehension of Catholic social principles. On the other hand, it was equally interested in helping Catholics to apply those principles to the American

20. Committee on Special War Activities, *Outlines of a Social Service Program for Catholic Agencies: Reconstruction Pamphlet #7, June 1919* (Washington: National Catholic War Council, 1919), pp. 3–4, 7. The CSWA said, "The war has brought to light certain limitations in our institutions which we should set ourselves to remedy during the reconstruction period" (ibid., pp. 4–5).

21. Cerny, "Monsignor John A. Ryan," p. 74.

22. Bernard J. Coughlin, *Church and State in Social Welfare* (New York: Columbia University Press, 1965), p. 30; Betten, *Catholic Activism*, p. 33.

scene." It aimed particularly at instructing the clergy in the hope that they would in turn explain the Catholic social tradition to their congregations.[23]

In 1919 and throughout the 1920s, the department's message always had a Progressive accent, and with good reason. When the Social Action Department was organized in 1919, John A. Ryan was appointed the director of its industrial relations division, with the power to formulate policy and to issue statements on industrial problems in the name of the bishops. Ryan used his post to advance a program of Catholic social action that bore the stamp of his own Leonine and Progressive thought. This twin ideological base endowed the SAD's social pronouncements with both a passion for the cause of industrial democracy and a noticeable bias in favor of the rights of labor.[24] As the nation turned resolutely away from reformism in the 1920s, the department's outspoken commitment to the causes of labor and reform made it and the church particularly vulnerable to criticism. It was to the credit of both Ryan and the bishops that the events of 1919 and the criticisms that were leveled at the church as a result of her actions during the year did not shake their resolve to further the cause of social reform. Throughout the strikes and the unrest, the church, Ryan, and the NCWC stood officially and vocally on the side of labor. As Edward Roddy notes, "And so it was in 1919–20: abandoning its 'masterly inactivity' at long last, the hierarchy appeared to plunge headlong into the receding sea of Progressivism. The Bishops' Program, the establishment of the National Catholic Welfare Council, the courageous defense of trade unionism and the ridicule of the red hysteria could not but surprise and shock

23. Cerny, "Monsignor John A. Ryan," pp. 112, 107. See also William J. Lee, "The Work in Industrial Relations of the Social Action Department of the National Catholic Welfare Conference, 1933–1945" (M.A. thesis, Catholic University of America, 1946), p. 3; Betten, *Catholic Activism*, pp. 148–49.

24. O'Brien, *American Catholics and Social Reform*, p. 121; Thomas J. McDonagh, "Some Aspects of the Roman Catholic Attitude toward the American Labor Movement, 1900–1914" (Ph.D. dissertation, University of Wisconsin, 1951), p. 8. Raymond McGowan of the Social Action Department said, "The aim throughout has been to make Catholic social teaching known and practiced. Since Catholic social teaching is distinctly favorable to the working people, the NCWC is distinctly favorable to the working people" ("The Program and Activities of the National Catholic Welfare Council," *Annals of the American Academy of Political and Social Science* 103 [1922]: 133).

many Americans."[25] Americans were in for yet more surprises. The church continued to pursue its reformist and prolabor course.

The NCWC weathered the first test of its social resolve and continued to identify the church with the cause of reform. The church had stood by labor in the steel strike and had acquitted herself creditably in the battle against what Ryan called autocratic capital. More challenges lay ahead, however. In their ambitious efforts to break the power of the unions, the National Association of Manufacturers and others involved in big business determined to press for an open-shop policy in American industry.

In the open-shop drive, which employed the same patriotic rhetoric that had been used by capital in the strike-torn summer of 1919, business was vicious, determined, and well-organized.[26] The business community founded and financed the publication of the *Open Shop Review* to advertise its goals and to advance its cause. Through this journal and a sophisticated public relations campaign, the businessmen tried to convince the nation of the rectitude of their intentions and of the radical nature of labor's demands. Business left no stone unturned in its drive to influence public opinion and garner support for its position. Accordingly, the open-shop philosophy was presented as the "American Plan," and the *Review* staunchly maintained that by denying labor the right to organize, business was defending the freedom of all Americans and of laborers in particular. Of course, the manufacturers defined freedom in a narrow and essentially economic sense, following the reasoning of the classical economists. Therefore, in defending freedom, they were really defending the industrialists' right to enter into free contracts with laborers and the laborer's right to sell his labor in the marketplace for whatever price his work would fetch. The National Association of Manufacturers maintained that a union shop or a closed shop prevented market forces from freely deter-

25. Roddy, "Catholic Newspaper Press," p. 271.

26. Leuchtenberg says, "In the post war years, business launched a determined campaign to break unions where they existed and to maintain the open shop where they did not. In 1920, President Eugene Grace of Bethlehem Steel announced that even if 95 percent of his workers belonged to a union, he would refuse to recognize it" (*Perils of Prosperity*, p. 98).

mining wages. Reformers and laborers found glaring faults in this classical economic position. They were quick to point out that such a free contract arrangement violated natural law morality because it treated the worker as a commodity and thus outraged and compromised his human dignity. Capital was unmoved by such protests.

To be fair to the capitalists, it must be noted that they believed that through their paternalistic care they could provide for the workers' needs more effectively and with far less contentiousness than could the unions, which were by nature a combative lot. Thus the leaders of big business offered their own antidote to industrial unrest—a form of welfare capitalism that sought to answer and even to anticipate workers' demands for improvements in wages and working conditions. In a sense, as Morrell Herald notes, the development of this concept bore witness to a sense of "social responsibility and trusteeship" on the part of management.[27] Though perhaps laudable, the paternalism that was evident in such schemes was not acceptable to the reformers or to the workers. They realized that the businessmen were refusing to recognize that the workers had natural rights. The businessmen preferred to think in terms of charity and to congratulate themselves on their enlightened benevolence. They did not want to be accountable to anyone, least of all to the working classes. The laborers wanted justice, not charity, and saw the unions as the only agencies with enough potential power to force capital to recognize and grant their rights.

While this battle heated up, the sun had already begun to set on Progressivism, and as a nation exhausted by exhortations to reform settled back toward normalcy, the Social Action Department led by Ryan sprang into action against the open-shop drive. In marked contrast to his earlier coolness, Ryan developed a greater cordiality toward unionism. Before the beginning of the open-shop drive, Ryan had displayed a consistently classic Progressive approach to reform, placing his hope in legislation rather than in unionist action. In this preference, Ryan had been guided by his own principle of expediency: in the Progressive

27. Morrell Herald, "Business Thought in the Twenties: Social Responsibility," in *The 1920's: Problems and Paradoxes,* ed. Milton Plesur (Boston: Allyn and Bacon, 1969), p. 119.

heyday, it had appeared that reform legislation in line with Leonine principles offered greater possibilities for change than did labor agitation simply because the nation and the government were favorably disposed to such a course. In the postwar period, as the government's interest in reform wavered in Wilson's declining years and disappeared under Harding, the possibility of effecting social reform through legislation diminished. Expediency operated again. In the quest for social justice, Ryan and, by extension, the church, were bound to support those agencies whose activities seemed to offer some possibility of social improvement. In the 1920s, the unions, even in their straitened circumstances, seemed to be the only agencies with enough power to bring about change. Therefore, through that decade, Ryan increasingly committed himself and the SAD to their cause. His underlying commitment to social justice endowed his prolabor words and actions with the same passion that had characterized his earlier work for reform legislation.

Proceeding on the belief that the open-shop drive was a gross violation of the canons of justice, Ryan took aim against business: "These industrial autocrats profess to be in favor of an open shop, to give to the man who does not belong to the union opportunity to work when and where he pleases. They refuse to deal with the union in any sense. More than that, in the steel industry, there is an association one of whose functions is to see that only non-union foremen are employed; that the non-union foremen as far as possible do not employ any union men. In other words, their open shop means a closed shop against the union."[28]

Ryan did not keep these thoughts to himself. On 20 November 1920, he issued a statement under the SAD's auspices defending the unions and denouncing the employers. He mocked the employers for hiding their real motives "behind the pretence of American freedom," and, taking his cue from the propaganda of the business community, which maintained that the unions were plotting a socialist overthrow of the American system, he accused them of being America's true fomenters of radical agitation because of their blind intransigence.[29] Ryan's at-

28. Ibid.

29. "Open Shop Drive Is Called Menace," *Textile Worker,* November 1920,

tacks on business did not let up. In 1920–21, he and the SAD canvassed manufacturers throughout the country to ascertain their motivations for supporting the open-shop drive. In their responses to Ryan's questionnaire, the employers made it clear that they were moved by a desire to destroy the unions and not a commitment to sacred American liberties. Ryan promptly published the results of his survey and drew howls of criticism from the business community. Ryan and his department did not stand alone in their opposition to the open-shop drive. As Edward Roddy notes, the Catholic press "courageously attacked the 'American Plan' or 'open shop' crusade in the face of widespread business hostility. Never before had so many Catholic editorial pages rung with liberal, pro-labor sentiments as in these twilight months of the Progressive era."[30] The church was presenting a united front against the power and pretensions of big business.

The reactions to these conspicuously public Catholic actions on behalf of labor, which would have been unthinkable before the publication of the Bishops' Program of Social Reconstruction of 1919, were diverse. Although Progressivism was in decline, those Progressives who endured welcomed the action taken by the NCWC. The liberal journal *Justice* praised the Social Action Department for unmasking the antiunion bias that lurked beneath the patriotic rhetoric of the open-shop drive and came to the defense of the department when business accused it of being radical in its sympathies. The *Survey* joined *Justice* in its warm words of praise for the forthright stand of the department.[31] In the cold and unfriendly climate of the 1920s, the Progressives took delight and comfort in the companionship of the bishops, their former adversaries.

As could be expected, the warmest and most conspicuous supporters of the SAD's actions were the embattled unions. Labor welcomed the SAD's 10 November 1920 statement criticiz-

---

p. 498; "'Open Shop' Drive Denounced by Great Religious Body," *Federal Employee*, 27 November 1920, p. 4.

30. Roddy, "Catholic Newspaper Press," p. 255.

31. "Catholic War Council against Open Shop," *Justice*, 18 February 1921, p. 2; Jay Lovestone, *The Government—Strikebreaker: A Study of the Role of the Government in the Recent Industrial Crisis* (New York: Workers' Party of America, 1923), p. 19.

ing the open-shop drive with gratitude and praise. The *Textile Worker* informed its readers: "The present movement, the NCWC statement says is not aimed so much for the creation of the open shop, but the destruction of unionism and the right of collective bargaining. The abolition of the unions would be retrogression, the council holds, and subject the workers to utter dependency upon the employers of labor."[32] The *Brotherhood of Locomotive Firemen and Enginemen's Magazine* exultantly informed its brethren that "the principle of the living wage and collective bargaining in industry is aggressively supported by the National Catholic Welfare Council of the Roman Catholic Church" and referred its readers to the bishops' program for a fuller treatment of the church's stand.[33] San Francisco's *Labor Clarion* took pleasure in pointing out that "the Church is opposed to the closed anti-union shop (by explicit deliverance) and implicitly opposed to the closed union shop if established by force" and concluded that labor had found an ally in its fight against business.[34]

If labor was heartened by the NCWC's general open-shop statement, it was overjoyed by Ryan's publication of his survey of the motivations of the industrialists in their pursuit of the open shop. *Labor* reported: "The Department of Social Action of the National Catholic Welfare Council has forced the National Association of Manufacturers into a corner and forced it to admit that it really desires to cripple the unions. . . . Those who spoke for the Manufacturers' Association were compelled to admit that they were waging warfare against labor organizations and that their so-called 'American Plan' was camouflage

32. "'Open Shop' Drive Is Called a Menace," p. 498.

33. "The Church and Democracy," *Brotherhood of Locomotive Firemen and Enginemen's Magazine,* 1 July 1920, p. 11. Labor's reaction was as extensive as it was warm. The *Brotherhood of Locomotive Firemen and Enginemen's Magazine,* 1 January 1920, covered Ryan's lectures as well as the statement on the open shop. The *Federal Employee,* 27 November 1920, p. 4, reproduced the Social Action Department's statement and commended it to its membership. The *Railroad Trainman,* May 1921, praised the SAD; the *Textile Worker,* November 1921, published Cardinal O'Connell's thoughts on industrial relations; the national labor newspaper, *Labor,* 8 January 1921, and 15 January 1921, praised the NCWC; and the *Labor Clarion* of San Francisco, 26 November 1920, published the entire SAD statement of 10 November 1920.

34. Lynn T. White, "The Church and Industrial Relations," *Labor Clarion,* 1 September 1921, p. 56.

to hide their real purpose." The *Textile Worker* rushed the same news into print and informed its readers of the results of the Ryan survey: "You think the open shop campaign is aimed at the abuses of the closed shop. Is it? The Catholic Welfare Council asked all the agencies behind the campaign whether they would enter into collective bargaining agreements with the unions. Without exception they replied 'No!' Some were frank enough to admit that the open shop campaign was aimed at the destruction of the unions." The unionists were especially happy because the church had access to newspapers whose probusiness learnings closed their pages to the unions.[35] Thus their views and fears were able to get a fair hearing and the unions benefited from having their case presented by a moral and ostensibly impartial agency.

Labor leaders were in desperate need of such public relations miracles in 1920. Accordingly, without guile but with a sense of realism, urgency, and persistence, labor leaders continued to point out to the public that the arbiters of morality in America supported them in their battle with capital. Indeed, labor tied its hopes and its cause as closely as possible to religion and religion's God. In writing of the NCWC's open-shop stand, Lynn White said in the *Labor Clarion:* "The Church cannot escape the responsibility imposed upon it as the steward in time of certain social principles which it believes to be eternal in their validity. These principles it did not originate. It received them from the lips of Him whom it reveres as Lord and Master . . . these principles are believed by the Church to be the ultimate basis of that social order which alone can abide because it conforms to God's will for the race." White's implication was clear: God and His church were ranged on the side of labor in opposition to the open-shop drive, which violated human justice and the divine will. White was not alone in pursuing this reasoning. The *Railroad Trainman* developed the same argument, and the *Textile Worker* rejoiced that "the great moral forces of the coun-

35. "Churchmen Smoke Out Open Shoppers as Union Raiders," *Labor,* 12 February 1921, p. 1; "The Open Shop: 'The American Plan of Employment,'" *Textile Worker,* June 1921, p. 146. Lawrence Todd of the *Seamen's Journal* noted that the church's words had caused the *Washington Post* to alter its stand on the open-shop drive ("Our Washington Letter," *Seamen's Journal,* 24 November 1920, p. 8).

try—the Churches and their leaders" had thrown in their lot with the forces of labor. It invited the public to form its own conclusions regarding the rectitude of the businessmen's stance.[36] Labor believed that its position was immeasurably enhanced as a result of the church's support.

Labor was not the sole beneficiary of this new relationship. As a result of the Church's advocacy of its cause, labor became a strong and vocal defender of the American church. When *Industry*'s editor, Henry H. Lewis, launched a vicious attack upon the SAD for its open-shop statements, the *Railroad Trainman* sprang to the church's defense. To Lewis's contention that the statements were issued without any investigation or evidence to back them up the *Trainman* retorted, "However, they have investigated, they have weighed the evidence and they are fair. How so? Clergymen come in intimate contact with all their people. . . . They say no word of evil against any one class. They condemn radicalism in labor and they condemn radicalism in the employers." The national union newspaper, *Labor*, spoke up in defense of the church: "The third criticism that he [Lewis] made was to the effect that ecclesiastical organizations frequently discuss industrial subjects without sufficient knowledge of the facts. This is the superior and patronizing attitude so often taken by so-called 'practical men.' The truth is that, as a rule, clergymen who make pronouncements in this field know the facts only too well."[37] Labor plainly valued its new friend and repaid the church's advocacy of its position with passionate fidelity.

While the representatives of labor and the remnants of the reformist camp exulted at the NCWC-SAD's strong advocacy of the cause of labor, the business community fumed. The capitalists were stung by the apparent defection of one of their oldest and most conservative allies. They did not intend to let the

36. White, "Church and Industrial Relations," p. 47; "The Churches vs. the Open Shop," *Railroad Trainman*, May 1921, p. 274; John P. Frey, "Eliminate Industrial Waste," *Textile Worker*, November 1921, p. 398. The same article appeared in the *American Federationist*, the organ of the American Federation of Labor.

37. O. Playfair [pseud.], "On the Great Open Shop Controversy," *Railroad Trainman*, May 1921, p. 274. "Churchmen Smoke Out Open Shoppers," p. 572.

church go unchallenged. Their response was twofold. In their continuing efforts to gain the benefits the church's moral authority would lend to their campaign against labor, the advocates of the open shop used the *Open Shop Review* to publish snatches of Roman Catholic statements that seemed to endorse their position.[38] The statements of that great Republican and friend of capital, Archbishop John Ireland, and of the violently antilabor Father Molyneux found their way into the pages of the *Review,* which also managed to find and publish a remark of Cardinal Gibbons that suited its cause: "James Cardinal Gibbons is quoted in Pamphlet No. 1, the National Association of Manufacturers as follows: 'The right of the non-union laborer to make his own contract freely and perform it without hindrance, is so essential to civil liberty that it must be defended by the whole power of the government.'" Even Pope Leo XIII was pressed into service to champion the cause of the open shop: "But these words of Pope Leo XIII in his famous 'Encyclical on the Condition of Labor' are well worth our reflection: 'Associations of every kind and especially those of working men, are now far more common than formerly . . . there is a good deal of evidence which goes to prove that many of these societies are in the hands of invisible leaders and are managed on principles far from compatible with Christianity and the public well-being, and that they do their best to get into their hands the whole field of labor and to force workmen either to join them or to starve.'"[39] Capital thought such statements were powerful antidotes to the radical poison infecting the American Catholic Church.

Despite these brave efforts to prove that the best thought of the church favored the open-shop movement, the business community was plainly chagrined that the churches were vocally and publicly arrayed against them. Writing for *Industry,* Henry H. Lewis explained the reason for capital's nervousness and annoyance:

38. William O'Connell, Address, 7 March 1920, in *Open Shop Review,* April 1920, pp. 134–35.

39. Open Shop Department of the National Association of Manufacturers, *Open Shop Encyclopedia for Debators* (N.p.: National Association of Manufacturers, 1922), pp. 276, 266.

> Cleraly to appreciate the astounding nature of this charge [that the open shop would destroy unionism in America] against the integrity and humanity of the American businessmen in general it is necessary to understand that the religious organizations making the charges are in a position, because of their representative character, to impress the great army of Catholics and Protestant clergymen as well as many lay members. . . . It has been said that the councils really represent the policy and beliefs of small groups instead of the great body of Churchmen. That is as may be, but the fact remains that both Councils have been authorized by their respective Churches and function under certain dispensations.

Business was uneasy because the institutional status of the Federal and National Catholic Welfare councils made their statements potent shapers of public opinion against capital and its cause. Accordingly, *Industry* took it upon itself to expose the radicalism of the clergy and to refute the seriously misguided clergymen's charges, which were based on "ignorance of practical conditions."[40] *Industry* took to its task with extraordinary vigor and lambasted the churches in issue after issue for their wrongheaded support of subversive unionism. Business was visibly and vocally annoyed that in its desperate battle with labor, the churches and specifically the Catholic Church refused to cooperate with its campaign.

The events of 1919 and 1920 taught the nation, labor, and capital some important lessons about the church's role in industrial America. The bishops' program had announced the church's intention to become involved in social issues, and throughout the strikes the depth and focus of the church's commitment to social justice became clear. By the end of 1920, it was plain to all that the church was deeply committed to the cause of labor. Moreover, through the establishment of the Social Action Department, the church made it clear that her future social involvement would go beyond the publication of occasional statements like the Knights of Labor Memorial of 1886 and the program of 1919. Indeed, in the formation of the department, the church institutionalized her commitment to both the social education of American Catholics and the cause of reform. The church had gone beyond the expedient approach of 1886 to a more principled advocacy of social reform. In the 1920s, the

40. "The Great Open Shop 'Controversy,'" *Industry,* 1 January 1921, pp. 2, 5.

newly articulated foundation for the church's position and the institutional apparatus of the NCWC and the SAD would allow the program of social action to survive the cold winds of conservative reaction.

The received wisdom is that American Progressivism was killed by the war. Such a belief, however, would seem to be somewhat shy of the truth. Certainly the dawn of peace found the reformers still eager to carry on their crusade for social reform with a confidence born of their war triumph. The war did not kill reform. It did not even chasten the reformers. If anything, it whetted their appetites for new and greater conquests. The problems of peacetime, however, seemed to overwhelm them. Clarke Chambers recites a litany of events that taxed their ability to hope: "Industrial warfare, the collapse of the unions in the great strikes of 1919, the harassment of aliens and dissenters, inflation, the politics of normalcy, the striking down of child labor and minimum wage legislation by the Supreme Court, the Harding scandals,—these followed hard and fast."[41]

External pressures, however, only partially account for the enervation of the formerly vital Progressive movement. Herbert Margulies maintains that "greater stress has been placed on the erosion of the movement from internal causes. From this perspective, the war was at most only an accelerating agent in the process of dying, but the death of Progressivism was nevertheless natural, not inflicted from outside." To understand and appreciate Margulies's position, it must be remembered that the Progressive movement was from the start a mosaic, a loose coalition of elements held together by a shared belief in the values and virtues of middle-class culture and dedicated to the building of a democratic, classless, but actually middle-class society. During the war, the more socially minded Progressives had shifted to the left in their beliefs, espoused a class-oriented analysis of social conditions, and begun to employ a class-conscious rhetoric in their public statements. In so doing, they dropped some of the movement's traditional distrust and vocal opposition to the cause of labor and became active supporters of the unions against the menacing power of big business. This leftward movement placed a severe strain on a "loose coalition

41. Chambers, *Paul U. Kellogg and the Survey,* p. 77.

[that] was inherently unstable." The middle-class infrastructure of the movement could not sustain a wholesale shift to the more radical stance espoused by the social wing of the movement. As William Leuchtenberg notes, "A middle class movement hostile to interest-group politics, Progressivism was shocked by the militancy of labor in 1919, and many Progressives aligned themselves with property-conscious conservatives."[42] The Progressive movement faltered and declined, then, as a result both of internal weaknesses and external events and pressures.

It must not be assumed, however, that as the nation settled in to an era of greater complacency and relative indifference to reform, the reform impulse totally died. During the 1920s, there was a significant regrouping of forces, or a realignment of agencies. From this new coalition, there emerged a new urban liberalism that hearkened back to the institutional reforms of 1917–19 in its formulation of plans for the future.[43] The reform alliance of the 1920s resembled the evanescent coalition that emerged during the war and endured into the first year of peace, but it was chastened by the defeat of idealism and the defection of the government. Therefore, through the 1920s, as William Leuchtenberg notes, the new reform movement was "less interested in the moral reformation of men and more in using the power of the federal government to provide specific economic and social benefits." Although the reformers of the 1920s hoped, as did the Progressives, for government action to aid the cause of reform, the government's coolness to their proposals

42. Herbert F. Margulies, "Recent Opinion and the Decline of the Progressive Movement," in *The 1920's: Problems and Paradoxes*, ed. Plesur, pp. 40, 52; Leuchtenberg, *Perils of Prosperity*, p. 126.

43. Ellis W. Hawley says, "The years 1917–1919 have become significant not only for their impact on liberal reformism and their responses to developments abroad but also for their institutional innovations and especially for their contributions to New Era designs for economic, social and international order" (*Great War*, p. 231). Stanley Shapiro concurs: "But the war also produced a political movement which historians, bedazzled by the story of its prosecution, have largely ignored. Between 1917 and 1920 an important attempt was made to formulate a new reform program and forge a new reform alliance in the United States. Although evanescent, that movement illustrates the war's positive influence on Progressives generally—its 'therapeutic' effect, as Randolph Bourne put it, and its special impact on the intellectual elite of Progressivism" ("Twilight of Reform," p. 349).

forced them to seek other means to bring about the realization of their dreams. As Otis Graham points out, "Voluntary associations in the social welfare and social service movements remained in existence and continued their struggles on behalf of labor legislation, social insurance, public housing and adequate relief."[44] These voluntary associations lobbied assiduously for the attainment of the possible and never forgot the reform triumphs of the war years. Indeed, with their late Progressive predecessors they adamantly insisted that the war, with its imposition of government controls and its erection of the War Labor Board, had provided the nation with a workable apparatus for social amelioration that also provided the blueprint for the future.[45] As Ellis Hawley says, the reform saga of 1917–33 "is a story of men deeply influenced by the organizational experience of a democracy at war and seeking, against various obstacles, to draw from that experience a set of liberal ordering mechanisms capable of coordinating an expanding organizational economy and fostering peaceful progress in the social and international spheres."[46] In many ways, it is also the story of failure. The problem was that the national cohesion that allowed such mechanisms to work during the war was born of crisis. Liberals would have to await yet another crisis before their hopes would be realized and the unfinished work of economic reform could be taken up again.

In the meantime, the faithful remnant continued to cherish the ideal of industrial democracy even as they worked for more possibilist and less idealistically based reforms. In the depths of reform's nadir, Glenn Plumb, the reform-minded counsel for the railroad brotherhoods, raised the ghost of the ideal and sang its praises. Plumb saw the age as the typical Progressive idealist would—as an unfortunate but temporary hiatus on the evolu-

44. Leuchtenberg, *Perils of Prosperity*, p. 137; Graham, *Great Campaigns*, p. 116.

45. John S. Smith says, "For the hard core of the nation's reformers those who remained active after the great majority of the Progressives accepted the return to 'normalcy,' the war labor administration was an important breach in American tradition. The war labor program of the federal government seemed to them to give reality to what had before been only theorizing" ("Organized Labor and Government in the Wilson Era, 1913–1921: Some Conclusions," *Labor History* 3 [1962]: 279).

46. Hawley, *Great War*, pp. 226–27.

tionary road to the establishment of the ideal of democracy: "Now . . . the progress of democracy is temporarily halted by the inability or the unwillingness of privileged classes to go forward with the general advance of humanity." Plumb issued a poignant call to all Americans to repudiate industrial autocracy and to return to the traditional democratic mission: "The action taken by the founders of the American nation exactly marks out the course for us to follow in the present crisis. They reconstructed their political institutions in accordance with the fundamental principles that, for the very nature of humankind, must govern all the relations of individuals to each other. These are the principles of democracy."[47]

Uttered in defeat, these words, which enshrine Plumb's Progressive idealism, demonstrate the congruence between American reform and Ryan's Catholic social thought. Plumb's words vindicated Ryan's claims and his struggle to make the church realize that she had nothing to fear from the reformers. In addition, this similarity between the two systems of thought enabled the church to embrace the Progressive vision of reform with a vehemence that bordered on the quixotic during the 1920s. A further examination of Plumb's words makes the church's embrace of the American reform tradition even more understandable. Plumb called attention to the Declaration of Independence as the source of America's inspiration and the guide for its social life: "The Declaration of Independence—accepted by the ablest American jurists as our first and most fundamental Constitutional document—defines the rights of men, and declares that 'for the securing of these rights, governments are instituted among men.' These rights are not defined in political terms. Politics has to do with governments, and government, according to the Declaration, is only for the purpose of securing rights that are inherent and inalienable—that are not created by government, and that would exist if there were no government." Plumb believed that the American social contract was founded on natural law and that the government had a positive role to play in the social life of the nation: the protecting and securing of natural rights. In turning his attention

47. Glenn E. Plumb and William G. Roylance, *Industrial Democracy: A Plan for Its Achievement* (New York: B. W. Huebsch, 1923), p. 15–16.

to the industrial sphere, Plumb said that "governments are instituted for the securing of the inherent and inalienable rights of individuals, among which are included industrial rights."[48] These words could have been written by Ryan. They give eloquent testimony to the natural law foundations that underlaid the Progressive movement's desire to effect the final establishment of democracy. It is no wonder then that the church felt at home with Progressivism and made its crusade her own. The urgency born of the natural law foundations of Progressivism and the reformist ideal of democracy lived on into the 1920s and formed an ideological bridge between the old reform movement and the new urban liberalism.

In some ways, then, the emergent reform alliance of the turbulent 1920s shared some of Progressivism's vision and favored some of the earlier movement's methods. With the earlier reform impulse, the new liberalism was wholeheartedly committed to the ideal of democracy, looked to the government as the most effective agent for the promotion of reform, and believed that the wartime experiments in the regulation of the economy and the mediation of industrial disputes were blueprints for the future of industrial life in America. In one significant way, however, the new liberalism differed markedly from the earlier movement. The utter failure of reconstruction chastened the reformers. The government had defected from the reform cause and had become an instrument of reaction. In addition, through its brilliant—even stunning—victory over labor and reform, business had shown how crucial it was to appreciate and use power. Therefore, the liberals of the 1920s were shorter on idealism, more committed to possibilist goals, and more appreciative of and skillful in the use of power than their predecessors. They showed a new and enduring openness to a continuing alliance with labor. Realism had once more dawned—however painfully—on the reformers. In many ways, the Social Action Department of the National Catholic Welfare Council may be seen as a case study of the ways in which realistic reformism, with its roots in the Progressive past, managed to survive the 1920s.

The SAD was more or less the product of the Bishops' Program of Social Reconstruction of 1919. The program had sig-

48. Ibid., pp. 50, 55.

naled the church's emergence from silence on social issues in such a public way that abandonment of the social sphere would have been disastrous for its image. Therefore, in partial fulfillment of the promise contained in the program, the hierarchy had formed the SAD to provide a forum for an ongoing Catholic reflection on and critique of social problems. At first, the program served as a kind of Magna Carta for the work of the SAD. As time went on and the Progressivism with which the program was at one fell into disfavor, the SAD's actions lost some of the crusading zeal announced by the plan. Ryan explained the shift in strategy by saying that the church was not ready for such a radical program. With his fellow reformers, Ryan turned his attention to more immediate social problems and goals, and under Ryan's leadership, so did the department. Sensing that the unions were the only hope for forcing reforms upon the industrial system and chagrined that the government was becoming more hostile to the unions, Ryan turned the SAD into a vocal advocate for the rights of labor.[49] In that context, he championed the cause of labor in the open-shop controversy.

Even as Ryan was defending the unions against their business and governmental adversaries, he tried desperately to move both the labor leaders and the rank and file toward a more militantly reformist stance, to prod the unions into becoming a force for reform. As Neil Betten notes, "Ryan continued to urge unions to transcend material goals traditionally desired by the AFL and to acquire a social vision. He wanted the AFL to support government measures to aid the worker, including legislation for which Ryan traditionally fought: the child labor amendment, government supervision of bituminous coal, etc." In addition, reflecting his residual Progressivism, Ryan "urged the AFL to make greater claims on management" and demand some share in its workings.[50] Finally, because Ryan understood that the cause of reform was hostage to power, he pleaded with the AFL to broaden its power base by welcoming into its ranks the great numbers of industrial workers whose presence would add immeasurably to labor's power effectively to bargain with industry

49. Abell, *American Catholicism and Social Action*, pp. 204, 212; Betten, *Catholic Activism*, p. 38.

50. Betten, *Catholic Activism*, pp. 38, 40.

for reforms and concessions. When the AFL rebuffed Ryan's pleas, the SAD became a virtual midwife at the birth of the Congress of Industrial Organizations. Thus Ryan's defense of labor grew partly out of his belief that labor had a right to organize and partly out of his conviction that the cause of reform in a conservative age would best be served by the development of a powerful and reform-minded labor movement.

As a means both to further the social education of Catholics and to advance the cause of reform among the ranks of labor and capital, the SAD founded the Catholic Conference on Industrial Problems in 1922. As Karl Cerny notes, "The purpose of the organization was to interest Catholics—employers and employees—in studying Catholic social principles and discussing the problems involved in applying them to American industry."[51] This educational work was to be carried on in a noncontroversial manner. In pursuit of this goal, the conference met once a year between 1922 and 1928. Thereafter, several meetings were held each year at a variety of locations so as to expose larger numbers of Catholics to the church's social teachings. Although the stated purpose of these conferences was the advancement of Catholic social consciousness, the guiding vision behind them was Progressive: the conferences sought to discover and create a community of interest between labor and capital so that the industrial world could function on the basis of cooperation, mutual respect, and selflessness.[52] Ryan's old hope for industrial democracy was still alive, and he wished to demonstrate its luminous benefits to both parties in the industrial process.

For all its efforts to cajole labor into a more reformist stance, the SAD was, like its companions in the emerging liberal alliance, decidedly and publicly prolabor. This new attitude was not lost either to the general public or to the labor and capitalist camps. Capital became increasingly exasperated by the church's stand and vocal in its criticism, whereas labor was elated.

As the decade grew older, however, unionists and their allies became more selective in their praise for the churches in general and for the Catholic Church in particular. Jerome Davis, a

51. Cerny, "Monsignor John A. Ryan," pp. 109–10.
52. Betten, *Catholic Activism*, p. 40.

regular contributor to the *World Tomorrow,* complained, "Few of us would deny that the churches are noble institutions serving humanity. The Federal Council of Churches, the National Catholic Welfare Council, the Jewish groups and the various denominations issue social creeds which usually champion industrial democracy. Once the pronouncement is made, little is generally done by the local congregation to make it effective." The teamster leader Daniel Tobin had great praise for Ryan and for Cardinal Gibbons's work but bitterly pointed out that "among the large number of clergymen in the Catholic Church there are but a few who have had the courage to express themselves in favor of the trade union movement while many of them are totally opposed to organized labor in America." James Meurer was even more pointed in his criticism: "My opinion is that the people never left the Church, but that many Churches have left the people for a smug seat in the clouds of self-righteous contentment, where the lowly Nazarene would most likely get his head cracked by a burly policeman if he attempted to interfere." Tobin's criticism was more specific. Despite Ryan's strenuous efforts, he found Catholicism to be the biggest laggard in labor advocacy: "I am a member of the Roman Catholic Church . . . I am more dissatisfied with the position of the Catholic Church toward labor than I am with the position of many of the Protestant or non Catholic Churches."[53] Toward the end of the 1920s, labor was once again voicing the criticism and demands it had made in the prewar period. Although Ryan and the Social Action Department had done great work to advance the cause of prolabor reform, the educational work committed to his department was far from over.

The labor leaders were not the only ones who found fault with the department. The bishops also criticized Ryan's work,

53. Jerome Davis, "A Class Church and a Churchless Class," in *Labor Speaks for Itself on Religion: A Symposium of Labor Leaders throughout the World,* ed. Jerome Davis (New York: Macmillan, 1929), p. 23; Daniel Tobin, "Can the Church Be Led Back?" in ibid., pp. 62–63; James H. Meurer, "Has the Church Betrayed Labor?" in ibid., p. 34. Arthur Wharton said, "Just what Labor thinks of the Church is probably influenced in part by deductions based on what many believe to be the indifference of the Church toward labor. If there is antipathy toward the Church by Labor, it is due largely to the failure of the Church to study the Labor Movement" ("What the Church Needs to Be Saved," in ibid., p. 89).

but for a strikingly different reason. Whereas labor believed that the church was not vocal enough in its support of reform, the bishops were angered because they believed that Ryan and the Social Action Department were too noisy and controversial in their statements. Episcopal displeasure was especially aroused by the seemingly radical stand taken by the SAD on the federal child labor amendment. The Central Verein and the Jesuit weekly *America* were vociferous in their denunciations of the proposed amendment and correspondingly critical of Ryan's stand for it. Among the hierarchy, the assault on the amendment and on the SAD's advocacy of it was led by the powerful archbishop of Boston, William Cardinal O'Connell, who opposed it because he felt it went counter to Catholic and American traditions. O'Connell used the church to defeat the hated law in Massachusetts. Sermons were preached, statements were issued, and the people were instructed to vote against the measure. When the SAD issued a statement supporting the law, O'Connell was furious. When Ryan had the temerity to enter O'Connell's see city to promote the amendment, O'Connell was outraged. O'Connell wrote to the archbishop of Baltimore, Michael Curley, and demanded that Ryan be silenced.[54] Curley showed O'Connell's letters to Ryan and advised him to exercise caution in the future but refused to comply with O'Connell's demands.

Chagrined that he was unable to silence Ryan through episcopal diplomacy, O'Connell determined to go further. The NCWC was the source of Ryan's claim to authority. Therefore, in league with Denis Cardinal Daugherty of Philadelphia and Archbishop John J. Keane of Dubuque, O'Connell sought to have Rome suppress the NCWC and its Social Action Department and thus rid the American church of the source of contagion. Fortunately, the move was turned back as a result of a concerted drive by the leaders and supporters of the NCWC.[55]

54. See Vincent A. McQuade, *The American Catholic Attitude on Child Labor since 1891: A Study of the Formation and Development of a Catholic Attitude on a Specific Social Question* (Washington: Catholic University of America Press, 1938), pp. 82, 79; William O'Connell to Michael Curley, 2 November 1924, Ryan Papers Ref. N–Po, Box B2-41, ACUA.

55. After precipitating this crisis, O'Connell wrote to Raphael Cardinal Merry Del Val to complain of the "politics" that were destroying the church: "There

The episcopal discontent with Ryan's activities, however, revealed the vulnerability of the uncanonical NCWC. The council depended for both its existence and its effectiveness on the continued goodwill of the bishops. At the same time and perhaps paradoxically, O'Connell's attack bore witness to the strength of the NCWC and the importance of its unity for the social justice ministry of the American church. The NCWC's and, by extension, the SAD's power to affect public opinion lay in the national belief that it represented the entire American hierarchy and that consequently the hierarchy approved of all its statements. In his work, Ryan used this impression, and O'Connell deeply resented the presumption that he agreed with Ryan's radical views. Therefore, he wished to destroy the agency that derived its moral authority from his and his fellow bishops' position in the church and in the nation. Finally, the episcopal discontent with Ryan and with one of the proposals of the bishops' program shows that in the conservative 1920s, as Aaron Abell notes, "the hierarchy had lost interest in its own Program, or that part of it which called for Federal intervention in industry."[56]

Throughout the 1920s, Ryan and other leading Catholic social theorists continued to work for Catholic acceptance of the key idea that the state should take an active role in promoting social justice. For instance, in analyzing the causes of the social problems that beset the nation during the decade, William J. Kerby maintained that America's excessive reverence for a laissez-faire economy had created a weak and irresponsible government: "Now this outcome of competition would have been prevented or greatly modified if we had not lived under a state whose philosophy and policies prevented it from interfering. The individualistic state based on the policy of large economic freedom as to contract, enterprise, property, industry, was hindered very greatly by its constitution and traditions from curbing the

---

is all around about an intangible something which would seem to emanate from too much politics, diplomacy and intrigue—too much mingling with affairs which don't concern us. . . . How different in the wonderful days of Pio X!—when the chief concern was God, and when . . . politics and free masons were kept in their places!" (William O'Connell to Raphael Merry Del Val, 1921, O'Connell Papers, Correspondence, Merry Del Val, 1921–29, AAB).

56. Aaron I. Abell, "The Bishops' 1919 Program," *Social Order* 12 (1962): 118.

strong or aiding the weak." As a result of the domination of the government by the strong, Kerby lamented that America had given birth to a system in which "human rights seem shorn of all respect when industry holds life more cheaply than profits, and industrial power absolves itself from the restraints of Christian faith." Kerby pleaded for a change of political philosophy. He reminded his readers, in Leonine terms, that "poverty is a plight of the state. Its victims do not enjoy the realization of justice. They are baffled. Rights defined in law are not secure. New laws, demanded by the conscience of the time, are delayed. More effective representation of the poor before legislatures and courts is required."[57] Kerby was adamant in his demand that the government, in fulfillment of its natural law role, take action to effect improvements in social conditions.

Kerby and Ryan were not alone in their efforts to rehabilitate state intervention in Catholic eyes. To those Catholics who believed that the political and economic spheres should be governed by a laissez-faire philosophy, John O'Grady pointed out that "Catholic social thought during the past century is, to a large extent, a protest against economic liberalism. The principles expounded by Catholic thinkers and leaders are utterly at variance with the principles advocated by liberal economists." Parker Moon was more explicit: "The Catholic teaching on this point is clear. Leo XIII in his great Encyclical explicitly stated that it is not merely the right, but the duty of the Government to pass whatever laws are needed to preserve order, to protect family, to afford working men the opportunity for the practice of religion."[58] Thus, throughout the decade of the 1920s, American Catholic social theorists did their best to make it clear that the central Progressive-Leonine principle of the bishops' program—that the state was impelled by its natural law duty to enter into the area of social amelioration—was a hallowed part of the Catholic tradition.

In their educational work, Ryan and his colleagues managed to endow not only the principle of state intervention but also

57. William J. Kerby, *The Social Mission of Charity: A Study of Points of View in Catholic Charities* (New York: Macmillan, 1921), pp. 12, 25, 56, 131.

58. John O'Grady, *The Catholic Church and the Destitute* (New York: Macmillan, 1929), p. 80; Parker T. Moon, "Catholic Social Action," in *Catholic Builders of the Nation*, ed. C. E. McGuire (Boston: Continental, 1923), p. 219.

the program itself with a semicanonical status in the American church. Moreover, with the promulgation of *Quadragesimo Anno* by Pius XI in 1931, Ryan believed that he had further warrant for pleading for this semicanonical status both for the program and for the principle of state intervention for the cause of social justice.[59] Ryan adamantly believed in and defended the unity of thought, sentiment, and method that linked the program to the encyclicals.[60] He argued that the program represented an American expression of the Catholic social tradition. By claiming a place in the tradition for the document, Ryan and his confreres buttressed its moral authority, disengaged it from its historical setting, and used it and the method it both employed and represented as an authoritative referent for advocating specific social programs in the 1930s.

As a result, by the time the Depression descended on America, there was a clearly articulated Catholic position in favor of state intervention for the attainment of social justice. The church was therefore ready with its prescription for the alleviation of the social distress of the Depression. As Ryan had previ-

59. See, for instance, the NCWC news release of 29 May 1939: "Recalling the two great encyclicals, *Rerum Novarum* and *Quadregesimo Anno*, Msgr. Ryan said that the first document, 'did not receive adequate consideration until almost 28 years after it had appeared.' While its teaching and influence found expression and recognition in the Bishops' Program of Social Reconstruction and the Pastoral Letter of the entire American hierarchy in 1919, he said, for some 40 years, 'economic reform made little progress in the halls of legislation'" (Ryan Papers, Ryan Ref. N–Po, Box B2-41, ACUA). He also continued to hammer away at the idea that on the basis of papal thought, the idea of state intervention for the cause of social justice be accepted by American Catholics: "It may be useful at this point to take notice of the misgiving expressed by some Catholic social students with regard to legislation as a method of reform. These persons are of the opinion that a new social order can come about only through changes in the hearts of men. . . . Not all social salvation he (Pius XI) said is to be hoped from State intervention, but the destruction of a variety of associations that once flourished between the State and individuals renders legislation indispensable for the establishment of a new social order. According to Pius XI, therefore, a large part in the reconstruction of the social order is to be played by the State and legislation" ("Legislation and a Christian Social Order," address to the Social Action Congress, Cleveland, 12 June 1939, Ryan Papers, Writings, 1935–40, Box B2-28, ACUA).

60. See John A. Ryan, "'Reconstructing the Social Order' and the Bishops' Program of Social Reconstruction," 15 December 1931, News Release, Ryan Papers, Ryan Ref., Ed–G, Box B2-38, ACUA.

ously presented Leonine thought to the Progressives, during the New Deal he explained Leo's and Pius XI's thought to a nation reeling under the blows of social devastation. In addition, he used his old Progressivist understanding of Leo's thought to justify the New Deal to Catholics. He was especially anxious to justify the wide-ranging use of state powers to effect social change: "In passing it might be observed that the principle of State intervention laid down by Pope Leo would easily justify all the legislative measures that have been adopted by Congress since the advent of the New Deal." Ryan fairly canonized the New Deal and its architect: "The teaching of these two Popes . . . can readily be compared with the Roosevelt policies. . . . The New Deal is not socialistic. It would retain private ownership of the instruments of production but would compel private owners to use their possessions in such a way as to promote the general interest and the common good. It would extend, as already intimated, the regulative function of the State over industry for the sake of the weaker classes, the Forgotten Men and likewise for the benefit of society as a whole."[61] To Ryan, Roosevelt seemed a sage. He agreed with the popes. He agreed with Ryan.

Given Ryan's enthusiastic embrace of the New Deal, it would be tempting to brand him an opportunist. Such a designation would be somewhat wide of the truth. Ryan believed that theory had to be redeemed and its truth proven by its successful application to actual conditions. Hence he was extraordinarily sensitive to circumstances and possibilist means as well as to principled goals. Although Ryan and the Social Action Department found it expedient to support trade unions during the 1920s, as Karl Cerny notes, "Despite its greatly increased interest in the trade union movement, the Department nevertheless believed that the possibilities of trade union action in achieving a reform

61. Ryan, "Pope Leo's *Rerum Novarum,*" p. 139, 132. Ryan also said, "Pope Leo declared that the state should especially concern itself with the welfare of the poorer classes, the working classes, and in general, that it is the business of the state to intervene in social and industrial life whenever the interest of the community or of any particular class cannot be safeguarded by private individuals and associations" ("Catholic Principles and Roosevelt Policies," in his *Seven Troubled Years,* p. 132).

program were limited. . . . Only governmental activity seemed to provide any reasonable prospect of insuring a decent livelihood for all American labor."[62] Ryan had never abandoned his Leonine-inspired idea that the government should involve itself in the work of establishing the reign of justice.[63] With the onset of the Depression, it appeared opportune to return to the earlier advocacy of state intervention with one essential difference. The Progressive Ryan had envisioned intervention by state governments, whereas the New Deal Ryan favored federal action. The nation seemed to agree that since reckless business practices had brought on the Depression, the government should right the situation. As in 1917, social crisis proved to be the midwife of social reform.

In these changed circumstances, there was a tremendous revival of interest in the bishops' program.[64] The nation seemed ready to admit the faults of American capitalism and to accept the need for government intervention for which the program called. As a result, forgetting for the time that the program was historically conditioned and Progressive in its preference for local and state intervention rather than for federal measures, Ryan and others began to lament the failure to adopt the program and to see it as the essential blueprint for all New Deal legislation. In 1932, for example, at the threshold of the New Deal, Burke extolled the virtues of the program and told the nation that the Depression could have been avoided if the bishops' words had been heeded in 1919. Taking deadly aim at the unbridled industrialism and individualism that had led the nation to economic ruin, Burke said that "the present unhappy condition of human society is due to the fact that for long decades the supreme dignity and rights of man have been ignored and dethroned." In the throes of the Depression he praised the wisdom of the program and its sponsoring bishops: "They so acted in the hope that proclaiming natural rights and duties, urging Christian principles of a sound social order and making specific recommendations thereunder would help the nation during the after war

62. Cerny, "Monsignor John A. Ryan," pp. 157–58.
63. See ibid., pp. 159–60.
64. Ryan, *Social Doctrine*, pp. 149–50.

years to walk in justice," and chided the nation for its failure to adopt the bishops' plan.[65] That failure had contributed to the economic distress of 1929.

A tendency developed to keep a kind of score card on the successful enactment of the program's proposals. In 1939, Edward Mooney, the archbishop of Detroit, was proud to announce that of the eleven proposals contained in the document, ten had been enacted as laws during the New Deal era. The bishops appeared to have been prescient. Ryan fairly crowed to announce, "Notable observers have since said that if the recommendations made by the Bishops had been put into effect, the depression that developed in 1929 would not have been so deep or so widespread, and that the groundwork would have been laid for the measures that have now been adopted to combat the continuing depression." Ryan and the NCWC were not alone in calling attention to the bishops' wisdom. Roosevelt's attorney general, Frank Murphy, said, "It is a matter not for vanity but for gratitude and future inspiration . . . that the Catholic faith has contributed much to the progressive movement. Fourteen years before the Administration of President Roosevelt came into being, the need for many of the reforms achieved in the last six years was brilliantly stated in the 'Bishops' Program of Social Reconstruction!'" The wisdom of the program was being recognized, and it and the church were being located in the mainstream of American reform. Archbishop Mooney assured the document a place in the Catholic social canon when he said, "Even if that goal [fulfillment of reform hopes] had not been reached, readers would still be able to find in the program much that is useful in the statement of Catholic social principles and in the application of these principles to many spheres of our economic life. Indeed it is not too much to say that the Bishops' Program is of permanent value."[66]

65. John J. Burke, "Encomium," p. 2, 1932, and "Social Justice," 1932, p. 1, Burke Papers, Writings on Social and Economic Justice, Paulist Fathers' Archives.

66. Ryan, "Legislation and a Christian Social Order," p. 1; "20th Anniversary of the Bishops' Program for Social Justice Finds Many of Ideas Adopted," NCWC News Release, 6 February 1939, Ryan Papers, Ryan Ref. Box B2-36, ACUA; Frank Murphy, Address to the Second Annual Convention of National Catholic Social

Fortified by these endorsements, Ryan confidently used the program's long-range proposals for the establishment of industrial democracy as the basis for a call for more radical changes in the social order than were possible from the enactments of its shorter-range proposals. Reasoning that "we cannot evade the obligation of proposing a fundamental substitute for the present system," and calling to mind that Pope Pius XI sanctioned a radical reform of social structures in *Quadragesimo Anno,* Ryan called for "labor sharing in management and profits, public housing and a wider distribution of ownership."[67] Ryan was both urgent and insistent in his calls for radical social change and confident that as the New Deal's legislative measures had proved the wisdom and feasibility of the program's short-term reform proposals, so also bolder New Deal actions to implement industrial democracy would in the long run be heralded as the ultimate solution to social ills. In all of Ryan's confident crowing, it is clear that during the Depression, he was resurrecting the program as a part of the American Catholic canon of social teaching and further that, twenty years after its appearance, Ryan was still using the document to effect and celebrate a reconciliation between the Catholic and American reform traditions.

Not all the praise and the extravagant claims for the place of the program in the American reform tradition emanated from the Catholic camp. On 17 October 1938, Attorney General Robert Jackson said in an address to the National Conference of Catholic Charities: "Liberal political thinking in America had been profoundly influenced by the Bishops' Program of Social Reconstruction." Jackson was lavish in his praise of the document, claiming that the program "accurately outlines the social objectives of the political liberals of today." He told his audience that the Social Security system had been foreshadowed by the program's call for a comprehensive program of social insurance, and he sought to effect a reconciliation between Catholic social

---

Action Congress, 19 June 1939, Ryan Papers, Ryan Ref. N–Po, Box B2-41, ACUA; Edward Mooney, "Introduction to the 20th Anniversary Edition of the Bishops' Program of Social Reconstruction," Senate Document 79, 76th Cong., 1st sess., 1939, p. 3.

67. John A. Ryan, "Two Programs of Social Reconstruction," address, Ryan Papers, Writings Miscellaneous, Box B2-24, pp. 5, 9, ACUA.

thought and New Deal policies.[68] Jackson's speech was a tour de force. He welcomed the church into the American reform tradition with a warmth that delighted the American Catholic people. Significantly, in doing so, he used the same document that Ryan had used to claim the church's right to a place in the American reform camp: the Bishops' Program of Social Reconstruction. Nearly two decades after its publication, the bishops' plan was achieving the hope for which Ryan had dreamed: the reconciliation of the two traditions to which he was heir. Unfortunately, Jackson's praise and Ryan's New Deal claims for the program have led to some confusion on the proper categorization of the program.[69]

Although Ryan's desire to represent the program as a harbinger of New Deal measures is understandable, the reasoning behind his claims is faulty because it loses sight of the historical conditioning of the program. The document bore all the hallmarks of late Progressivism, a movement that, though it pointed to and was related to the urban liberalism that began to flourish later in the century, was nonetheless derived from classic Progressivism. The short-term reform measures advocated by the program clustered around and were directed to the achievement of the three reformist goals enunciated by Benjamin P. Dewitt: the insurance of a humane life and the erection of a welfare and regulatory state. Further, in thoroughly Progressive fashion, there was evident in the spirit and measures of the document a heartfelt belief in the efficacy of legislation as the ultimate and ultimately satisfying vehicle of reform. In this regard, as with most Progressive plans, as Aaron I. Abell notes, the program "was designed to operate chiefly on the state, only

68. Robert J. Jackson, "Social Justice under Our Constitution: Catholic Social Teaching Used as New Deal Guide," address at National Conference of Catholic Charities, 11 October 1938, pp. 1, 2, Ryan Papers, Box B2-36, ACUA.

69. Not all Catholics were willing to acknowledge the wisdom of the program or its architect even during the Depression. William O'Neill, the president of General Tire and Rubber, wrote to Bishop Karl Alter to protest Ryan's continued use of the authority of the bishops to advance his own ideas of radical reform that were contained in the program. O'Neill fairly howled when he said, "Are we not perhaps, turning to the protestant way, when we receive from our clergymen what, from any but expert and experienced students of the labor problem, can only be their own private economic tub-thumpings?" (O'Neill to Alter, 25 August 1939, ADT). He denounced Ryan as a "Tugwell in a cassock patronized by the 'United Front' of communism."

incidentally on the federal level." As a result, Abell concludes that "the Bishops' Program belongs to the Progressive era in outlook as well as in time," rather than to the New Deal era.[70]

The long-range reforms envisioned by the program—the establishment of cooperative stores and of industrial democracy—were equally Progressive in inspiration. In enunciating these seemingly radical goals, Ryan and his colleagues were motivated by the typically reformist dream of extending rather than destroying the middle class. In addition, in their explication of the rationale behind the program and their arguments concerning the feasibility of reform, the proponents of the bishops' program pursued a line of argumentation that was thoroughly at one with Progressive reform logic. Ryan and his confreres looked to the war and its expedient social measures to discern the direction the nation should follow to realize the establishment of a more just social order. Finally, the bishops' program displayed a typically Progressive moral earnestness and a dogged optimism that in the era following the Great War, the morality and altruism of wartime would dominate public life and thus smooth the way to the creation of a more just and humane society.

In summary, one would have to agree with Neil Betten that the program "was a truly Progressive document."[71] In retrospect, this episcopal embrace of the Progressive cause was somewhat ironic because Progressivism withered at the very moment when its adherents expected it to capture America. The decline of reform fervor in the 1920s, however, should not detract from the document's significance and importance as a Progressive statement. Its publication marked the emergence of the Catholic Church from its self-imposed isolation from the decidedly Protestant tradition of American reform. Indeed, through the program, the church arrived at a surprisingly and shockingly—even spectacular—public advocacy of precisely that Progressive stance which the bishops had feared before the war. This hierarchical embrace of the cause of reform was momentous in the event and even more important in its consequences. The ideological equation of American reformism and

70. Abell, ed., *American Catholic Thought,* p. xxx; Abell, "Bishops' 1919 Program," p. 117.

71. Betten, *Catholic Activism,* p. 37.

Leonine Catholicism that underlay the program and its measures assured American Catholics of the value of their specifically Catholic social reflections for American life and awakened them to the Catholic heritage at the same time that it called their attention to the principled natural law bases upon which that tradition was founded. As a result, American Catholics began to perceive themselves as the true guardians and interpreters of the meaning of America's natural law ideas of social responsibility, particularly in the area of industrial relations. Consequently, Catholics in the 1920s and thereafter became quixotically passionate in their advocacy of social justice. As a result, the Social Action Department of the National Catholic Welfare Council became one of the prime guardians of the Progressive heritage during the socially stagnant 1920s because of its director's firm belief that American reformism and Leonine social Catholicism were one in thought and in strategy.

Although the church's new and official identification with the cause of American reform was important, the effects of the program's publication on the church herself were even more important, both within the universal Catholic communion and on the American religious scene.

Before 1919, the American church had assiduously avoided involvement in social issues and thus found herself out of step with her sister churches of Europe. Even Leo XIII's *Rerum Novarum* had failed to create a groundswell movement toward social involvement in the American church. In the years between 1891 and 1919 a few voices urged a more articulate and positive Catholic stand on social issues, but these were lonely voices indeed, working without the benefit of the all-important hierarchical sanction that would give force to their words. Thus, as David O'Brien points out, "The publication of the Bishops' Program constituted a distinct advance on earlier American Catholic social thought and it gave authoritative sanction to the work of a few active Catholic reformers."[72] Hence the program was important for the church first because it broke her long silence on social issues and second because it did so in a way that was both public and authoritative. As Aaron Abell notes, the public and official nature of the document "suggested that

72. O'Brien, *American Catholics and Social Reform,* p. 42.

henceforth the hierarchy was willing to exercise a continuous and systematic oversight of Catholic social action." Karl Cerny argues that "the developments of 1919 were symbolic of the importance that the Bishops assigned to the spread of Catholic social principles."[73] If this was the case, what were the Catholic social principles which the program exposed, and what position did and does the program occupy in the Catholic tradition?

It is clear from his writings that John A. Ryan believed that the program was thoroughly Leonine both in its inspiration and in its provisions. If Ryan was correct, it could be argued that the program was significant for the church because it signaled an American Catholic appropriation of the Leonine social heritage. Several considerations seem to verify Ryan's contentions and thus validate such a claim: first, in writing the program and later in his defenses of it, Ryan made it clear that he based his ideas on his understanding of the Catholic tradition of natural law morality; second, Ryan followed a thoroughly Leonine method of seeking and articulating ways of translating natural law principles into a modern industrial idiom so that this traditional morality would have current critical force; third, in all of his apologetic writings about the program, Ryan followed the Leonine neo-Thomistic approach that appreciated both the historical conditioning of Thomas's insights and the elasticity of his method and the liberation that came from acknowledging Thomas as an example of the efficacy of sympathetic and sensibly adaptable thought. Thus, in method, Ryan was thoroughly Leonine and the program was clearly an example of the use of such a method. In laying claim to the program's Leonine pedigree, Ryan went well beyond a general claim for methodological inspiration. He justified almost all of the Progressive particulars of the program as essentially Catholic or sanctioned by Catholic thought by appealing to Leo's statements on the moral responsibility of the state to intervene for the establishment of a socially just economic order. In this endeavor, Ryan perhaps overstated his case and did not adequately reflect Leo's fears of an omnicompetent state. Nonetheless, he was Leonine and he did the church the enormous favor of dispelling somewhat the tra-

73. Abell, "Bishops' 1919 Program," p. 109; Cerny, "Monsignor John A. Ryan," p. 115.

ditional Catholic fear of state activity in the social and economic spheres. In addition, through the program, Ryan managed to remake the image of the church in an industrial society. As a result, the American church became more at home with Leonine thought and Leonine-inspired social action in such a public way that the church had to abandon forever the masterful social inactivity of the past. This was a contribution of inestimable and timeless importance.

As a Leonine and Progressive document, then, the bishops' program remade the image of the American church in two key areas and signaled a rapprochement between the Catholic and American reform traditions. In addition, the document and its method of publication announced the American Catholic acceptance of the American denominational settlement. The sophisticated publicity campaign that announced the publication of the program betrayed a new attitude on the part of the church. Abandoning its previous passivity with regard to public opinion, which was based on a belief that Catholicism's character as the one "true church" would serve to lure non-Catholics to the fold, the American church began an aggressive campaign to carve out a place for herself in the competitive denominational marketplace of American religious life. With their document, the bishops signaled their willingness to compete with other churches and ideologies for the affections of the working classes and to compete with the Federal Council of Churches of Christ for the right to claim moral leadership in the nation. The publication of the document was merely the opening salvo in the church's long struggle to establish her claim to moral leadership. At the time of the program's promulgation, many Protestants acknowledged the church's pioneering work and called upon Protestant America to meet the Catholic challenge. Through the work of the Social Action Department, Catholicism continued to press her claims, and with telling results. In 1945, writing for the *Christian Century,* Harold Fey told his Protestant brethren that in the fight to win industrial workers, the Catholic Church was far outstripping the Protestant churches. He attributed Catholicism's success to the National Catholic Welfare Council's provision of a unified agency for coordinating Catholic work; to labor's realization that "the Roman Catholic Church as such is committed to the idea that it is labor's right and duty to organize into unions, to develop cooperatives and other means of self-help"; and to the papal encyclicals and the Bishops' Program of Social Reconstruction of 1919 that provided the church with a rationale for social reform.[74] Fey advised his coreligionists to learn from and compete with their Catholic counterparts and adversaries. Clearly, the bishops' program marked a Catholic acceptance of religious competition in American society.

On balance, then, the Bishops' Program of Social Reconstruction was a remarkable document, for its publication signaled the maturation of the American Catholic Church. With the program, the church entered into the American religious and social mainstreams as well as that of Leonine Catholic social action. She had at last become a progressive and Progressive force in American life.

74. Harold E. Fey, *Can Catholicism Win America?: A Series of Eight Articles Reprinted from the Christian Century* (Chicago: Christian Century Reprints, 1945), p. 13. "The Catholic plan for changing the industrial order has three objectives: security, ownership and partnership. It is no accident that stability is its first requisite. Ownership for workers gives them a stake in society and partnership a share in the control of the industrial process. This plan is a composite created from the encyclicals of Leo XIII, Pius XI and Pius XII, supported by the American Bishops' Program for Social Reconstruction of 1919" (ibid.).

Bibliography

ARCHIVAL SOURCES

The Archives of the Catholic University of America, Washington, D.C.

The Archives of the Catholic University are the repository of two important collections for this study: the Archives of the National Catholic War Council and the John A. Ryan Papers. The holdings of these two collections are as follows:

The Archives of the National Catholic War Council consist of 215 boxes of material, of which approximately 135 boxes are directly relevant to this study. Among these materials are the following:

The Rockford File of Bishop Peter J. Muldoon of Rockford, Illinois, the chairman of the Administrative Committee of the NCWC: 10 boxes. This file is especially important for this study because the archives of the Diocese of Rockford are closed to the public.

The Executive Secretary's File: 16 boxes.

The File of the Committee on Special War Activities: 10 boxes.

The File of the Reconstruction Committee of the CSWA: 43 boxes.

The Historical Materials File: 10 boxes.

The Minutes of the meetings of the Administrative Committee, the Executive Committee, and the Committee on Special War Activities: 9 boxes.

The John A. Ryan Papers consist of 56 boxes.

Other Archival Sources

The Archives of the Diocese of Toledo contain some of the personal papers of Bishop Joseph Schrembs, one of the members of the Administrative Committee of the NCWC. These holdings, however, are scant. The Archives of the Diocese of Cleveland, which hold the bulk of the Schrembs papers, contain no materials directly relevant to this study.

The Archives of the Diocese of Rockford contain the personal papers of Bishop Peter J. Muldoon. The archives are, however, closed to the public. Fortunately, upon Muldoon's death in 1927, the Reverend John J. Burke, C.S.P., removed all the materials in the bishop's possession that dealt with the work of the NCWC.

The Archives of the Archdiocese of Boston contain the personal papers of William Cardinal O'Connell. O'Connell was an implacable foe of Ryan and the work of the Social Action Department of the NCWC, but his personal papers contain few references to the work of the NCWC.

The Archives of the Paulist Fathers, New York City, contain an extensive collection of John J. Burke's papers. These papers, however, are largely personal in nature, and yielded very little that was pertinent to this study.

PERIODICALS

America
American Catholic Fortnightly Review
American Catholic Quarterly Review
American Child
American Church Monthly
American Federationist
American Industries
American Journal of Sociology
American Labor Monthly
Annals of the American Academy of Political and Social Science
Ave Maria
Biblical World
Boston Pilot
Brooklyn Tablet
Brotherhood of Locomotive Engineers' Journal
Brotherhood of Locomotive Firemen and Enginemen's Magazine
Catholic Action
Catholic Charities Review
Catholic Telegraph (Cincinnati)
Catholic World
Central Blatt and Social Justice
Century Magazine
Christian Century
Commoner
Commonweal
Current Opinion
Dial
Ecclesiastical Review
Electrical Workers' Journal
Federal Council Bulletin
Federal Employee
Forum
The Good of the Order: A Fortnightly
Harper's Weekly
Hartford Catholic Transcript
Hearst's International
Independent
Industry
Intercollegiate Socialist Review
International Socialist Review
Justice
Labor
Labor Clarion
Labor Record
LaFollette's Magazine
Law and Labor
Liberator
Literary Digest
Locomotive Engineer's Journal
Machinists' Monthly Journal
Manufacturers' Record
Methodist Review
Metropolitan Magazine
Miners' Magazine
Mining Congress Journal
Monthly Labor Review
Nation
National Catholic War Council Bulletin
Nation's Business
Newman Hall Review
New Republic
New World (Chicago)
New York Call

New York Post
New York Times
Open Shop Review
Outlook
Pittsburgh Catholic
Public
Railway Conductor
Railroad Trainman
Reconstruction: A Herald of the New Time
Review
Salesianum
Seamen's Journal
Shoeworkers' Journal
Social Service
Survey
Tablet
Textile Worker
Typographical Journal
United Mineworkers' Journal
Wall Street Journal
Western Catholic (Quincy, Illinois)
Western Watchman
World Tomorrow
World's Work

WORKS BY JOHN A. RYAN

Alleged Socialism of the Church Fathers. St. Louis: B. Herder, 1913.

"Americanism in Industry." *Annals of the American Academy of Political and Social Science* 90 (1920): 126–30.

"Anonymous Critics of the Bishops' Reconstruction Programme." *Catholic Charities Review* 3 (1919): 163–65.

"Are Wages Too High?" *Catholic Charities Review* 6 (1922): 116–18.

"Assaults upon Our Civil Liberties." *Catholic Charities Review* 7, no. 2 (1923): 17–19.

A Better Economic Order. New York: Harper and Bros., 1935.

"A Bill of Rights for Labor." *Catholic Charities Review* 6 (1922): 87–89.

"The Bishops' Pastoral as Others See It." *America,* 22 March 1919, p. 224.

"The Bishops' Program of Social Reconstruction." Address delivered at Sydney Mines, N.S., 29 July 1921. Ryan Papers, Writings Miscellaneous, Box B2-24, ACUA.

"The Bishops' Program of Social Reconstruction." *American Catholic Sociological Review* 5 (1944): 25–33.

"Capital and Labor." *Textile Worker* 8 (1920): 488–96.

"Cardinal Mermillod and the Union of Fribourg." *America,* 6 June 1931, pp. 200–201.

The Catholic Church and the Citizen. New York: Macmillan, 1928.

"Catholic Doctrine in Industrial Relations." Class Notes. Ryan Papers, Socio-Politico, Box B2-35, ACUA.

"Catholic Laymen and the Labor Problem." Address (ca. 1928). Ryan Papers, Writings Miscellaneous, Box B2-24, ACUA.

"Catholic Principles and Roosevelt Policies." In his *Seven Troubled Years: 1930–1936: A Collection of Papers on the Depression and on the Problems of Recovery and Reform.* Ann Arbor: Edwards Bros., 1937.

Catholic Principles of Politics. With Francis J. Boland. New York: Macmillan, 1940.

"Catholicism and Social Action." Address delivered at Our Lady of the Elms College, Chicopee, Massachusetts, 3 February 1939. Ryan Papers, Writings, 1935–40, Box B2-28, ACUA.

"The Church and Radical Social Movements." Lecture, n.d. Ryan Papers, Writings Miscellaneous, Box B2-24, ACUA.

"The Church and the Social Question." Lecture, n.d. Ryan Papers, Writings Miscellaneous, Box B2-24, ACUA.

The Church and Socialism and Other Essays. Washington: University Press, 1919.

"The Church and the Workingman." *Catholic World,* September 1909, pp. 776–82.

"Church Unchanging on Social Questions." Class Notes on Catholic Social Teaching, n.d. Ryan Papers, Ryan Ref., A–Ch, Box B2-36, ACUA.

"Civic and Political Morality." *Catholic Action,* September 1933, pp. 9, 12.

"Completing the Record." *Catholic Charities Review* 4 (1920): 177–78.

The Constitution and Catholic Industrial Teaching: Social Action Series #8. New York: Paulist, 1937.

"Correspondence," with Conde Pallen, *Winona Courier* 12, no. 3 (August 1921): 21–35.

Declining Liberty and Other Papers. New York: Macmillan, 1927.

"A Depressing Revelation of Capitalist Conscience." *Catholic Charities Review* 5 (1921): 14–15.

Distributive Justice: The Right and Wrong of Our Present Distribution of Wealth. New York: Macmillan, 1916.

"The Economic Philosophy of Aquinas." In *Essays in Thomism,* edited by Robert E. Brennan, O.P. New York: Sheed and Ward, 1942.

"The Encyclicals and Social Justice." Address, 10 May 1936. Ryan Papers, Writings 1935–40, Box B2-28, ACUA.

"Industrial Relations." *Catholic Charities Review* 4 (1920): 279–80.

International Economic Life: A Preliminary Study Presented to the Catholic Association for International Peace by the Committee on Ethics and Economic Relations. New York: Paulist, 1934.

"Introductory: Some Other Reconstruction Programs." Typed notes. Ryan Papers, Correspondence 1939 (L–Z), Box B2-18, ACUA.

Journal. Ryan Papers, Box B2-32, ACUA.

"Judge Gary on Labor Unions." *Catholic Charities Review* 5 (1921): 194–95.

"Judicial Nullification of a Minimum Wage Law." *Catholic Charities Review* 6 (1922): 356–57.

"Labor and the Law." *Catholic Charities Review* 6 (1922): 11–15.

"Labor-Sharing in Management and Profit." *Catholic Charities Review* 4 (1920): 46–49, 71–74.

"Legislation and a Christian Social Order." Address to the Social Action Congress, Cleveland, 12 June 1939. Ryan Papers, Writings, 1935–40, Box B2-28, ACUA.

A Living Wage: Its Ethical and Economic Aspects. New York: Macmillan, 1906.

"Living Wage Repudiated." *Catholic Charities Review* 6 (1922): 8.

"The Message of the Encyclicals for America Today." In *Children of the Uprooted,* edited by Oscar Handlin. New York: George Braziller, 1966.

"The Moral Obligation of Civil Law." *Catholic World,* October 1921, pp. 73–86.

"The Need of Legal Standards of Protection for Labor." *American Labor Legislation Review* 11 (1921): 221–26.

"The New Industrial Revolution." In his *Seven Troubled Years, 1930–1936: A Collection of Papers on the Depression and on the Problems of Recovery and Reform.* Ann Arbor: Edwards Bros., 1937.

"The New Morality and Its Illusions." *Catholic World,* May 1930, pp. 129–36.

The New Norm of Morality: Defined and Applied to Particular Actions. Washington: National Catholic Welfare Conference, 1944.

"A New Theory of Political Sovereignty." *Catholic World,* November 1917, pp. 237–43.

"Next Steps in Industrial Democracy." Address, n.d. Ryan Papers, Writings Miscellaneous, Box B2-24, ACUA.

"The Open Shop Controversy." *Catholic Charities Review* 5 (1921): 87–89.

"Our Present Problems of Industrial Reconstruction." Address, n.d. Ryan Papers, Writings Miscellaneous, Box B2-24, ACUA.

"Pope Leo's Rerum Novarum." In his *Seven Troubled Years, 1930–1936: A Collection of Papers on the Depression and on the Problems of Recovery and Reform.* Ann Arbor: Edwards Bros., 1937.

"Pope Pius XI and a New Social Order." *Catholic Action,* June 1934, pp. 14–15, 18.

"A Practical Philosophy of Social Work." *Catholic Charities Review* 4 (1920): 242–45.

"Profiteering and the High Cost of Living." *Catholic Charities Review* 4 (1920): 179–80.

"A Programme of Social Reform by Legislation." *Catholic World,* July 1909, pp. 433–44; August 1909, pp. 608–14.

"The Purpose of the State." *Catholic World,* March 1921, pp. 803–14.

Questions of the Day. 1931. Reprint. Freeport, N.Y.: Books for Libraries Press, 1967.

"Radical Labor and Autocratic Capital." Address for a Knights of Columbus convention, n.d. Ryan Papers, Writings Miscellaneous, Box B2-24, ACUA.

"The Railroads Reject the Living Wage." *Catholic Charities Review* 5 (1921): 224–25.

"Railway Labor Agreement." *Catholic Charities Review* 5 (1921): 155–56.

"The Railway Labor Board Fails Again." *Catholic Charities Review* 6 (1922): 320.

"'Reconstructing the Social Order' and the Bishops' Program of Social Reconstruction." NCWC Social Action Department Press Release XXVI, 15 December 1931, Ryan Papers, Ryan Ref. Ed–G, Box B2-38, ACUA.

"The Right of Self-Government." *Catholic World,* December 1918, pp. 314–30, and January 1920, pp. 441–54.

"The Rights of the Citizen." *Catholic World,* March 1922, pp. 781–86.

"Significance of Encyclical's Commemoration." *Catholic Action,* May 1936, p. 4.

Social Doctrine in Action: A Personal History. New York: Harper and Bros., 1941.

"Social Justice in the World Today." Address, n.d. Ryan Papers, Writings Miscellaneous, Box B2-24, ACUA.

"Social Legislation and a 'Constitutional Crisis.'" *Survey,* 14 February 1914, pp. 626–27.

Social Reconstruction. New York: Macmillan, 1920.

"The Social Teaching of Saint Thomas Aquinas." Address, July 1928. Ryan Papers, Writings Miscellaneous, Box B2-24, ACUA.

Socialism: Promise or Menace. With Morris Hillquit. New York: Macmillan, 1914.

"Some Effects of *Rerum Novarum.*" *America,* 25 April 1931, pp. 58–60.

"Some Principles of Social Reconstruction." *Everybody's Magazine.* Ryan Papers, Scrapbook 1901–45, ACUA.

"Some Problems of Minimum Wage Legislation." *Catholic Charities Review* 6 (1922): 223–26.

"Some Problems of Social Reconstruction." Class Notes for Marygrove College Summer Session, 24 June–2 August 1929. Ryan Papers, Socio-Politico, Box B2-35, ACUA.

The State and the Church. With Moorhouse F. X. Millar. New York: Macmillan, 1922.

"The State and Social Distress." *Catholic Charities Review* 4 (1920): 3–8.

"The Supreme Court Outlaws the Secondary Boycott." *Catholic Charities Review* 5 (1921): 50–51.

"The Teaching of the Catholic Church." *Annals of the American Academy of Political and Social Science* 103 (1922): 76–80.

"To Keep the Record Straight." *Catholic Charities Review* 4 (1920): 137–41.

"The Two Papal Encyclicals on Labor." Address, n.d. Ryan Papers, Writings Miscellaneous, Box B2-24, ACUA.

"Two Programs of Social Reconstruction." Address, n.d. Ryan Papers, Writings Miscellaneous, Box B2-24, ACUA.

SECONDARY SOURCES

Abell, Aaron I. "American Catholic Reaction to Industrial Conflict: The Arbitral Process, 1885–1900." *Catholic Historical Review* 41 (1956): 385–407.

———. *American Catholicism and Social Action: A Search for Social Justice, 1865–1950.* Garden City, N.Y.: Hanover House, 1960.

———. "The Bishops' 1919 Program." *Social Order* 12 (1962): 109–18.

———. "The Catholic Church and Social Problems in the World War I Era." *Mid-America* 30 (1948): 139–51.

———. "The Catholic Factor in Urban Welfare: The Early Period, 1850–1880." *Review of Politics* 14 (1952): 289–324.

———. "Monsignor John A. Ryan: An Historical Appreciation." *Review of Politics* 8 (1946): 128–34.

———. "Origins of Catholic Social Reform in the United States: Ideological Aspects." *Review of Politics* 11 (1949): 294–309.

———. "The Reception of Leo XIII's Labor Encyclical in America, 1891–1919." *Review of Politics* 7 (1945): 464–95.

———, ed. *American Catholic Thought on Social Questions.* Indianapolis: Bobbs-Merrill, 1968.

Abrams, Ray H. *Preachers Present Arms: A Study of the War Time Attitudes and Activities of the Churches and the Clergy in the United States, 1914–1918.* Philadelphia: Round Table Press, 1933.

Adams, Graham, Jr. *Age of Industrial Violence, 1910–15: Activities and Findings of the United States Commission on Industrial Relations.* New York: Columbia University Press, 1966.

Ames, Edward Scribner. "Religion in the New Age." In *America and the New Era,* edited by Elisha Friedman, pp. 285–300. New York: E. P. Dutton, 1920.

Baker, Ray S. *The New Industrial Unrest: Reasons and Remedies.* New York: Doubleday, Page and Co., 1920.

Batten, Samuel Zane. "The Churches and Social Reconstruction." *Biblical World* 53 (1919): 594–617.

Becnel, Thomas. *Labor, Church and the Sugar Establishment.* Baton Rouge: Louisiana State University Press, 1980.

Bell, Bernard I. "And Now That the War Is Over." *American Church Monthly,* March 1919, pp. 608–14.

———. *The Church's Work for Men at War.* Milwaukee: Morehouse, 1919.

Bernstein, Irving. *A History of the American Worker, 1920–1933: The Lean Years.* Boston: Houghton Mifflin, 1960.

Betten, Neil. *Catholic Action and the Industrial Worker.* Gainesville: Florida State University Press, 1976.

Billington, Ray A. *The Protestant Crusade.* New York: Macmillan, 1938.

Bleid, Benjamin J. *Three Archbishops of Milwaukee.* Milwaukee: N.p., 1955.

Boase, Paul H. *The Rhetoric of Christian Socialism.* New York: Random House, 1969.

Boyle, John P. "Peter E. Dietz and the American Labor Movement." M.A. thesis, Catholic University of America, 1948.

Braeman, John, Robert H. Bremner, and David Brody. *Change and Continuity in Twentieth Century America: The 1920's.* Columbus: Ohio State University Press, 1968.

Broderick, Francis L. *Right Reverend New Dealer: John A. Ryan.* New York: Macmillan, 1963.

Brooks, John Graham. *Labor's Challenge to the Social Order: Democracy Its Own Critic and Educator.* New York: Macmillan, 1920.

———. *The Social Unrest: Studies in Labor and Socialist Movements.* New York: Macmillan, 1903.

Brophy, Mary L. *The Social Thought of the German Roman Catholic Central Verein.* Washington: Catholic University of America Press, 1941.

Brown, Thomas N. *Irish-American Nationalism.* Philadelphia: J. B. Lippincott, 1966.

Browne, Henry J. *The Catholic Church and the Knights of Labor.* Washington: Catholic University of America Press, 1949.

Bruce, Robert V. *1877: Year of Violence.* Chicago: Quadrangle Books, 1959.

Bruni, Gerardo. *Progressive Scholasticism.* Translated by John S. Zybura. St. Louis: B. Herder, 1929.

Bryan, William J. "Applied Christianity." *Commoner,* May 1919, pp. 11–12.

———. "A Constructive Program." *Commoner,* May 1919, pp. 9–10.

Buenker, John D. *Urban Liberalism and Progressive Reform.* New York: Charles Scribner's Sons, 1973.

Burke, John J. "Special Catholic Activities in War Service." *Annals of the American Academy of Political and Social Science* 89 (1918): 213–20.

Burner, David. "1919: Prelude to Normalcy." In *Change and Continuity in Twentieth Century America: The 1920's,* edited by John Braeman, Robert Bremner, and David Brody, pp. 3–32. Columbus: Ohio State University Press, 1968.

Camp, Richard L. *The Papal Ideology of Social Reform: A Study in Historical Development, 1878–1967.* Leiden: E. J. Brill, 1969.

Carroll, Mollie. *Labor and Politics: The Attitude of the American Federation of Labor toward Legislation and Politics.* Boston: Houghton Mifflin, 1923.

Carter, Paul A. *The Decline and Revival of the Social Gospel: Social and Political Liberalism in American Protestant Churches, 1920–1940.* Ithaca: Cornell University Press, 1954.

Cerny, Karl H. "Monsignor John A. Ryan and the Social Action Department." Ph.D. dissertation, Yale University, 1954.

Chaffee, Edmund. *The Protestant Churches and the Industrial Crisis.* New York: Macmillan, 1933.

Chambers, Clarke A. *Paul U. Kellogg and the Survey: Voices for Social Welfare and Social Justice.* Minneapolis: University of Minnesota Press, 1971.

———. *Seedtime of Reform: American Social Service and Social Action, 1918–1933.* Minneapolis: University of Minnesota Press, 1963.

Cleveland, Frederick A., and Joseph Schafer. *Democracy in Reconstruction.* Boston: Houghton Mifflin, 1919.

Coale, James A. "The Church and Labor." *Biblical World* 54 (1920): 354–62.

Cochran, Thomas C., and William Miller. *The Age of Enterprise: A Social History of Industrial America.* New York: Macmillan, 1960.

Coffin, Henry Sloane. *In a Day of Social Rebuilding: Lectures on the Ministry of the Church.* New Haven: Yale University Press, 1918.

Cohen, Julius H. *An American Labor Policy.* New York: Macmillan, 1919.

Cohen, Warren I. *The American Revisionists: The Lessons of Intervention in World War I.* Chicago: University of Chicago Press, 1967.

Coleman, John A. "Vision and Praxis in American Theology: Orestes Brownson, John A. Ryan and John Courtney Murray." *Theological Studies* 37 (1976): 3–40.

Committee on the War and the Religious Outlook. *The Church and Industrial Reconstruction.* New York: Association Press, 1920.

Commons, John R. *Races and Immigrants in America.* New York: Macmillan, 1907.

Commons, John R., Selig Perlman, and Philip Taft. *History of Labor in the United States, 1896–1932.* Vol. 6: *Labor Movements.* New York: Macmillan, 1935.

Coughlin, Bernard J. *Church and State in Social Welfare.* New York: Columbia University Press, 1965.

Crawford, V. M. *Catholic Social Doctrine, 1891–1931.* London: C.S.G., 1945.

Croly, Herbert. "The Spirit of Reconstruction." *Catholic Charities Review* 3 (1919): 205.

Cronin, John F. *Catholic Social Principles.* Milwaukee: Bruce, 1950.

Cronin, John F., and Henry Flannery. *The Church and the Workingman.* New York: Hawthorne, 1965.

Cross, Robert D. *The Emergence of Liberal Catholicism in America.* Cambridge, Mass.: Harvard University Press, 1958.

Cuff, Robert D. "Herbert Hoover, the Ideology of Voluntarism and War Organization during the Great War." In *Herbert Hoover: The Great War and Its Aftermath, 1914–1933,* edited by Lawrence E. Gelfand, pp. 21–39. Iowa City: University of Iowa Press, 1979.

Curran, Charles E. "American and Catholic: American Catholic Social Ethics, 1880–1965." *Thought* 52 (1977): 50–74.

Curran, Robert E. *Michael Augustine Corrigan and the Shaping of Conservative Catholicism in America, 1878–1902.* New York: Arno, 1978.

Davis, Jerome. *Christianity and Social Adventuring.* New York: Century, 1927.

———. "A Class Church and a Churchless Class." In Davis, ed., *Labor Speaks for Itself on Religion: A Symposium of Labor Leaders throughout the World,* pp. 19–28. New York: Macmillan, 1929.

———. *Labor Speaks for Itself on Religion: A Symposium of Labor Leaders throughout the World.* New York: Macmillan, 1929.

Dennett, Tyler. *A Better World.* New York: George H. Doran, 1920.

Doran, Daniel E. "The Work of the National Catholic War Council." In *Catholic Builders of the Nation,* edited by C. E. McGuire, 2:272–84. Boston: Continental Press, 1923.

Drake, Paul H. *Democracy Made Safe.* Boston: LeRoy Phillips, 1918.

Dubofsky, Melvyn. *When Workers Organize: New York City in the Progressive Era.* Amherst: University of Massachusetts Press, 1968.

Eagan, John J. "An Employer's View of the Church's Function in Relation to Industry." *Annals of the American Academy of Political and Social Science* 103 (1922): 101–4.

Ebersole, Luke E. *Church Lobbying in the Nation's Capital.* New York: Macmillan, 1951.

Eddy, Sherwood. *Everybody's World.* New York: George H. Doran, 1920.

———. *Religion and Social Justice.* New York: George H. Doran, 1927.

Elder, Benedict. "'NCWC'—The Church in Action." *Catholic World,* September 1920, pp. 721–29.

———. *The Life of James Cardinal Gibbons, Archbishop of Baltimore, 1834–1921.* 2 vols. Milwaukee: Bruce, 1952.

Ely, Richard T. *Social Aspects of Christianity.* New York: Thomas Crowell, 1889.

Ernst, Eldon G. *Moment of Truth for Protestant America: Interchurch Campaigns following World War I.* Missoula: American Academy of Religion and Scholars' Press, AAR Dissertation Series 3, 1974.

Faunce, W. H. P. "The Church and Social Reconstruction." *Christian Century,* 5 June 1919, pp. 9–11.

Fenton, Edwin. "Immigrants and Unions, A Case Study: Italians and American Labor, 1870–1920." Ph.D. dissertation, Harvard University, 1957.

Finney, Ross L. *Causes and Cures for the Social Unrest.* New York: Macmillan, 1922.

Fitzpatrick, Edward A. "Social Progress and Political Administration." In *America and the New Era,* edited by Elisha Friedman, pp. 193–214. New York: E. P. Dutton, 1920.

Fitzpatrick, John. "The Bishops' Labor Programme." *National Catholic War Council Bulletin,* July 1919, pp. 9–10.

Flynn, George Q. *American Catholics and the Roosevelt Presidency, 1932–1936.* Lexington: University of Kentucky Press, 1968.

———. *Roosevelt and Romanism: Catholics and Diplomacy, 1937–1945.* Westport, Conn.: Greenwood Press, 1976.

Foner, Philip S. *History of the Labor Movement in the United States.*

Vol. 5: *The American Federation of Labor in the Progressive Era, 1910–1915.* New York: International Publishers, 1980.

Foster, William Z. *The Great Steel Strike and Its Lessons.* New York: B. W. Huebsch, 1920.

Fox, Mary H. *Peter E. Dietz, Labor Priest.* Notre Dame: University of Notre Dame Press, 1953.

Frank, Glenn. *America's Hour of Decision.* New York: Whittlesey House, 1934.

———. *The Politics of Industry: A Foot Note to the Social Unrest.* New York: Century, 1919.

Friedman, Elisha M. *America and the New Era: A Symposium on Social Reconstruction.* New York: E. P. Dutton, 1920.

———. *American Problems of Reconstruction: A National Symposium on the Economic and Financial Aspects.* New York: E. P. Dutton, 1918.

Fuchs, Josef. *Natural Law: A Theological Investigation.* Translated by Helmut Reckter and John A. Dowling. New York: Sheed and Ward, 1965.

Furfey, Paul H. *Love and the Urban Ghetto.* Maryknoll, N.Y.: Orbis, 1978.

Gavin, Donald P. *The National Conference of Catholic Charities, 1910–1960.* Milwaukee: Bruce, 1962.

Gearty, Patrick W. *The Economic Thought of Monsignor John A. Ryan.* Washington: Catholic University of America Press, 1953.

Gelfand, Lawrence E. *Herbert Hoover: The Great War and Its Aftermath, 1914–1923.* Iowa City: University of Iowa Press, 1979.

Gibbons, James. "Letter to the Hierarchy." 5 May 1919. *Ecclesiastical Review* 61 (1919): 10–16.

Gleason, Philip. *Catholicism in America.* New York: Harper & Row, 1970.

———. *The Conservative Reformers: German-American Catholics and the Social Order.* Notre Dame: University of Notre Dame Press, 1968.

Goldman, Eric F. *Rendezvous with Destiny: A History of Modern American Reform.* New York: Vintage, 1977.

Goldstein, David. *Socialism: Nation of Fatherless Children.* Boston: Union News League, n.d.

Goldstein, David, and Martha Moore Avery. *Bolshevism: Its Cure.* Boston: Boston School of Political Economy, 1919.

Gould, Lewis L. *The Progressive Era.* Syracuse: Syracuse University Press, 1974.

Gouldrick, John W. "John A. Ryan's Theory of the State." Ph.D. dissertation, Catholic University of America, 1979.

Graham, Otis L. *The Great Campaigns: Reform and War in America, 1900–1928.* Englewood Cliffs, N.J.: Prentice-Hall, 1971.

Green, Marguerite. *The National Civic Federation and the American Labor Movement, 1900–1925.* Washington: Catholic University of America Press, 1956.

Greenstone, J. David. *Labor in American Politics.* New York: Alfred A. Knopf, 1969.

Griffiths, Carl W. "Attitudes of the Religious Press toward Organized Labor, 1877–1896." Ph.D. dissertation, University of Chicago, 1942.

Griswold, Latta. "The Church and Reconstruction." *American Church Monthly,* August 1919, pp. 1034–47.

Guitton, Georges. "The Background of Rerum Novarum." *America,* 25 April 1931, pp. 56–57.

Halsey, William M. *The Survival of American Innocence: Catholicism in an Era of Disillusionment, 1920–1940.* Notre Dame: University of Notre Dame Press, 1980.

Handlin, Oscar. *The Children of the Uprooted.* New York: George Braziller, 1966.

———. *Race and Nationality in American Life.* Boston: Little, Brown, 1957.

———. *The Uprooted: The Epic Story of the Great Migration That Made the American People.* Boston: Little, Brown, 1952.

Hanna, Mary T. *Catholics and American Politics.* Cambridge, Mass.: Harvard University Press, 1979.

Hard, William. "The Catholic Church Accepts the Challenge." *Metropolitan Magazine,* January 1920, p. 27.

Harkness, Georgia. *The Methodist Church in Social Thought and Action.* New York: Abingdon Press, 1964.

Hawley, Ellis W. *The Great War and the Search for a Modern Order: A History of the American People and Their Institutions, 1917–1933.* New York: St. Martin's Press, 1979.

Hayes, Edward C., and Joseph Schafer. "Democratization of Institutions for Social Betterment." In *Democracy in Reconstruction,* edited by Frederick A. Cleveland, pp. 111–45. Boston: Houghton Mifflin, 1919.

Hays, Samuel P. *The Response to Industrialism, 1885–1914.* Chicago: University of Chicago Press, 1957.

Herald, Morrell. "Business Thought in the Twenties: Social Responsibility." In *The 1920's: Problems and Paradoxes,* edited by Milton Plesur, pp. 113–28. Boston: Allyn and Bacon, 1969.

Hicks, John D. *The Populist Revolt: A History of the Farmers' Alliance and the People's Party.* Minneapolis: University of Minnesota Press, 1931.

Higham, John. "The Mind of a Nativist: Henry F. Bowers and the APA." *American Quarterly* 4 (1952): 16–24.

———. *Strangers in the Land: Patterns of American Nativism, 1860–1925.* New Brunswick: Rutgers University Press, 1955.

Hobson, J. A. *Democracy after the War.* London: George Allen & Unwin, 1919.

Hofstader, Richard. *The Age of Reform: From Bryan to F.D.R.* New York: Vintage Books, 1955.

———. *The Paranoid Style in American Politics and Other Essays.* New York: Alfred A. Knopf, 1965.

Hopkins, Charles. *The Rise of the Social Gospel in American Protestantism, 1865–1915.* New Haven: Yale University Press, 1940.
Husslein, Joseph. "Popes' and Bishops' Labor Program." *America,* 14 June 1919, pp. 248–50.
———. *Social Wellsprings.* Milwaukee: Bruce, 1940.
———. *The World Problem: Capital, Labor and the Church.* New York: P. J. Kenedy and Sons, 1918.
Huthmacher, J. Joseph. "Urban Liberalism and the Age of Reform." *Mississippi Valley Historical Review* 49 (1962): 231–41.
Ireland, John. *The Church and the Modern Society.* Chicago: D. H. McBride, 1896.
Johnson, F. Ernest. *The New Spirit in Industry.* New York: Association Press, 1919.
———. "The Teaching of the Protestant Church." *Annals of the American Academy of Political and Social Science* 103 (1922): 81–85.
Johnson, F. Ernest, and Arthur E. Holt. *Christian Ideals in Industry.* New York: Methodist Book Concern, 1924.
Joyce, William L. *Editors and Ethnicity: A History of the Irish-American Press, 1848–1883.* New York: Arno, 1976.
Karson, Marc. *American Labor Unions and Politics, 1900–1918.* Carbondale: Southern Illinois University Press, 1958.
Kauffman, Christopher J. *Faith and Fraternalism: The History of the Knights of Columbus, 1882–1982.* New York: Harper & Row, 1982.
Kerby, William J. "How the Catholic Church Does It." In *Christianity and Social Adventuring,* edited by Jerome Davis, pp. 119–34. New York: Century, 1927.
———. *The Social Mission of Charity: A Study of Points of View in Catholic Charities.* New York: Macmillan, 1921.
Kinzer, Donald L. *An Episode in Anti-Catholicism: The American Protective Association.* Seattle: University of Washington Press, 1964.
Korman, Gerd. *Industrialization, Immigrants and Americanizers: The View from Milwaukee, 1866–1921.* Madison: State Historical Society of Wisconsin, 1967.
Krickus, Richard. *Pursuing the American Dream: White Ethnics and the New Populism.* Garden City, N.Y.: Doubleday, 1976.
Laux, J. J. (George Metlake). *Christian Social Reform: Program Outlined by Its Pioneer, William Emmanuel Baron von Ketteler.* Philadelphia: Dolphin, 1912.
Lee, William J. "The Work in Industrial Relations of the Social Action Department of the National Catholic Welfare Conference, 1933–1945." M.A. thesis, Catholic University of America, 1946.
Leo XIII. "The Christian Constitution of States." In *The Church and the State,* edited by John A. Ryan and Moorhouse F. X. Millar, pp. 1–25. New York: Macmillan, 1922.
———. "Law and Liberty." In *The Church and the State,* edited by John A. Ryan and Moorhouse F. X. Millar, pp. 234–43. New York: Macmillan, 1922.

———. "On the Condition of Labor." In *The Condition of Labor: An Open Letter to Pope Leo XIII,* edited by Henry George, pp. 119–57. New York: United States Book, 1891.

Leuchtenberg, William E. *The Perils of Prosperity, 1914–1932.* Chicago: University of Chicago Press, 1958.

Link, Arthur S. *Woodrow Wilson and the Progressive Era, 1910–1917.* New York: Harper, 1954.

Lippincott, Isaac. *Problems of Reconstruction.* New York: Macmillan, 1919.

Lovestone, Jay. *The Government—Strikebreaker: A Study of the Role of the Government in the Recent Industrial Crisis.* New York: Workers' Party of America, 1923.

Lovett, Robert M. *The Middle Class and Organized Labor.* New York: League for Industrial Democracy, 1940.

Lusk, Clayton, et al. *Revolutionary Radicalism: Its History, Purpose and Tactics: Being the Report of the Joint Legislative Committee Investigating Seditious Activities.* 2 vols. Albany: J. B. Lyon, 1920.

MacDonald, Fergus. *The Catholic Church and the Secret Societies in the United States.* New York: U.S. Catholic Historical Society, 1946.

MacIver, Robert M. *Labor in the Changing World.* New York: E. P. Dutton, 1919.

Mackenzie-King, W. L. *Industry and Humanity: A Study in the Principles Underlying Industrial Reconstruction.* Boston: Houghton Mifflin, 1918.

MacLean, Annie N. *Some Problems of Reconstruction.* Chicago: A. C. McClurg, 1921.

Maloney, William J. M. A. "The Contents of the Bishops' Labor Program." *America,* 12 March 1919, pp. 601–2.

Marshall, Charles. *The Roman Catholic Church and the Modern State.* New York: Dodd, Mead, 1928.

May, Henry F. *The End of American Innocence: A Study of the First Years of Our Own Time, 1912–1917.* New York: Alfred A Knopf, 1959.

———. *Protestant Churches and Industrial America.* New York: Harper and Bros., 1949.

McAvoy, Thomas T. "The Catholic Minority after the Americanist Controversy, 1899–1917: A Survey." *Review of Politics* 21 (1959): 53–82.

———. *The Great Crisis in American Catholic History, 1895–1900.* Chicago: Henry Regnery, 1957.

———. *A History of the Catholic Church in the United States.* Notre Dame: University of Notre Dame Press, 1969.

McCaffrey, Lawrence J. *The Irish Diaspora in America.* Bloomington: Indiana University Press, 1976.

McColgen, Daniel. *A Century of Charity: The First Hundred Years of the Society of Saint Vincent De Paul in the United States.* Milwaukee: Bruce, 1951.

McConaughy, J. W. "The Bishops and Industrial Civilization." *America*, 19 March 1919, pp. 629–30.

McCool, Gerald A. *Catholic Theology in the Nineteenth Century: The Quest for a Unitary Method.* New York: Seabury, 1977.

McCrow, Thomas K. "The Progressive Legacy." In *The Progressive Era*, edited by Lewis L. Gould, pp. 21–53. Syracuse: Syracuse University Press, 1974.

McDonagh, Thomas J. "Some Aspects of the Roman Catholic Attitude toward the American Labor Movement, 1900–1914." Ph.D. dissertation, University of Wisconsin, 1951.

McDonald, David J. *Union Man.* New York: E. P. Dutton, 1969.

McGowan, Raymond A. "Catholic Work in the United States for Social Justice." *Catholic Action* 18, no. 5 (May 1936): 5–11.

———. "The Program and Activities of the National Catholic Welfare Council." *Annals of the American Academy of Political and Social Science* 103 (1922): 130–33.

McKeown, Elizabeth. "The National Bishops' Conference: An Analysis of Its Origins." *Catholic Historical Review* 66 (1980): 565–83.

———. "War and Welfare: A Study of American Catholic Leadership." Ph.D. dissertation, University of Chicago, 1972.

McMahon, Charles A. "Bishop Muldoon's War and Reconstruction Services." *Illinois Catholic Historical Review* 10 (1928): 295–300.

McManamin, Francis G. "John Boyle O'Reilly: Social Reform Editor." *Mid-America* 43 (1961): 36–54.

———. "Peter Muldoon, First Bishop of Rockford, 1862–1927." *Catholic Historical Review* 48 (1962): 365–78.

McNamara, Sylvester J. *American Democracy and Catholic Doctrine.* Brooklyn: International Catholic Truth Society, n.d.

McQuade, Vincent A. *The American Catholic Attitude on Child Labor since 1891: A Study of the Formation and Development of a Catholic Attitude on a Specific Social Question.* Washington: Catholic University of America Press, 1938.

Messner, Johannes. *Social Ethics: Natural Law in the Modern World.* Translated by J. J. Doherty. St. Louis: B. Herder, 1949.

Meyer, Donald B. *The Protestant Search for Political Realism, 1919–1941.* Berkeley and Los Angeles: University of California Press, 1961.

Millar, Moorhouse F. X. "Scholasticism and American Political Philosophy." In *Present Day Thinkers and the New Scholasticism*, edited by John S. Zybura, pp. 301–41. St. Louis: B. Herder, n.d.

Miller, Robert. *That All May Be One: A History of the Rockford Diocese.* Rockford: Diocese of Rockford, 1976.

Miller, Robert Moats. *American Protestantism and Social Issues, 1919–1939.* Chapel Hill: University of North Carolina Press, 1958.

Moon, Parker T. "Catholic Social Action." In *Catholic Builders of the Nation*, edited by C. E. McGuire, pp. 209–28. Boston: Continental, 1923.

———. *The Labor Problem and the Social Catholic Movement in*

France: A Study in the History of Social Politics. New York: Macmillan, 1921.

Mooney, Edward. "Introduction to the 20th Anniversary Edition of the Bishops' Program of Social Reconstruction." Senate Document 79, 76th Cong., 1st sess., 1939.

Murray, Robert K. "Labor and Bolshevism." In *The 1920's: Problems and Paradoxes,* edited by Milton Plesur, pp. 129–46. Boston: Allyn and Bacon, 1969.

———. *The Red Scare: A Study in National Hysteria, 1919–1920.* Minneapolis: University of Minnesota Press, 1955.

Muste, A. J. "Labor's View of the Function of the Church." *Annals of the American Academy of Political and Social Science* 103 (1922): 112–16.

Nash, Roderick. *The Nervous Generation: American Thought, 1917–1930.* Chicago: Rand McNally, 1970.

National Catholic War Council. *The Church and Social Order: A Statement of the Archbishops and Bishops of the Administrative Board of the National Catholic Welfare Conference.* Washington: NCWC, 1940.

———. *National Catholic War Council Handbook.* Washington: NCWC, 1918.

———. *Outlines of a Social Service Program for Catholic Agencies: Reconstruction Pamphlet #7.* Washington: NCWC, 1919.

National Industrial Conference Board. *Problems of Industrial Readjustment in the United States: Research Report #15.* Boston: National Industrial Conference Board, 1919.

Niebuhr, Reinhold. "The Church and the Industrial Crisis." *Biblical World* 54 (1920): 588–92.

Noggle, Burl. *Into the Twenties: The United States from Armistice to Normalcy.* Urbana: University of Illinois Press, 1974.

North, Frank Mason. "The Church and Future Problems." *Christian Century,* 20 February 1919, pp. 8–10.

O'Brien, David J. *American Catholics and Social Reform: The New Deal Years.* New York: Oxford University Press, 1968.

O'Grady, John. *Catholic Charities in the United States: History and Problems.* Washington: NCCC, 1930.

———. *The Catholic Church and the Destitute.* New York: Macmillan, 1929.

Olds, Marshall. *Analysis of the Interchurch World Movement Report on the Steel Strike.* New York: G. P. Putnam's Sons, 1922.

Open Shop Department of the National Association of Manufacturers. *Open Shop Encyclopedia for Debators.* N.p.: National Association of Manufacturers, 1922.

Pallen, Conde. "A Belated Complaint." *Catholic Charities Review* 5 (1921): 271–72.

Pastoral Letter of 1919. *Pastoral Letters of the American Hierarchy, 1792–1970,* edited by Hugh J. Nolan. pp. 212–61. Huntington, Ind.: Our Sunday Visitor, 1971.

Perlman, Mark. "Labor in Eclipse." In *Change and Continuity in Twentieth Century America: The 1920's,* edited by John Braeman, Robert H. Bremner, and David Brody, pp. 103–46. Columbus: Ohio State University Press, 1968.

Plesur, Milton. *The 1920's: Problems and Paradoxes.* Boston: Allyn and Bacon, 1969.

Plumb, Glenn E., and William G. Roylance. *Industrial Democracy: A Plan for Its Achievement.* New York: B. W. Huebsch, 1923.

Pollock, Norman. *The Populist Response to Industrial America: Midwestern Populist Thought.* Cambridge, Mass.: Harvard University Press, 1962.

Pope, Liston. *Millhands and Preachers: A Study of Gastonia.* New Haven: Yale University Press, 1942.

Powderly, Terence V. *The Path I Trod.* New York: Columbia University Press, 1940.

Purcell, Richard. "John A. Ryan: Prophet of Social Justice." *Studies* 35 (1946): 153–71.

Quick, Herbert. *From War to Peace: A Plea for a Definite Policy of Reconstruction.* Indianapolis: Bobbs-Merrill, 1919.

Rager, John C. *Democracy and Bellarmine: An Examination of Blessed Cardinal Bellarmine's Defense of Popular Government and the Influence of His Political Theory upon the American Declaration of Independence.* Shelbyville, Ind.: Qualityprint, 1926.

Redechko, James P. *Patrick Ford and His Search for America: A Case Study of Irish-American Journalism, 1870–1913.* New York: Arno, 1976.

Reeve, Carl, and Barton Reeve. *James Connolly and the United States.* Atlantic Highlands: Humanities Press, 1978.

Reynolds, Lloyd, and Charles Killingsworth. *Trade Union Publications.* Baltimore: Johns Hopkins University Press, 1945.

Roddy, Edward G. "The Catholic Newspaper Press and the Quest for Social Justice, 1912–1920." Ph.D. dissertation, Georgetown University, 1961.

Rodgers, Daniel T. *The Work Ethic in Industrial America, 1850–1920.* Chicago: University of Chicago Press, 1978.

Roohan, James E. "American Catholics and the Social Question, 1865–1900: A Survey." Ph.D. dissertation, Yale University, 1952.

Rosenthal, Benjamin J. *Reconstructing America Sociologically and Economically.* Chicago: Arcadia, 1919.

Roth, Jack J. *World War I: A Turning Point in Modern History.* New York: Alfred A. Knopf, 1967.

Ryan, Daniel J. *American Catholic World War I Records.* Washington: Catholic University of America Press, 1941.

Ryan, James H. "The New Scholasticism and Its Contribution to Modern Thought." In *Present Day Thinkers and the New Scholasticism,* edited by John S. Zybura, pp. 342–68. St. Louis: B. Herder, n.d.

Sanks, T. Howland. "Liberation Theology and the Social Gospel: Variations on a Theme." *Theological Studies* 41 (1980): 668–82.

Saposs, David J. *American Labor Ideology: Monograph 3: Case Studies in Labor Ideology: An Analysis of Labor, Political and Trade Union Activity as Influenced by Ideology—Philosophic, Structural and Procedural Adaptations since World War I.* N.p.: University of Hawaii, Industrial Relations Center, 1971.

———. "The Catholic Church and the Labor Movement." *Modern Monthly,* May 1933, pp. 225–30; June 1933, pp. 294–98.

———. *Left Wing Unionism: A Study of Radical Policies and Tactics.* New York: Russell and Russell, 1926.

Schafer, Joseph. "The Historical Background of Reconstruction in America." In *Democracy in Reconstruction,* edited by Frederick A. Cleveland and Joseph Schafer, pp. 3–24. Boston: Houghton Mifflin, 1919.

Schlesinger, Arthur M. *Political and Social Growth of the American People, 1865–1940.* 3d ed. New York: Macmillan, 1941.

Scudder, Vida D. *The Church and the Hour: Reflections of a Socialist Churchwoman.* New York: E. P. Dutton, 1917.

Seller, Maxine. *They Seek America: A History of Ethnic Life in the United States.* N.p.: Jerome S. Ozer, 1977.

Shanabruch, Charles H. "The Catholic Church's Role in the Americanization of Chicago's Immigrants, 1833–1928." 2 vols. Ph.D. dissertation, University of Chicago, 1975.

Shannon, William V. *The American Irish.* New York: Macmillan, 1966.

Shapiro, Stanley. "The Great War and Reform: Liberals and Labor, 1917–19." *Labor History* 12 (1971): 323–44.

———. "The Twilight of Reform: Advanced Progressives after the Armistice." *Historian* 33 (1971): 349–64.

Sheerin, John B. *Never Look Back: The Career and Concerns of John J. Burke.* New York: Paulist, 1975.

———. *The Catholic Spirit in America.* New York: Dial, 1927.

Simons, Algie M. *The Vision for Which We Fought: A Study in Reconstruction.* New York: Macmillan, 1919.

Slosson, Preston W. *The Great Crusade and After, 1914–1928.* New York: Macmillan, 1935.

Small, Albion W. "Christianity and Industry." *American Journal of Sociology* 25 (1920): 673–94.

———. "The Church and Class Conflicts." *American Journal of Sociology* 24 (1919): 481–501.

Smith, John S. "Organized Labor and Government in the Wilson Era, 1913–1921: Some Conclusions." *Labor History* 3 (1962): 265–86.

Speare, Morris E., and Walter B. Norris. *Vital Forces in Current Events.* New York: Ginn, 1920.

Society of Industrial Engineers. *Industrial Reconstruction Problems.* New York: Society of Industrial Engineers, 1919.

Stang, William. *Socialism and Christianity.* New York: Benziger, 1905.

Stevenson, Elizabeth. *Babbitts and Bohemians: The American 1920's.* New York: Macmillan, 1967.

Stroh, Paul. "The Catholic Clergy and American Labor Disputes." Ph.D. dissertation, Catholic University of America, 1939.

Swing, Raymond. "The Bishops and an Economic Philosophy." *America*, 29 March 1919, pp. 631–32.

———. "The Catholic View of Reconstruction." *Nation*, 29 March 1919, pp. 467–68.

Taylor, Albion G. "Labor Policies of the National Association of Manufacturers." Ph.D. dissertation, University of Illinois, 1927.

Taylor, Alva. "The Church and Industrial Democracy: Quakers and Catholics." *Christian Century*, 17 April 1919, p. 13.

Thomas, Charles S. "Reconstruction Needs in Our Democracy." In *Reconstructing America: Our Next Big Job*, edited by Edwin Wildman, pp. 9–19. Boston: Page, 1919.

Tifft, Thomas W. "Toward a More Humane Social Policy: The Work and Influence of Msgr. John O'Grady." Ph.D. dissertation, Catholic University of America, 1979.

Toner, Jerome L. *The Closed Shop in the American Labor Movement*. Washington: Catholic University of America Press, 1941.

Vance, James S. *Proof of Rome's Political Meddling in America*. Washington: Fellowship Forum, 1927.

Vidler, Alec R. *A Century of Social Catholicism, 1820–1920*. London: S.P.C.K., 1964.

Walsh, Frank P. "The Significance of the Bishops' Labor Program." *National Catholic War Council Bulletin*, August 1919, pp. 18–19.

Walsh, James J. *The Thirteenth Greatest of Centuries*. New York: Catholic Summer School Press, 1907.

Walsh, Harry F. "The Function of the Church in Industry." *Annals of the American Academy of Political and Social Science* 103 (1922): 96–100.

———. *The Labor Movement: From the Standpoint of Religious Values*. New York: Sturgis and Walton, 1917.

Ward, Harry F. *The New Social Order: Principles and Programs*. New York: Macmillan, 1919.

———. *The Opportunity for Religion in the Present World Situation*. New York: Women's Press, 1919.

———. *The Social Creed of the Churches*. New York: Abingdon Press, 1914.

Ward, Richard. "The Role of the Association of Catholic Trade Unionists in the American Labor Movement." Ph.D. dissertation, University of Michigan, 1958.

Weeks, Estella. *Reconstruction Programs: A Comparative Study of Their Content and of the Viewpoints of the Issuing Organizations*. New York: Women's Press, 1919.

Werstein, Irving. *Shattered Decade, 1919–1929*. New York: Charles Scribner's Sons, 1970.

Whelpley, James D. *Reconstruction*. New York: Funk and Wagnalls, 1925.

Wiebe, Robert H. *Businessmen and Reform: A Study of the Progressive Movement.* Cambridge, Mass.: Harvard University Press, 1962.

Wildman, Edwin. *Reconstructing America: Our Next Big Job.* Boston: Page, 1919.

Williams, Michael. *American Catholics in the War: National Catholic War Council, 1917–1921.* New York: Macmillan, 1921.

———. "The Catholic Programme of Reconstruction." *National Catholic War Council Bulletin,* June 1919, pp. 8–10.

———. "The Possibilities of National Catholic Cooperation." In *Catholic Builders of the Nation,* edited by C. E. McGuire, pp. 285–99. Boston: Continental Press, 1923.

Yellowitz, Irwin. *Labor and the Progressive Movement in New York State, 1897–1916.* Ithaca: Cornell University Press, 1965.

Zybura, John S., ed. *Present-Day Thinkers and the New Scholasticism.* St. Louis: B. Herder, 1926.

Index